STORY OF A NATION

STORY
of a

MARGARET ATWOOD • MICHELLE BERRY

DIONNE BRAND • ROCH CARRIER

TIMOTHY FINDLEY • THOMAS KING

DAVID MACFARLANE • ANTONINE MAILLET

ALBERTO MANGUEL • HAL NIEDZVIECKI

JOHN RALSTON SAUL • MICHAEL TURNER

DEFINING *Moments*

IN OUR HISTORY

NATION

Preface by RUDYARD GRIFFITHS, *The Dominion Institute*

Introduction by CHRISTOPHER MOORE

Story of a Nation was initiated by

Westwood Creative Artists and The Dominion Institute

DOUBLEDAY CANADA

CANADIAN CATALOGUING IN PUBLICATION DATA

Main entry under title:
  Story of a nation : defining moments in our history

ISBN 0-385-65849-4

1. Canada—History—Fiction. 2. Short stories, Canadian (English).
3. Canadian fiction (English)—21st century. I. Title.

FC176.S85 2001   C813'.01083271   C2001-901032-X
F1026.6.S85 2001

JACKET AND BOOK DESIGN: CS RICHARDSON

Printed and bound in Canada

Published in Canada by Doubleday Canada, a division of Random House of Canada Limited

Visit Random House of Canada Limited's website:www.randomhouse.ca

FRI 10 9 8 7 6 5 4 3 2 1

The contributions of Margaret Atwood, Roch Carrier, Timothy Findley, Antonine Maillet, Alberto Manguel, and John Ralston Saul first appeared, in somewhat different form, in *The Globe and Mail*.

The Dominion Institute wishes to thank the following individuals for their support for the early reiteration of *Story of a Nation* as a *Globe and Mail* editorial series: The Honourable Sheila Copps, minister of Canadian Heritage; Richard Addis, editor of *The Globe and Mail*; Bruce Westwood, Westwood Creative Artists; and Michael A. Levine, solicitor at the law firm Goodmans.

Contents

PREFACE

WHAT DEFINES A COUNTRY? Is it the values a people share or the physical possession of some specific space or territory? Is it the memory of a common heritage or allegiance to a set of present-day institutions and ideals? These questions of identity are universal to all societies at all times.

What is remarkable about modern Canada, even to the casual observer, is the striking ahistorical character of our national identity. Through much of the twentieth century we chose to mark ourselves out as a "northern nation" defined by its endless lakes, vast interiors, and harsh arctic climes. Equally, when it came to giving expression to the values we shared in common, Canadians turned not to a common historical memory, as in Britain or America, but to a set of social institutions that were seen as manifestations of our national character. Medicare and social assistance became embodiments of a Canadian ethic of care, and the Charter of Rights and Freedoms the living representation of our respect for diversity.

For the vast majority of Canadians, the idea of the country as a sprawling geographic entity held together by shared institutions proved to be a potent and enduring basis for national community. Over the last quarter century, our sense of common identity has undergone a sea change. The combined forces of globalization and technological change, slowly, and then rapidly, began to undermine the touchstones that had animated our identity: the sense of ourselves as a country defined by its geography and institutions.

Canada, as we now never tire of telling ourselves, is one of the most "connected" societies in the industrial world. The very dream and reality of the virtual world has made it increasingly difficult to sustain the myth that we are a country defined by geography. With every instantaneous modem, cellular, and satellite connection between Vancouver, Inuvik, and St. John's, the physicality of Canada slips away. A similar unravelling of identity has occurred around our sense of being a nation that articulates its values through institutions. The permeation of the country's government and social conventions by a growing number of international financial protocols, such as GATT and NAFTA, has steadily eroded Canadians' belief that their institutions can be vehicles for collective self-determination. More and more young Canadians, rightly or wrongly, see the country's institutions as beach-heads for a global, corporatized vision of society that rings hollow with their yearnings for authenticity and belonging.

Simply put, Canada is now experienced by many of its citizens as a shrinking and porous community. Both of which are national attributes that, if unchecked, will preclude the very idea of a sovereign country. Against these trends towards dissimilation, Canada and Canadians are in the middle of a fascinating and perilous project of recrafting the foundations of a common identity. One of the hallmarks of this ongoing search for the basis of a new, robust national identity has been Canadians' sudden and intense interest in things historical. From the CBC's "A People's History" to the steady stream of non-fiction bestsellers on historical themes to the new sense of urgency surrounding Remembrance Day commemorations, Canadian history is enjoying an unexpected and far-reaching renaissance.

History and historical consciousness provide a powerful rebuttal to the carrion calls of globalization and technological change that the nation-state's time has come and gone. History gives us a renewed sense of place and context in a world where geography matters less and less. It provides the frames of reference to conduct a coherent national conversation when each of us is a complicated amalgamation of region, ethnicity, and gender. An increased historical awareness also provides what many Canadians feel is lacking in their highly mobile and autonomous lives: the raw materials to reimagine community by connecting one's personal narrative with the story of a larger whole. History and historical consciousness are ties that bind.

History is also a public space. It is not owned by a multinational corporation or by a government agency. At a time when the very notion of the public good seems under threat by the forces of globalization, historical memory is one of the last great reserves of collective imagination that we can tap into to more fully articulate who we are as a nation. The rash of new popular histories of Canada created by filmmakers, authors, and enthusiasts are indicative of how Canadian history has moved outside the ivory tower into mainstream social discourse to achieve just this end. And again, in a Canada where many of our institutions are permeated with agendas that lie beyond our borders, Canadian history is a rich terrain to reimagine a national identity that is an extension of our past, rather than a rupture with the traditions of tolerance and respect that stretch back to the country's founding.

At the beginning of the twenty-first century, we are very much a country in search of a new set of reference points to construct a common identity. This is a juncture in our national story fraught with opportunity and potential disaster. We either fail to renew a national vision and jettison some 250 years of hard-won lessons about what constitutes a just society, or we articulate a new identity founded on a basis more enduring and universal than outmoded notions of shared institutions and geography.

This is why *Story of a Nation* is such an important book. It takes Canadian history beyond its traditional treatment as an academic subject and reconfigures our past as a vehicle not only to understand where we have come from, but what our history means to us as a country today. It shows that history is narrative. That our past is not something transfixed in amber, but a story that is open to us to create and recreate in the image of the values we hold important as Canadians. Moreover, this process is a public activity open to everyone and not something to be left to government or corporate Canada.

Story of a Nation speaks to the seminal challenge that Canada faces in the twenty-first century. We either have the creativity to reimagine ourselves anew or what constitutes the country's identity will fall to global forces largely outside our control. While future historians will write the ultimate outcome of this contest of identity, our newfound sense of the importance of history—its ability to craft and sustain a common public memory—will be at the heart of the struggle for a new and vibrant Canadian nationalism.

Rudyard Griffiths

INTRODUCTION

WHERE DID HERE COME FROM? In 1993, when Douglas Glover brought out a novel of eighteenth-century loyalty and terrorism, *The Life and Times of Captain N.* (dedicated to his son, "that he might know the people who went before"), a reviewer felt obliged to write: "I'm loath to say that Douglas Glover has written a historical novel, though he has. Wait! Don't stop reading!"

How times change! (Fiction clearly has its own history.) Not long after, critical and popular success greeted *Away*, Jane Urquhart's novel of nineteenth-century refugees. Then it was the turn of Margaret Atwood's *Alias Grace*, about a servant and a murder in Upper Canada, and Guy Vanderhaeghe's *The Englishman's Boy*, about cowboys and movies in the west, and Anne Michaels's *Fugitive Pieces*, about the Holocaust and Toronto. Soon Wayne Johnston showed us, in *The Colony of Unrequited Dreams*, that a Canadian novelist could find international success with, of all things, the apprenticeship of Joey Smallwood.

So the writers in this collection, invited to create new stories on great events in the Canadian past, are joining a tradition in the making. It would be no surprise to McLennan, Maillet, Findley, Ondaatje, or Bowering, all of whom have built substantial fictions around past events. But at the end of the twentieth century, we began to recognize, with a kind of shock, just how often the most interesting fiction writers in Canada feel compelled to grapple with history. Gone is the belief that readers have to be tricked or cajoled to go along with them.

What's happening here?

Those of us who write non-fiction about history cannot help thinking that fiction about history might be . . . well, easier. When thin trails of evidence run out, when motives remain mysteriously opaque, hell, the novelists get to make it up! Their readers, after all, practise this thing called the suspension of disbelief. How nice would that be?

As several of the narrators in this collection remind us, no one suspends disbelief when they read a history book. Who "discovered" America? What were the causes of the First World War? Did the Roman Empire have to fall? Arguments never end, and we take for granted there must be another side to every interpretation. This is the hallmark of the genre: non-fiction never expects us to suspend disbelief. It is the literature of the kind of lived experience where meanings are multiple and uncertain and debatable. Non-fiction about history is less the story of the past than an argument about the past.

Novelists, mostly, have another ambition. Partly, they turn to history for the sheer pleasure of the scenes it offers. Any writer might be inspired by the fertile fields the Canadian past offers the imagination: to flesh out a character like Joey Smallwood; to speak in the diction of a nineteenth-century servant; or simply to have the opportunity to blow up one's home town in the greatest man-made explosion before Hiroshima. But there's more at play here than imaginations.

Once or twice in this collection, a historian seems about to emerge from beneath the skin of a novelist. But mostly, the fictional voice does not seek to debate the evidence or ignite arguments between alternatives. (The historical novel most likely to fall flat is the one with an afterword that declares, "I did research. Everything here is absolutely true, except the parts I made up.") Novelists succeed with history when they use their freedom of invention to the hilt, to construct voices and characters, memories and mythologies.

In these stories, our writers seek to make meanings out of history's arguments. Margaret Atwood and Antonine Maillet think us through death and loss in the great events of the 1750s. Roch Carrier encounters Québec's eternal conflict—habitant or voyageur—in the Klondike gold fever. Hal Niedzviecki finds common ground with a burned-out filmmaker among the young and downwardly mobile of sixties Rochdale. Alberto Manguel imagines the Red River settlement as "a bookish invention." Dionne Brand evokes the moods and music of a woman who confronted fifties racism in a Nova Scotia movie house. In the legacy of the world wars, Timothy Findley finds only bitter loss, and John Ralston Saul (creating a memoir rather than a fiction) encounters his father. Tom King suggests, hilariously, how even the dullest official documents carry explosive personal meanings for those who are supposed to be defined and confined by them. Michelle Berry, Michael Turner, and David Macfarlane evoke, in different times, youthful protagonists experiencing a special loss of innocence: the moment when one discovers history's events are also lived experiences.

We live—it's a cliché—in an era when everyone has his or her fifteen minutes, and "You're history!" is a casual dismissal of the out-of-fashion. It is not only the old who may feel themselves visitors to an alien planet running on Ritalin and Ecstasy. And there's no choice in the matter. Let the pace of change slow down a moment, and The Economy will collapse.

"How does one live in this world, with all these changes going on?" writer Daphne Marlatt once said, trying to explain the origins of her novel of early Vancouver, *Ana Historic*. "And one reaction to that question is, how did they manage it in the past?"

The past knows about change. Jane Urquhart's Irish and Guy Vanderhaeghe's cowboys were survivors of obliterated worlds, struggling to shape new myths in changed circumstances. So is Antonine Maillet's Bélonie in this collection. The faster we change, the more our novelists have sensed something in common with other people who have been bulldozed by history. Non-fiction histories tell us the meaning of any event must be debated, but fiction knows we can also create our meanings. So the historical novel re-emerges, less as a romance set in costume, more as an experiment in the making of meaning. It becomes a story to tell us where *here* came from, even as it vanishes.

For the present may be vanishing, but the past does not go away. At the beginning of the twentieth century, James Joyce's young modernist Stephen Daedalus imagined history was a nightmare from which to awaken. At the end of the century, Anne Michaels's Jakob rejects the dictum. Jakob has lived the twentieth-century nightmare, and he understands there is no forgetting. "History is amoral: events occurred. But memory is moral: what we consciously remember is what our conscience remembers."

Christopher Moore

STORY OF A NATION

Margaret Atwood

THE BOMBARDMENT CONTINUES

Translated from the French

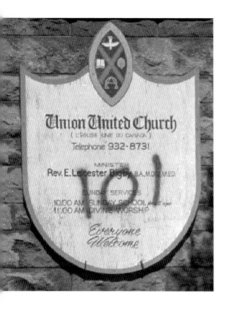

In Canada, we are so used to the split along linguistic lines—

the news in French is not the same as the news in English—that we have forgotten that, from the beginning of the European presence in North America, allegiances were arranged quite differently. Throughout the seventeenth century and until the fall of Québec in 1759 and the end of New France in 1760, sporadic wars were fought in the northeastern part of the "New World" between nations—French versus English—but also between religions; and this latter split was the more important, as it cut across both national and linguistic borders.

Two religions were at war: Roman Catholicism and what we may roughly call Protestantism, though the latter was not a monolith. New England was Protestant, of course, and New France was Catholic; but New England—which by the mid-eighteenth century included the garrison town of Halifax and the southeastern part of Nova Scotia—included many inhabitants who were not English in origin, and did not even speak English. It was the policy of the English government to settle

A sign on the wall of a United Church in Montréal's St-Henri Westmount district. The spray-painted "101" refers to the Québec language law that calls for unilingual French signs. 1996.

their Nova Scotian territory as quickly as possible with emigrants, from the British Isles to be sure, but also with any sort of Protestants they could get, rightly reasoning that these would be prepared to fight fiercely for the religious freedom offered to them by the English, and to avoid a return to the persecution they had experienced in their countries of origin.

The "Foreign Protestants" welcomed in Nova Scotia included many German-speakers—founders of such towns as Lunenburg—and also many Francophones. These latter were Huguenots, in flight from France, where Protestantism had had a rocky ride from the outset. Intermittent but ferocious warfare had gone on between the Catholics and those who had seceded from this faith until the Edict of Nantes granted a measure of toleration to the Huguenots in 1598. But matters were not settled, and the double-sided animosity continued. Protestants were excluded from New France in 1627, probably on the theory that New France—so constantly in conflict with New England—could not afford to have a lot of citizens in it who might in a pinch side with their co-religionists rather than with their co-nationals. Then, in 1685, the Edict of Nantes was revoked, and a great deal of pressure was put on French Protestants to convert. Celebration of their rites was prohibited, their children were seized and placed in convents and seminaries, they were fined and imprisoned; and a system of *dragonnades* was put in place, whereby soldiers were billeted on recalcitrant Protestant families with orders to disrupt, which in practice meant raping, pillaging, and destroying, as well as eating the family out of house and home. (Quite often these "dragoons" were Irish Catholics, who had been persecuted in their turn, and thus—according to Sartre's rule of thumb, explicated in *The Question*—would have known best how to go about it.) Things were so severe for Protestants in France at this time that they referred to their homeland as "the desert."

The combined effect of the revocation of the Edict of Nantes and the exclusion of French Protestants from New France was to drive these Protestants elsewhere. Colonies of them sprang up in Protestant Dublin, in Berlin, and in parts of England; but large numbers of them headed across the Atlantic to New England. Wherever they went, they brought their skills. The Huguenots were noted as merchants, cloth manufacturers, entrepreneurs, and bankers; and because New France had not welcomed them and their capabilities, it was deprived of their expertise, which went instead to the English—thus weakening New France by suppressing independence of thought and enterprise and keeping the population essentially feudal, leading to its eventual conquest. Needless to say, the French Protestants may not have been without a spirit of vengeance; it is noteworthy that Wolfe's army included some of them.[1]

It's intriguing to play What If with history. Had the Huguenots not been excluded from New France in 1627, Québec might not have fallen in 1759; if Québec had not fallen, the American Revolution would not have taken place, since the New England colonists could not have done without the support of England in any conflict with France; if the American Revolution had not taken place, Louis XVI would not have spent too much money helping the proto-Americans against the English, and American Republicanism would not have stirred things up, and there would not have been a French Revolution. So the two great revolutions of the eighteenth century—the granddaddies of all since—can trace their existence to an act of religious intolerance in Voltaire's remote and despised "few acres of snow." Oh, and as a side effect, there might never have been a Canada.

But in the century leading up to these events, French Catholics and English and Foreign Protestants were not the only forces in play during this slice of historical time: each side in the New France-New England conflict had its "Indian" allies. These were useful not only for pitched battles, but more especially for stealthy raids on the settlers of the other side. In the mid-eighteenth century, what is now New Brunswick was French Catholic territory, and the Malecite tribe were French Catholic

1. Michelle Gaudette, "Guerres de religion d'ici," in *Le Devoir*, July 26, 2000.

allies. These latter were encouraged to do whatever they could against the settlers brought to Nova Scotia by the English, and were promised rewards for their efforts. They had their own reasons too for raiding enemy settlements: like most tribes, theirs had been depleted by disease and warfare, and captured children, if young enough, could be adopted and raised as their own.

This is the background against which the following story is set. As far as its main facts go, it is entirely true. It came to me first through a family connection, involving intermarriage in the nineteenth century between the descendants of the murdered Louis Payzant and his widow Marie Payzant and the descendants of a Loyalist family which had fled New England at the time of the American Revolution—a revolution that was able to occur, paradoxically, because the threat of New France had now been removed. As a result of the fall of Québec, the Payzants were political and religious winners; though because of their exclusion from French society, they were eventually linguistic losers: they had to exchange their mother tongue for religious freedom. The Loyalists were political losers, but linguistic winners: they changed only their territory.

Such losses and gains, such compromises, such cross-cultural alliances, are not just a mark of today's Canadian society, but have been with us from the beginning.

THE BOMBARDMENT CONTINUES

(Translated from the French)

SEPTEMBER 8, 1759

The bombardment continues. Ever since July we have been under siege: the English are on Point Lévis, they cannot be dislodged, or so it is said in the town, and by the wounded soldiers who are brought in daily; and they batter away at us, slowly and methodically, in the dogged and maddening English way. They cannot climb the escarpment, the cliffs are too steep; they cannot breach the city walls as they are too thick; but they lob their cannonballs and incendiary missiles up and over and down onto our fine and well-built houses and the King's stone buildings like boys hurling rocks over a fence. It is a sort of continual and deadly jeering, and it is wearing the men here down because they cannot get at the English, any more than the English can get at them.

There will be the boom and then the crash, you never know where to expect it, and then the screams of the injured, and then there may be a fire, and the tumult and the yelling and running to and from with buckets to put it out. The miserable wet weather has in this respect been a help—at least the fires do not spread, as they would in a dry wind. But it is sad to see the destruction, and the wounds and carnage among the citizens, for whom I pray even though they are of the Devil's religion; and I hope they may yet be offered grace, and save their souls alive; and I cannot witness a fire without the vision of my own burning home rising before me on that dreadful night when I lost my dear husband; yet I thank God daily that you my dear children were saved alive, and I trust it was for some Divine purpose, and that all may yet be well.

I must write this hastily and in secret, but I do it for your sake, my children—should I die in the conflict and should you be spared, I should wish you to know a little of your dear Father, so ruthlessly murdered. I pray that God may forgive his killers, as they knew not what they did, but were set to act by others, and in pursuit of a war not their own.

SEPTEMBER 9, 1759

It is my task to help the Ursuline Nuns in caring for the wounded and the dying. They do not entirely trust me and so I am not permitted to comfort the afflicted, lest heresy seep in, and so my tasks are limited to adding up of the accounts, and the settling of their purchases, or such as can be made at this time, as I have much practice in this art, due to my experience in the cloth trade, which was also your Father's business; and it is in this way that I am able to obtain paper and ink, and to write this letter to you, when I am not observed. Sometimes I am sent to purchase food, though there is little enough of that to be had: old flour, sprouted barley, cabbages, salted cod, and not even much of that, and whatever wild game the Indians have managed to capture in the forests to the north of us; but the best must go to the soldiers. Soon we shall begin to eat the mice and rats, and I fear some have already begun to do this; and it is certain there are fewer stray dogs and cats than formerly. The English have the St-Laurent blockaded to the east of the city, so no ships make their way to us from France, even supposing the King to have sent any; though the general opinion is that we have been abandoned, and given up as a lost cause.

Our only hope is that we may receive a shipment of provisions from Montréal, as the land to the west of us has not yet been overrun by the English, or this is what is said by the scouts. But every day four or five of the English ships glide past us upriver with the tide, out of reach of our guns, and then glide down again as the tide reverses; and so it must be that they are pondering and observing, and planning in some way to cut us off from any fresh supplies, and then we must starve or surrender.

If only we might be granted an early winter—then, unless the English retreat, their ships would be frozen in, and crushed by the ice. When the cold sets in they will have to sail for home, or for some port in New England, tails between their legs, instead of burning the farms along the river shore as they do now, and pillaging the farmers—the unlucky *Canadiens*, the *habitants* as they call themselves, who come to the city if they can, and then there is even less food for us here.

But why do I say *us?* I am virtually a prisoner here, I must not forget that. Although I am allowed to walk about freely enough—where could I go, I cannot pass the walls of the city without observation, no more than any other soul here—they keep a sharp eye on me. They are not my friends at heart—even the Nuns, who have been as kind as their nature allows; even General Montcalm, who after you had been kidnapped and spirited away and hidden amongst the savage tribes, was—along with the Bishop—the means of having you restored to me, my dearest children.

SEPTEMBER 11, 1759

Now while time permits I must set down an account of the dismal events that left you fatherless, and were the cause of our journey to this place. Some of these sad scenes you will still remember, or the eldest children will; but my little Lisette, who was born in this place—of all this she is still happily ignorant.

Both your Father and I were born into the reformed faith, what is called by others the Huguenots. Those of our faith were once numerous in France, but in 1685—thirteen years before your Father's birth in Normandy—the King went back on his solemn promise, and revoked the Edict of Nantes, which had been our protection; and ever since that time we have been treated as little better than outlaws in that country, which we term amongst us the Desert. Our clergy were expelled, we ourselves were forbidden to worship, and were persecuted and imprisoned if we were caught doing so; our children were torn from us and sent to Roman Catholic schools or shut up in convents, for which we ourselves were forced to pay, at inflated prices. Drunken and violent soldiers—foreigners, some of them, savages with red hair, from Ireland, who did not even speak our language—were billeted with our families, at our expense, with orders to disrupt our households, destroy our goods, and corrupt our women and children, until we should bend under the weight of these afflictions and

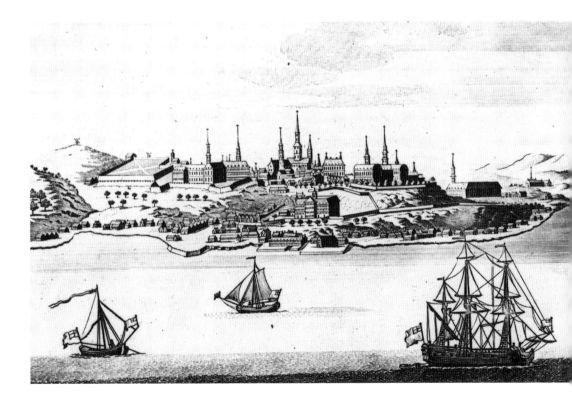

A perspective of Québec City, 1759. Engraved by Halett.

abjure our faith. Many fled, and sought shelter in England or the Netherlands or other countries, or across the seas; many died, both in prison and out of it.

Your late and much lamented Father, Louis Payzant, was of a respectable merchant family in Caen. I was his second wife, the first having died under dreadful circumstances having to do with these same inflictions and persecutions, which your Father would never discuss as it gave him too much pain. He then bravely determined to flee with his eldest daughter, who had been released from the convent where she was shut up, to attend her mother's funeral, in order to spare her from the fate intended for her, that is, that she should be forced to become a nun or to marry a husband of their choosing. This he did in secret, having hidden the two younger children with families outwardly Roman, but truly of our faith; leaving behind him sufficient of his goods to discharge any debts, for he was always honourable in his business dealings; and thus he became a religious fugitive, as such were called, and a hunted man, and could not return to France without great risk.

He went to the island of Jersey, ruled by the English, and re-established his business there; and my family having previously fled, and I having some experience of the trade in cloth, which was also your Father's, it was there we became acquainted, and were married, and where my four children were born, and the three little ones taken by God.

But the coast of France was not far away, and times were uncertain, and war between France and England never far away; in which case the Channel Islands would be menaced; and if they were taken, reprisals against your Father would have been severe. Thus when an offer was made by the English, of free land in their colony of Nova Scotia to any of the Protestant faith who would agree to emigrate, and to settle there, your Father after judicial investigations decided to remove us to that place, where he thought we would be safer; a vain hope in retrospect, but who could have foreseen it at the time? For in all things concerning the future, we see but through a glass, darkly.

At first all went well. We set sail in the summer of 1753, with our servants,

and much merchandise, and passed three years in establishing ourselves on the main-
land, after which time your Father had chosen what seemed to him the most advanta-
geous place for a trading post, namely, an island in Mahone Bay, easy of access by
boat and defended on all sides by water. After much exertion and many arrangements,
and considerable expense, our new home was freshly completed, and we installed in
it, by the May of 1756; and we tired but thankful, were fast asleep on the 8th of that
month, a date I will forever keep in memory as being the most unhappy of my life.

At midnight, hearing the dogs bark, your Father seized his musket and went
to the door and opened it, and fired into the air to warn and frighten any intruder;
whereupon he was on the instant shot through the heart, and fell on our very thresh-
old. I rushing to him in terror, was thrust away from him by the hands of a group of
Indians, unknown to us, but as it later proved of the tribe of the Malecites, set on by
the French from the coast north of New England—termed by them Acadia—who
had promised them payment for both scalps and prisoners, war having indeed broken
out as your Father had foreseen. They scalped your Father, waving the freshly bleeding trophy aloft, then broke into the room of our poor Servant, whom they murdered
in cold blood—both her and her two-year-old son, whose brains they dashed out by
swinging him by the feet against the wall; and they killed also the eleven-year-old boy
who had been forced to guide them to our island; it being generally their habit, when
on such excursions, to dispose of any who would be of no further use to them, and
who might not fetch a ransom.

In an agony of fear I gathered you together, my dear children, expecting that
we were to die at any minute; while, yelling horribly, the invaders proceeded to ran-
sack our goods and merchandise. Why we were spared by them I do not know; it was
a Divine mercy; perhaps we were saved by our language, they being confused by
finding the tongue of their allies spoken in the territory of their enemies, and thinking perhaps that some mistake had been made. For whatever reason we were herded
into their canoes, while they set fire to the house which had been our purpose and
goal; and the last view I had of it was of the raging pyre that consumed both your

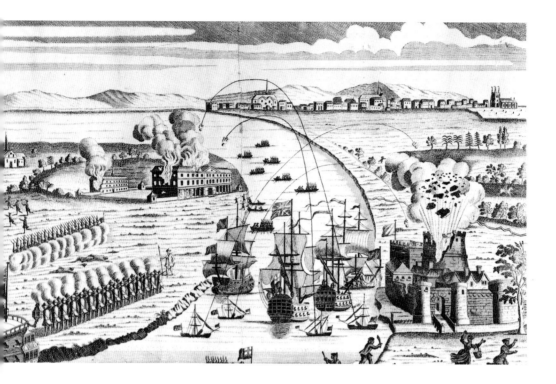

dear Father's corpse, and all our hopes together.

We were taken by secret ways through English territory and around the Bay of Fundy, under threat of death should we attempt to escape or give warning; and I was given to understand that if the youngest children could not stand the journey, or proved too troublesome and impeded our progress, they would be killed on the spot; but we were not otherwise ill-treated. At last we came to a French mission, called Sainte-Anne's, where we were presented with much satisfaction to the Jesuits resident there.

The Indians wanted to keep the children, for it is in this way that they replenish their numbers, their tribe having been much depleted both by illness and by the raids of the English—or so it was explained to me by the priests, who bargained on my behalf, as they took pity on my forlorn state; and indeed I was half mad with grief and horror, and had only preserved my sanity through your Father's memory and the need to protect you and to preserve your lives. At length it was decided that

The Siege and Taking of Québec with a View of the Glorious Battle before the Town, 1759. Engraving.

the Indians were to have two of the children, the other two remaining with the Jesuits; who said it was the best they could do, and assured me the children would not be harmed, but would be adopted by the Indians, and treated as their own, children being much valued among them. With this consolation I had to be content; and I was sent overland on another arduous journey to the city of Québec, bereft of both husband and children; and in that place I was at first imprisoned, and then placed with the nuns; and it was there my dear Louise was born, named for her Father and the only vestige of him remaining to me.

I considered it the lesser of evils to abjure my faith in order that Lisette might be baptized, and might remain with me; for otherwise she would be taken away; and after that I strongly petitioned to have the other children returned to me, in which after a time I was successful, promising that the boys would be sent to school to the Jesuit Academy here.

And now, my children, you know all; and having survived the past, we must await the future, with whatever fortitude we may muster; and I pray secretly each night, in the words of my true faith, for your safety and welfare.

SEPTEMBER 14, 1759

It is not possible, yet it has happened.

Yesterday morning, the 13th of September, when the sun rose—no, it had not yet risen. When the sky became light—but how can I report an occasion that I myself did not witness? But the accounts that I have heard state that suddenly, there was the English army—so all agree—as red as blood in their scarlet uniforms, drawn up in formation outside the walls of the city and ready for battle, where a scant eight hours previously there had been nothing but a farmer's field. Our good General—I may call him good now, for he is dead and never showed himself maliciously towards me and my children, but instead took pity on our misfortunes—our good General Montcalm is reported to have said, "I see them where they have no business to be." It must have been a very sudden surprise to him—how had the English come up the steep cliffs, in the middle of the night, past our sentries? It was like an act of sorcery—as if the Devil himself had flown up with them, one Englishman at a time—and our soldiers, being superstitious, were dismayed: perhaps their General Wolfe had made a bargain with the Evil One, it was whispered. He was known to be redheaded, which was thought to be a sign of an inclination towards the Satanic faction—

The Death of General Wolfe, ca. 1776. By Benjamin West from the Coverdale Collection of Canadiana.

or so these poor creatures thought. One of the Nuns told me that. As for the Indians, they said Wolfe must have a magic bone, and that success in the battle to come would depend on somehow getting this bone away from him and burning it. All of what I set down here is rumour, but with any besieged as long we had been, and as hungry as we were by then, rumour has the force of a cannon. What we could all tell was that General Wolfe and his men now stood between us and any hope of provisions arriving from Montréal.

General Montcalm decided to give battle. He decided to take the entire garrison force and ride out and engage. What else could he have done? He could have waited, I suppose; but it was only the middle of September, and winter could be a month or two away, and we might all be dead by then.

We saw them marching out through the gates; the Indians too, although these did not march but were intended for skirmishers and snipers. Perhaps it was one such that killed General Wolfe, for he too is now dead.

We saw them marching out, and although Jean went up onto the ramparts to watch, that is all we knew until our own army in disarray came flying back, the enemy on their heels. The English had withstood the shock of our attack, some of them lying down so that the shot went over their heads, and had held their own fire until our men were quite close; whereupon all discharged their guns at once, which turned the tide. It was like a bolt of lightning and a thunderclap, and the effect was momentous. In the noise and confusion our ranks were broken, and once such a flight begins it becomes general. Nor is it a question of bravery, as often there is not enough time for that. Battles for the earth, as battles for the soul, are often determined in an instant—or so my dear Louis used to say, and he had some knowledge of such things.

And now we are penned up inside the city, with the English in control of all approaches and our General dead. Fear and uncertainty hold sway; some of the Indians have slipped away under cover of darkness, as they evidently do not like their chances. The Nuns are tending the wounded, those who have been brought in; I fear that many still lie on the field, a prey to wolves and to the tender mercies of our foes.

STORY *of* a NATION

When not engaged in these duties the Nuns are on their knees—I believe they have not slept for days—they are convinced the English will run us through, or worse, the children too. I pray as well, using the words that are necessary but with other words in my heart; and the same God must hear us both, as there is only One.

SEPTEMBER 18, 1759

Yesterday the city was surrendered. The flag of France was lowered and that of the English was raised. I ought to have been glad, because now I will be free; we will all be free, my dear children, and may leave this place where we were brought against our wills, after so much suffering. All that it will be necessary for me is to reveal my true religion to the English leaders, and tell my story to them, and I am sure I will be allowed to return to Nova Scotia to claim your Father's land, which I will do for your sakes; although I would not have the heart to settle there, on that island now forever haunted; but will sell it, and take us elsewhere to some new place where there is no blood in the soil.

Yet whatever I do, I find I must betray something. Here in this city—in what was but yesterday New France, but is no longer, and has no name—I was at least able to speak a language that all around me could understand. True, it was also the language of the Desert—of those who drove us from our native soil, who oppressed and persecuted us, who stole our children and forced them to renounce their faith, who tortured and imprisoned us and did not stop at murder; but it was my own language too and the language of my prayers. Whereas there, I will be among foreigners of all kinds; and worse, I will face an inevitable and melancholy reality— that you, my own children, will grow up speaking nothing but English, a hard and stubborn and wooden language I will never be able to master sufficiently to make my meaning plain in it.

It cannot be helped. As Scripture says, we are but strangers and sojourners on this earth; and must look to the life to come, where all will speak in the same language, and will understand the tongues of angels.

I will keep this account for you, my children, and place it in good hands in our new home, if by God's grace we shall arrive at one, wherever it may be found; and should I die I trust that it will be delivered to you, when you are old enough to read it; and that it will provide you, if not with comfort, at least with understanding. And in the meantime I sign myself,

Your eternally loving mother,

Marie Payzant

NOTES

The source for the account of the battle was John Keegan's excellent book, *Fields of Battle: The Wars for North America* (Knopf: New York, 1996). I was first told about Marie Payzant by my aunt, Joyce Barkhouse. There are various accounts of Marie Payzant's ordeal; I have relied on the well-researched paper by Linda G. Wood, "Marie Payzant of France, Lunenburg and Falmouth," presented at Acadia University, 1997. The proceeds from this story will go to the drastically besieged Woodcock Fund, care of the Writers' Trust.

Antonine Maillet

THE GREAT DISTURBANCE
ACCORDING TO BÉLONIE

Don't look for this story in books—you're liable to find it and that would be a pity.

All the headings, the titles and subtitles, statistics, the dates and theses and antitheses, have gnawed at its mystery and flooded its soul. And a story without a soul does not deserve to cross the bar of Time. Yet this story is alive, alive in body and soul, buried somewhere in some refractory and stubborn memories, and it's waiting. Waiting for storytellers who don't tell history the way historians do, that is, as it happened, but in their own way, the only true way, which is the one that you want to hear.

I've dug it out bit by bit, violating the most reluctant consciences, taking an axe to the hard heads of some old folks who wanted nothing but to go to sleep in peace . . . To sleep? Oh no, not that! Not before you hand down to the son of the son of your son the scraps of history that your father's father's father handed down to you one winter night.

And so, link by link, I went back to my ancestor Bélonie, who was nearly a

Winslow reading the Proclamation for the Expulsion of Acadians. A wood engraving on paper, late nineteenth–early twentieth century.

hundred years old in 1770 and all decked out for his final journey, sure that no one would ever come back to hound him as he stood at the edge of his grave and try to extract his last memories.

MEMORIES THAT WENT BACK TO THE 1713 Treaty of Utrecht, which had permanently sealed the fate of a country that the French and English kings had been fighting over for a century, flinging charters back and forth across the Channel that changed the name of Acadia to Nova Scotia, then back to Acadia, to Nova Scotia, to Acadia again . . . a promised land that no king of France or England had yet laid eyes on but that Bélonie dreamed of passing on to his descendants.

Dreamed of until 1755.

Alas! In one night a single calamity had taken everything away. At the age of seventy-five, Bélonie had seen his house, his barns, and his harvests go up in flames, and he'd seen half his people perish. The other half went into exile on an English ship that in less than two days was engulfed in the eye of a hurricane. At the prow of a vessel that was taking him to a foreign land along with the remainder of his compatriots, Bélonie watched his lineage disappear on the horizon. After that he was merely an old man.

Fifteen years later that same old man would gather up Pélagie in her cart to bring her back from exile to the land of Acadia. A stubborn, cantankerous old man. Why? Why leave Georgia? Why go back to an Acadia now dead and bereft of descendants? Because, Pélagie, Bélonie had already made a pact with the Grim Reaper. If he were to travel up the coast of America again, it would be in the cart of Death, not that of the living. But Pélagie, who had survived half her people, was determined to bring them home come hell or high water and despite God, the Devil, and Fate. In the end she managed to cram into her cart—against his will—that bundle of flesh and shrieks and memory who had just enough time to tune his creaking with the clattering of the wheels before he blinked at the dark coach, without doors or lanterns and drawn by six blazing black horses that had been travelling the world since the beginning of time: the cart of Death.

"If nobody's ever seen it, who can say if that cart is black?"

Bélonie doesn't answer Pélagie. He is determined not to waste his spit on pointless questions. There's not a man alive who's ever seen Death, yet everyone knows it. Has anyone ever seen the Devil with his horns, the archangel Saint Michael leaning on his spear? Bélonie would haul his own cart, like it or not, Pélagie, all the way to lost Acadia. The dead were more numerous than the living and they too deserved to spend their eternity in the Promised Land.

The old man, brailed in the midst of the rigging and paraphernalia for the journey, grumbles.

"Promised Land, eh? Hasn't kept any promises. Who's going to inherit this Acadia that's been burned to its roots, raped, obliterated, wiped off the face of the earth? Does anyone still dream of it? Certainly not Bélonie, who was unable to rescue a single descendant from the calamity. They were all swallowed up, mowed down to the last of the offspring, an infant whose eyes were barely open. He would return to the ancestors with the others, but in the funeral cart, the one that Bélonie was pulling, unbeknownst to the others, that was joined to Pélagie's convoy by an invisible thread. And they're off to the north, all the dead!

Pélagie doesn't respond to the old crackpot's muttering, she continues to haul scraps of Acadia the length of an America that can't even hear the creaking axles of her cart. She'll make her way on foot, through forests and swamps, in search of a piece of earth in which to plant her roots that are more unkempt than drifting water weeds. Like the others, Bélonie will bury his memory-laden bones there. Memories! As for memories, Bélonie, you've got twenty more years of them than the oldest of the survivors, more than Charles's Charles, more than Anne-Marie-Françoise, than Gimpy Célina, you're an indispensable link in the transmission which, if it weren't for you . . .

"History can get along without me," mumbles the grouch. "I'm not saying anything, there's no need for the dead to testify. I'm no longer of your world. You wanted me to be part of the convoy at any price? Too bad! The Grim Reaper, whose dark cart is transporting all my descendants, their names inscribed on my own tombstone, will be my only travelling companion. Hee!"

Life was moving dead ahead on that September morning at Grand Pré, and it let us plunge into a bottomless crater. Memory was returned to the earth. What a shame! Bélonie would have had so many stories to tell!

It was a century and a half since Champlain and Marc Lescarbot founded the Neptune Theatre and the Order of Good Cheer at Port Royal to help get through the first winters without losing heart. And then, little by little, the plot of land becomes a property and the land becomes a country. A hundred years of good living on free and fertile soil where generations of Bélonies built *aboîteaux*, those dams that would let them steal the land from the ocean, they filled cellars and attics, sang at High Mass on Sunday, danced at their children's weddings, passed on from throat to throat the oldest words from France, words that borrowed a lilting intonation and a rugged accent from the wind and tides of a new climate. It was a life that was constantly recreating itself, every morning. For all eternity.

An eternity that comes to a sudden stop one September morning. To the amazement of the wise old patriarchs and the prophets of good fortune, history now collapses, tearing up pacts and treaties, locking men inside the church at Grand Pré where they'll be read a letter from His Joyous British Majesty who absolves them of their treason and ships them without due process to the land of exile. An entire people deported along the coast of America, from Georgia to New England. All right! Into the marshes, the woods—and we'll remake our lives as best we can.

Bélonie muses that events have unfurled at such a pace on this September morning, he hasn't had time to shake off his ancestral beliefs or learn a new way of looking at the world, that in fifteen years he's been unable to adopt a new country which was rammed down his throat against his will. After they've cut off his roots and stripped his buds, he's now being asked to remember . . . But what is he to do with a muzzled memory? He had seen the last of his race sink into the sea, he'd seen the child swept away before his eyes were open . . . That was when the old man lost his memory.

"Bélonie! Bélonie!"

Someone shakes him, interrupting his reflections.

"Bélonie! There's somebody asking for you—a young fellow named Bélonie, son of Thaddée son of Louis son of Bélonie. He's just landed in the Salem marshes. And he says that . . ."

The old man raises his head and stares hard at the newcomer.

"Thaddée . . . son of Louis . . . son of Bélonie . . . ?" Pélagie clears a path through the bystanders and puts her hand on the old man's shoulder. The patriarch is nearing his hundredth birthday, mustn't upset him with some tall tale. There are no more Bélonie descendants, but the messenger dares to confront Pélagie. He pushes aside the young apparition who claims to be a direct descendant of the Grand Pré Bélonies.

"Seems he was picked up at sea a good fifteen years ago, by Captain Beausoleil in person. And he's been sailing the seven seas ever since."

Though Bélonie listens as hard as he can, creases his eyes, scrunches up his face around his nose, he can't grasp it. Because the impossible cannot be fathomed. History doesn't repeat itself and it doesn't run backwards. An eddy's not created in the same wake twice.

And Pélagie says:

"Come on, Bélonie, try to remember. That youngster who was lost at sea— what was his name?"

"Didn't have a name . . . wasn't even baptized."

Just then the young man breaks away, approaches the old man, and before Pélagie has time to let him know that Bélonie isn't deaf, shouts in his ear:

"I was baptized for days and days, so they say, before Beausoleil's sailors fished me out of my wicker basket that was floating on the sea off Sable Island. So they say."

All eyes are fixed on Bélonie. A long silence hangs in the air. Then they turn

to the newcomer who hastens to reply to the numerous question marks darting from them.

"So what happened was, it took them years to trace back where I came from. They'd even decided to call me Moses-saved-from-the-water. Then one day Captain Beausoleil brings a full cargo of deportees back from the West Indies to take to the Gaspé Peninsula . . ."

"The Gaspé? Why would he take them to the Gaspé?"

"Why? Because back then the Gaspé Peninsula was still French, that's why."

"What d'you know about it?"

"Quiet, you. Let the man talk."

The young man smiles, snorts, and resumes:

"Now, one of the deportees was an old, old woman who remembered that from the coast of Sable Island she'd seen with her own eyes the witch of the wind swallow up a ship with all hands."

"The hurricane!" stammers Old Bélonie.

Little by little, all the carts listen to the very end of the tale of the young survivor, the sole survivor of the famous shipwreck, a child who had emerged

Exile of the Acadians from Grand Pré from G.D. Warburton, "The Conquest of Canada,"
(London, 1850). Wood engraving on paper.

miraculously safe and sound from the mouth of the hurricane. The old woman who'd been deported to the West Indies was all set to swear an oath that after the storm had passed, she'd spotted a basket adrift on the water. She'd tried to get hold of it but the sea was stronger.

"She's the one who recognized my wicker cradle in the hold of Beausoleil's boat. And told me that I must be the son of Louis son of Thaddée son of Bélonie. And that very day she named me after the first of my line."

The centenarian turns to look at the funeral cart, and for the first time in fifteen years, he thumbs his nose majestically at the Grim Reaper. Hee!

For days at a time, the older Bélonie takes his great-grandson aside, out of range of inquisitive ears, and talks to him. Talks till his own mouth is parched. Time is short. His memory came back to him all at once when he locked eyes with his one and only heir. But not for long. He made too strong an undertaking to the Reaper fifteen years ago, he knows that she won't give him a lot of rope *dumeschui*.

"*Dumeschui*, Grandpa?"

"Means 'from now on.' You have got to pack these words inside that skull of yours, young fellow—words that the south wind's liable to carry away. Words so old that only ancient mouths still know how to say them without skinning them alive."

Now Young Bélonie will have to learn to tell tales like an old man. The sole offspring of a long lineage, a young scalawag barely fifteen years of age, every day came back with bulging eyes and mouth agape from the bushes where the patriarch took him. Away from the caravan of carts, the old man kneaded the youth's memory and imagination like a baker kneading his bread. There's no time to waste. In the centuries to come Young Bélonie would be charged with transmitting the only legacy that was saved from the calamity of 1755: memory.

Tell the story, Bélonie.

About the refusal to swear unconditional loyalty to the king of England.

About the fire in the church and the dwellings nestled all along the French Bay, also known as the Back Bay.

About an entire people packed into the holds of ships, individuals who hadn't finished getting in their last crops.

About children torn from their mothers' arms and mothers from the arms of their men, a number of whom would be shot at point-blank range as they headed for the woods.

About families broken up and abandoned on inhospitable shores, often driven back towards the sea, wandering along the coast between Maryland, Pennsylvania, the Carolinas, Georgia.

About the Thibodeau family who'd got separated from Pélagie's convoy to embark on the grand adventure of Louisiana where already some Landrys, Martins, and Cormiers were hiding.

About Pélagie's dream of bringing the remains of her family back to their ancestral land after fifteen years of exile, of hitching them to the side panels of her cart despite resistance by the fearful and the lazy, despite the risk of famine, cold, epidemics.

About the slow ascent towards the Promised Land, on tiptoe so as not to waken the sleeping bear. A caravan that takes the back roads up the coast of America, quietly, unbeknownst to history which in those years had its head turned more to skirmishes between the English colonies and the mother country. To the point that when the bells of Philadelphia rang to celebrate American independence, the Acadians hiding in the bushes heard a death knell.

Old Bélonie falls silent. He won't have enough time to tell the rest. His great-grandson, may God grant him life, will be the only one to know the outcome of this epic of a people already sidelined by history. But history alone does not decide on a people's fate. Life that stirs in the guts, that rubs against the hearts to which remnants of feelings cling, that lights up brains steeped in memories they can't shake off—life is sometimes stronger and more persistent than Fate. Get that into your thick skull, Young Bélonie. Because the old man will not continue. He's made a date . . .

The patriarch turns his head towards his cart, the one that's transporting his tombstone. Let her come now. Old Bélonie isn't a man to keep a lady waiting. And along comes the Lady.

"Is it you, Bélonie?"

"Get out of my way and let me in."

"Are you in that big a hurry?"

"I'm aching to know."

"To know?"

"To know the end of the story I've been given the job of telling."

"I'll keep quiet, you won't learn a thing."

"I don't expect to hear it from you."

Silence.

"You fooled me, you miserable creature, making me think I was the last of my line. But the Bélonies won't disappear with the babbling old crackpot of a drivelling fool of a stripper of the memory of a people. History can pipe down if it doesn't feel like opening the pages that make its great book creak. We can get along without history."

"You aren't even in my cart yet and you're already rambling!"

"I've got one foot on the step of your cart, and besides, I know. I know that memory will be passed on from household to household, from century to century, from Bélonie to Bélonie. The story will be told."

"But all of you to the very last will end up in my cart, you know that perfectly well."

"In the past, they'd have all told the story."

The Reaper swoops her scythe under the feet of the centenarian who has just enough time to wink at life and send out a final "Hee!"

Old Bélonie could go now. By the fireside, Young Bélonie would tell it to his son Bélonie, the third to bear the name, who would tell it to Thaddée, son of Bélonie, who would tell it to Bélonie, son of Thaddée, who would pass it on to Louis, son of Bélonie Maillet, who is my cousin.

And my cousin repeated the same remark that had been left hanging by his father Bélonie, fifth to bear the name, who expired in the manner of every male of his line: with a wink at life before he set his left foot—for good luck—on the step of the cart of Death.

A remark that's two centuries long.

To the stars, two centuries is nothing. No more than it is to the eyes of history, which have seen the birth and decline of Mesopotamia, Egypt, Greece, and Rome, and for more than two thousand years, exhausted itself following the rise and fall of a western world lashed by political and religious storms. With the convulsions of empires and the dizzying leaps of civilizations, history was much too busy to look into the affairs of a few scattered families shivering in the face of their first winter deep in the Memramcook Valley. History looks down on the world from too high up to take notice of Pélagie's heirs who every morning aspire to nothing more than making it through till evening, till the next day, a day at a time, during a chronicle that is also known as "little history," so little that it doesn't even dare to raise its eyes to the big history which hasn't deigned to notice, through the mist from the marshes strewn along the American coast, the return of the native-born to the land that gave them birth.

Young Bélonie alone understood and he announced that the Great Disturbance was over and that they'd just entered the small one.

Still, the throaty voice of the Bélonies, husky and rugged, could only make itself heard to those seeking relatives, who could have been called chroniclers or even genealogists if they'd had such pretensions; for every one of them had at his fingertips, backwards and forwards both, his ancestral line going back sixteen or thirty-two generations, and didn't stumble over even one great-grandmother who'd died in childbirth.

They could tell you that on the day after Pélagie, along with what's left of her cart, is laid in her grave in the Tantramar Marshes, her daughter Madeleine takes a compassionate look at her twin brothers flopped on the moss of a hill that's known

in the local language as a *montain*. Charles and Coco are tired of searching for a horizon that's been slipping away from them ever since they left Georgia ten years ago, cursing the life that had brought them into this world and burying their memories deep inside them so it would never come back to haunt their sleep. The children of Acadia no longer know where they are, they can no longer find the places where they used to live, which the enemy took over a quarter-century before. They turn their heads to the south, the east, the north, then freeze there like recumbent statues carved into the everlasting rock.

The storyteller Young Bélonie is gazing at these final witnesses of a moribund past when he sees their sister Madeleine stand up, grab hold of an axe, and fell her first tree.

"What I'm doing," she says, "I'm planting the posts for our house. Get up, you lazybones! The future lies ahead."

And the lazybones tear themselves away from their pedestal, breathe the damp air of the Memramcook Valley, and turn in every direction in search of a future that may perhaps respond to their children's desperate call.

While waiting and hiding from the prowling enemy, they clear an ungrateful

The Expulsion of the Acadians. By Charles Copeland.

land, they work the soil with a wooden plough, they plant, harvest, store, and gaze with envy at the great *V* of the wild geese that go back up north every spring. And each of them says that a wild goose that takes the trouble to fly so high, so far, has surely sensed the proper place to build its nest in full security.

"Gédaïque," cry the geese, "come to the Sea of Gédaïque . . . come to Barachois, to Grand Digue, to Cocagne . . . Come and settle in Bouctouche and Richibucto . . . Go up, go north, towards Tracadie, Caraquet, Miscou . . . Come, come! Disperse!" cry the wild geese.

And so after the chapter on the Deportation comes the one on the Dispersal of the Acadians. They make their way along the coast, dragging their household across the ice in winter or burrowing deep in the woods as a precaution so they won't be vulnerable to enemy attack.

"If you settle near waterways, cut down the trees around your houses. You'll be like wild animals, leaving yourselves without cover so you can see hunters approaching from a distance."

Says a wise old man.

Is that the reason then why so many dwellings along the coast are so oddly exposed? Yes, for that reason and also to exploit every plot of arable land: the fields at the edge of the woods for oats, clover, and hay; the space in front of the house for the vegetable garden that will provide the soup.

But each man knows that the surest way to stand up to time, which wears away as well as building up, is to fill it up as it's draining away. For a couple who are dying out, twelve or fifteen offspring come to eat from their bowl. And why not seventeen or twenty in the next generation? Besides, the winters are long and night comes early in northern lands . . . So we see the Goguens marrying Després, the Bourgeois marrying Landrys, the Richards marrying Caissies, the Légers marrying Girouards and Arsenaults, the Maillets marrying Allains, Cormiers, Bourques, and the LeBlancs marrying everybody. A flock of frisky youngsters who swarm about and mate and start to go timidly out onto their doorsteps to sniff the weather. And one day someone says the weather's fine and they can take a chance and emerge from the woods.

This happens in 1880.

"Little history" isn't written in millennia like the other kind, it's passed on by word of mouth, day by day. And yet the history of Acadia gives the impression that it wants to be played out a century at a time.

A century after the return of Pélagie who brought her people home, the descendants of the carts go out on their front steps and shout from one property to the next, from island to promontory to peninsula:

"Any of our people over there? Have you got any Thibodeaus, Robichauds, Collettes, Savoies with you? Where have all the Godins and the Bastaraches got to?"

And Chéticamp tells Caraquet that a branch of the Chiassons have settled on Cape Breton Island like they did on their northern peninsula; and Baie Sainte-Marie sends their stream of Belliveaus and Comeaus flying in the face of their cousins on the land; and the Arsenaults on Prince Edward Island—which was called Île Saint-Jean way back when —extend their arms to those who had fled the English redcoats a century earlier and found refuge on the Gaspé Peninsula.

"Where are the Maillets?"

"Over here!"

"Where's that?"

"On Île Madame! And along St. Mary's Bay."

"And they're all over Back Bay!"

"We're everywhere!" yells Thaddée, son of Louis son of Bélonie.

And they all understand that it's high time for a family reunion.

There's been so much said about the national convention of 1881! Foreign historians have talked about it, and come-from-away journalists and historiographers and sociologists, even some archeologists who tried to unearth the fossils of a vanished tribe. But no one thought of inviting the Bélonies to speak, though they were the only ones who saw the reunion at Memramcook with their own eyes, the way it was lived by the ordinary people of the land.

"Memramcook called its children from all over," said one of them. "And from all over, the dispersed appeared from between those little mounds of sand called *buttereaux*, and the *montains*, stepping over fences, springs, and *aboiteaux*. They came on foot or by sleigh, wearing caps or hard hats or top hats; they came in delegations or in family groups, fiddles under their arms and mouth organs in their back pockets. All of them from the Great Disturbance a century and a half before."

No one could believe their eyes when they saw so many people coming to celebrate their rebirth, one short century—one long century—after they'd been wrenched from the grave of deportation. Each one tapped his neighbour on the shoulder and asked how he'd made so many children in just three generations.

"Twenty-two for Hilarion Haché, but with two wives."

"That's nothing. Philémon Boudreau made nineteen with just one."

"Twenty-three from one marriage for handsome Xavier Doucet. We should put up a statue for that one."

"No need to put anything up for him, he does pretty well on his own."

"Oh!"

By then the convention was off to a good start, in the manner of the country. It would go on for two days, three if you count the conclusion which concluded again and again with:

"Come for a visit!"

"See you in a while!"

"I'm in the fifth house after the bushes, along what they call Four House Road."

But before scattering once again, Acadia had time to give herself a patron saint, Our Lady of the Assumption, who had watched over Louis XIII three centuries before; a flag, the French tricolour flanked by the star of the sea in the blue part, to show her line of descent while setting the new people apart from the old one; and a national anthem, "Ave Maris Stella," which makes Acadia the only country in the world outside the Vatican that sings its glory in Latin—and doesn't understand a word of it.

And so, thus armed, Acadia could set out to search for her soul and to conquer her freedom. She had a hundred years to give herself a church, schools, the rights of full-fledged citizens. A hundred years is a short time to assert the existence of a people; but it's long for those who have a sense of time and the habit of playing with history. In the face of a wolf, the fox has no choice but to try and outsmart him. When you're armed with neither claws nor teeth you learn to use cunning, to scheme, to surprise, to slip in through the slightest opening, to make others laugh if need be.

There was once a people looking for a bishop. That people, who had lost its sovereign, who'd had only the king of France and the pope in Rome as guides and masters, turned towards the Church. But the Church had to go through the bishop and the Acadian bishop—was Irish. How could they get a bishop from Rome whose name was Robichaud, Melanson, LeBlanc—without going through the hierarchy? How to get around the archbishop of Halifax? How to tell Rome that the faithful who spoke French wanted to pray in their own language?

"Go and tell the pope," suggests the most intrepid.

"But how? Who's going to talk for us in Rome?"

"Say, what's the name of the parish priest in Scoudouc?"

"It's Father . . ."

It's Father Jean l'Archevêque—an archbishop in name if not in fact—as another non-bishop might be called René Lévesque. And he goes to Rome and he introduces himself as Archevêque de Scoudouc and he asks for an audience with the pope. And he tells Pius X that he is none other than the humble parish priest of Scoudouc whose existence Pius X isn't even aware of though he'll learn that day about the existence of a people who've been faithful to his Church for over three centuries. And apparently Rome burst out laughing and promised a bishop to this people who were poor but clever.

And that's how history gets written when it eavesdrops at the doors of legend.

Then someone tells Acadia that it should learn how to vote, in spite of those who try to frighten them in the manner of the Ku Klux Klan. One of the Bélonies even realizes there are enough of them to tip the balance if they all vote the same way. Oh, what are you getting mixed up in, Bélonie! If there's one people in the world who won't have its electoral behaviour dictated, it's this one, which is quite unabashedly descended from the medieval period when the parade of madmen and the game of king for a day were invented as a way of scoffing at power. The Acadians would go to the polls out of duty and self-interest, but above all for their own enjoyment. Because the squabbling between Grits and Tories on election eve would be one of the greatest entertainments these theatre lovers would allow themselves. The crudest insults, the most colourful comebacks in their dramatic repertoire, come from political confrontations between neighbours when both their parties are sure they won't win anything in the election the next day.

Until 1960, when Acadia wins with the election of Louis Robichaud.

She wins schools, the recognition of her language and rights, and finally, her university. She wins the admiration of her fellow countrymen from sea to sea on the day she founds a law school where British Common Law is taught, translated into French—a first—to offer a fair and honourable defence to a small people who just the day before were fighting in English against a mayor called Leonard Jones and the Moncton City Hall. An arduous battle if ever there was one, but an artful one as well. The battle between fox and wolf. He who is without teeth to bite has to settle for cunning. For laughter too, if possible. And on two continents, everything seemed possible to the students of 1968.

In France, General de Gaulle, with great military pomp, faced down thousands of students who had taken to the streets to demand more openness and freedom. In Moncton in the middle of the night, a pyjama-clad Mayor Jones faced down a delegation of three students who were bringing him as a gift the symbol of their gratitude: the head of a pig. To demand the right to speak their language with impunity.

Then came 1980, bicentennial of the death of Pélagie who was buried in the Tantramar Marshes, at the crossroads of Acadia. Two short—or two long—centuries. Long enough to give her descendants time to ponder and manipulate her history, then to write it. For in the meantime, Acadia had gone from an oral to a written tradition, from anonymity to recognition. Another few years and recognition would take the form of opulent reunions that would rally her children scattered around the world. Thousands of Acadians, descendants of Acadians, friends of Acadians,

Remains of Old Fort Louisbourg, Nova Scotia.

Acadians through marriage, Acadians who don't know that they're Acadians, first cousins, second cousins, third, and sixth cousins who've materialized on three continents and who knows how many countries—they all came home in 1994 to prepare for the grand celebration in 2004, four centuries after Champlain's arrival at Port Royal.

If Old Bélonie had known when he passed on to his great-grandson the sole heritage to escape the calamity of 1755—memory—if he'd been able to guess what the thousands of descendants of the carts would do after two centuries, he wouldn't have thumbed his nose at the Grim Reaper who'd been scoffing at him from her dark cart; he'd have delivered a kick in the ass!

(Translated from the French by Sheila Fischman)

Alberto Manguel

AN ACT OF ATONEMENT

(The Red River Colony, 1826)

The American continent is a bookish invention.

The Europeans who arrived with (and after) Columbus barely saw the land they thought they had discovered. Instead, they believed they recognized in the people and the forests of the so-called New World a geography, a mythology, a fauna, and a flora which had been described in vivid detail in countless travel books. The names of the lands they invaded reflected their reading: El Dorado, the city of gold; the Amazon, kingdom of the warrior maidens; Patagonia, the realm of giants with huge feet (in Spanish, *Patagones*). The early chronicles of the conquistadores describe dragons, basilisks, unicorns, manticores, flying serpents, and sirens, all part of the American landscape. On one of his voyages, near the island that one day would be called Cuba, Columbus saw a mermaid (probably a manatee), and after duly noting its appearance, he added with a touch of regret: "But they are not as beautiful as we have been led to believe."

So powerful were these literary influences (even in men who read little but were born in cultures where the Book held the truth) that the Spanish Office of Indies, under pressure from the Holy Inquisition, decreed an embargo on all books of

An Ojibwa woman and her child, Red River Settlement, Manitoba, 1858.

fiction imported to the colonies. The measure was stronger in its intent than in its effectiveness: works of fiction poured into the Americas where Don Quixote and Orlando, Robinson Crusoe and Gulliver, acquired a vast and devoted following.

In spite of the caution of the Spanish officials, the invaders came with their libraries. It is a small point of honour for me that the first town established in the Americas with its own library was my native Buenos Aires, in 1580, when the Adelantado Don Pedro de Mendoza founded it for the second time, not far from where the natives had reduced the earlier settlement to ashes. In an enlightened gesture, Mendoza offered his books to the new settlers, among whom was Rodrigo de Ahumada, brother of Saint Teresa of Avila. There is a copy of a vague collection of sermons, printed in Cadiz in 1530, that bears the signature of Mendoza on the flyleaf and that I was able to hold in my hands some thirty years ago, with talismanic pleasure, in the old National Library of Buenos Aires, imagining that someone who had embraced Saint Teresa had also touched those same yellow pages.

The old metaphor that sees a library as the memory of a people seems especially true in young countries such as Canada, since it includes not only the experience of both early and recent newcomers but also the wisdom of the peoples who were here long before books came into being. For me, the landscape of Canada is less the picture-postcard image of our wilderness (for all its persistent beauty) than the extraordinary and brave libraries that, in spite of the imbecility of governments, federal and provincial, continue to survive across our country. My map of Canada is dotted with such bastions: the generous and comfortable Metro Library in Toronto (where, after Mike Harris's budget cuts had forced a reshuffle of the sections, I was told by an exhausted clerk that "Literature is now History"); the tiny, beautiful Memorial Library in Calgary, constantly threatened with closure; the vast new Reference Library in Vancouver, as popular as a mall; the erudite Municipal Library of Winnipeg; the venerable Bibliothèque de la Ville de Montréal; the wonderfully efficient National Library in Ottawa; the Jesuit College Library in Québec City that dates back to 1635; the cosy Municipal Library of Owen Sound, Ontario; the friendly

Library of Campbell River, British Columbia; the stately Halifax Library; the Thomas Fisher Rare Book Library, the Judith Merril Science-Fiction and Fantasy Library, the Osborne Collection of Children's Literature—all three in Toronto; dozens of struggling university libraries . . . It will surprise no one to discover that the Great Canadian Event that fired my imagination was the foundation (and destruction) of one of the first libraries in English Canada.

The earliest Canadian library of which we have documentary proof is the one that belonged to Marc Lescarbot, a French scholar who arrived in Port-Royal, Nova Scotia, in 1606, and there is evidence of a children's library established some fifteen years later by Marie Rollet Hébert in Québec City, where the good woman read to the young from the lives of saints and from compilations of cautionary tales.

In English Canada, though there were attempts at setting up libraries such as the one described in my story, the first permanent Red River Library was founded twenty-one years after the great flood, in 1847, by Colonel Crofton. Peter Fidler's books (which miraculously escaped the flood) formed part of this new library. All the facts in the story (except for the burning of the Sankt-Katharienenthal Library, a place that owes much, in my imagination, to the great Abbey Library of Sankt Gall) are true, including that of the Swiss mercenary army serving in India under a British flag and then coming to the Red River Settlement. Most of the information concerning these events can be found in W. L. Morton's entertaining *Manitoba* (2nd edition, 1967).

AN ACT OF ATONEMENT
(The Red River Colony, 1826)

THE MAN WHO ARRIVED at the Red River Colony in 1821 had left his village near the Rheinwaldhorn, embarked on the *Ausdauer* from Hamburg, crossed a desolate Atlantic for several monotonous months, and after landing in some dismal port along the St. Lawrence, had crossed the vastness of the Great Lakes, paddled (or rather, been paddled) along brown and ill-tasting waters, often having to haul the boat against the current through low-lying and slippery mudbanks for endless days, until he reached a Scottish hamlet sometimes known as Point Douglas, from where he had tracked south to the site the late Lord Selkirk had envisioned as a new Thule, near the junction of the Red and Assiniboine rivers.

Weariness did not blur the strangeness of the place. Back home, the fir trees and lakes complemented one another, framing the Swiss landscape against the background of imposing but never quite overwhelming mountains. Here, instead, the land had no frame, no order. Trees grew scattered in every direction or not at all, allowing only patches to spring up in odd corners, as if mange had crept over the endless red earth. There were strips and puddles of dark water everywhere that swelled or shrank according to the mood of the clouds. The coast of either river (who could tell which was which?) seemed ripped out of the land by a hand shaking with palsy, and the very horizon that would have defined a space innocent of mountains wavered in a haze of heat, smoke, and clouds of mosquitoes.

Everything he touched was dry as dust, and yet smelled rotten.

To the other Swiss immigrants, he had said that his name was Erich; they accepted this with indifference, since to them every village in their mountains was like their own, and even if they had never set foot in another, they knew that each had its church, its school, several herds of brown cattle, and a dozen or so Erichs. He had arrived in their village on the day the notice had been posted by Lord Selkirk's agents on the door of the Reformed Calvinist church, inviting able-bodied men to be the settlers of a new land, "rich, vast, and peaceful." A terrible winter and more than the customary number of dead convinced a handful of them that the call for adventure was a sign from Heaven to leave their cursed home. Throughout the region, even the spring had not brought relief: several cows had fallen sick and given birth to stillborn calves, a blight had smitten the cabbage crop, and the archbishop's library in the Abbey of Sankt-Katharienenthal had been severely damaged by a mysterious fire.

The other immigrants never asked Erich why he wanted to join them. They packed crates with clothes, tools, a few musical instruments. His bag contained only a second pair of trousers, three or four shirts, and several books. The pastor asked him to join them in prayer. He did, repeating the words his father had taught him. Then a group of about twenty young men left the village in the wake of a loaded cart, while the old people stayed behind, saying nothing.

By the time he arrived in the Red River Colony, the settlement was already ten years old. Along the riverbanks, the earlier settlers had laid out thin strips of farming land, and a few clusters of huts (they reminded him of the low barns where the cattle were kept in winter) huddled in one or two sheltered places. Most of those settlers were Scottish; a few were Métis, others were French, Poles, and Germans; a fair number had come from Lower Canada. Several were Swiss: they had arrived a few years earlier as part of the De Meurons, a mercenary regiment that had served under a British flag in India, had been called to fight in the War of 1812, had been disbanded after the fighting ended, and then had been reassembled by Lord Selkirk himself to punish the Métis and their allies who, under the leadership of Cuthbert Grant, had attacked the settlement at Seven Oaks in 1816. According to those who escaped, Grant and his army had shot down twenty-one settlers and, so that the killing should have the importance of a symbol, had mutilated the corpses. Selkirk's revenge was less symbolic than bureaucratic: almost as a formality, he took a few prisoners among the Métis; he then sent them, escorted by a handful of his Swiss soldiers, back to the Red River, where they were joined by the reluctant Seven Oaks survivors. Selkirk believed in the prayer book's prophecy of a brotherhood of men; the men who had once been enemies and were now forced to share the common life of the colony appeared less certain of such a promise, and each group kept to itself, in resentment, distrust, and cautious hope for its neighbours' misfortune.

In this uneasy atmosphere, the newcomers gravitated towards their fellow countrymen who gave them a reluctant welcome and let them fend for themselves. With the energy of beginners, the young men started to build low log shanties in the style of the new country, and to prepare the land for cultivation. At this last they proved useless. In their villages they had been trained as artisans or shopkeepers, herdsmen and lumberjacks, keeping at most a cabbage patch, and they knew nothing of ploughing, sowing, and reaping.

Among the families of the De Meurons, a few of the young men found women willing to marry them and teach them the rudiments of farming. It was a slow and painful learning: the weather was always too hot or too cold, the mosquitoes and deer flies drove the newcomers mad in summer and the damp icy winds drove them mad in winter. Those who tried herding, as they had in their village, found that here their skills were useless: the cattle, imported from the United States, were different from the gentle herds of their home meadows; they were both wilder and weaker, and suffered from the dogs and prairie wolves. Also, feeding the herds in winter was difficult, since the traditional fodder, a mixture of oats and barley, was hard to come by, and they had to rely on hay harvested in the summer and bought from neighbours either unwilling to sell, or who decided to charge such high prices that the transaction became impossible. On a fixed date in late July or early August (fixed to prevent anyone from enjoying an unfair advantage), the heavy grass was cut around the ponds and marshes to store away in the barns as fodder. But there was rarely enough, and the animals went hungry in late winter and early spring. The men who knew their Bible remembered the story of Job, and silently wished that the bargain between the Devil and the Almighty would soon come to an end.

Those who learned to plant wheat would sow it after three months, moving with the other men through the rank stalks, armed with sickles and scythes, and followed by the women and children who did the raking, binding, and stooking, their hands cut and bleeding. The flour gave a loaf that was blacker and harder than the one from their village, and throughout the years Erich spent in the Red River Settlement, it was the smell and taste of the softer bread that he missed most.

The wife he chose from among the few young women available was the eldest daughter of a captain who had collapsed with influenza shortly after their arrival in the New World. She was seventeen years old, large and blonde and silent. Her grandfather had served with the Swiss mercenaries in India, and fought under Lord Cornwallis in the Third Mysore War, laying siege to the city of Seringpatam, from where he had returned with a limp right arm and an embroidered Belagula standard that now hung over the hearth. She rarely smiled but taught him, in a dialect her father had almost forgotten and she never quite learned, how to till the soil and how to harvest. Erich proved even slower than the others in the task, and after two winters of suffering from the meagre results of badly managed summers, his wife told him that they would now plant potatoes instead and keep a milk cow in the yard.

In the evenings, the men would drink in the makeshift tavern set up by an enterprising Irishman who had not been welcome among the Scottish settlers. Erich joined them once or twice, so as not to draw attention to himself by his absence, and then stopped attending their gatherings. To his wife's surprise, he proved to be good at carpentry and quickly built several sturdy and handsome bits of furniture for the small house, including a glass-fronted bookcase for his brief library and a Dutch cupboard for her kitchen. By the light of a tallow candle, he would read from the books

he had brought, memorizing the words he thought he no longer knew by heart. This was, for him, an act of expiation, though he did not call it that. He never told anyone what he was doing, especially not his wife since, for him, she belonged entirely to that new and alien place that he did not want to infect with the experience of the old. She, in turn, paid no attention to his books. While he read, repeating over and over the words to himself, she would sew or bake, or tend to the cow or store the potatoes in the cellar, or sometimes just sit in her chair, staring at the fire. Occasionally a word would escape him, but she would not look up.

Thanks to the labours of his wife, Erich was spared much of the hardships of the settler's life. Locusts, which had a few years earlier devastated the crops,

Encampment on the Red River. H.Y. Hind Expedition, 1857–58.

returned in smaller numbers and seriously damaged the harvest, but their potato field was untouched. A disease brought (it was said) from the West afflicted the cattle, and a fair number had to be slaughtered for fear of the infection spreading; their milk cow was unharmed. Slowly Erich and his wife settled into a quiet routine of work and silence. He longed for new books. She never said what she longed for.

Two years after his arrival, Erich heard from one of the Métis women who came to buy their potatoes that a Protestant missionary and his wife had built a church and a school a few miles to the west, in Kildonan. Erich decided to visit it. He did not tell his wife why he was going; they rarely gave or expected explanations from one another. He merely told her that he would not be back before the next week.

In Kildonan he went straight to the church to ask for the new minister. Unlike the great log houses built in the manner known as the "Red River frame," the church was a graceless log building with a rickety steeple, that served both the Anglicans and Presbyterian Scots who sullenly stood at the pews on Sundays, muttering their prayers: the Scots offended that the new missionary spoke no Gaelic, the Anglicans distrustful of a man who spent too much time with the Indians and the Métis. On the morning of his arrival, Erich found that the church was empty. A small boy directed him to "the school," another log building as drab and dark as the church. He found the missionary at his desk.

During the two years since he had arrived at the settlement, Erich had picked up a few words of English (with a strong Scottish rolling of *r*s) and a few less of French (in the slow Métis lilt), and in a mixture of these he spoke now to the Reverend David Jones. What words he could not remember or never knew, he supplied in his thick *Schwyzerdütsch*. That first talk did not last long, and the Reverend Jones tried to listen carefully. To make sure that he had not misunderstood too much of it, he repeated it back to his visitor.

Erich's father had acquired, over the years, a fair collection of some fifteen books that were kept under lock and key in the bedroom. Though he was a carpenter by profession, the old man's passion had always been those arduously acquired volumes which he lovingly inspected every morning and every night. He compared the sharp black Gothic letters to carvings and admired the handicraft with which they had been cut. On Fridays, after supper, he would pull out one of the books and read from it to the children, and so it was that, week after week, Erich became acquainted with the marvellous adventures of Ulysses, the man who said his name was Nobody; with Plutarch's gossipy and parallel lives; with the coarse and comic tales of Heinrich von Wittenweiler; with the patriotic Swiss songs of Johann Caspar Lavater. Sometimes the father read from the Bible and sometimes from Von Morstein's *Martyrology*.

Erich's father was an experienced carpenter and when the abbot of Sankt-Katharienenthal required new bookcases for the abbey's famous library, an emissary was sent with the abbot's authority to engage his services. For three months Erich's father had laboured in the gold and pink room that housed the abbot's treasures, and in between the sawing and the sanding, he asked to see (and was shown) many of the precious volumes. A few of his own books had illustrations, simple woodcuts or steel engravings depicting Simplicissimus on his travels or one of Virgil's shepherds under a flowering bush. But here were intricate, meticulous marvels in all the colours of nature, showing tiny scenes from the life of our Saviour; the delicate landscapes visited by valiant travellers and inhabited by men with the heads of dogs and others who carry their head under the arm, like good Saint Denys; the joyful adventures of King Alexander the Great, known as Iskander; the precise architecture of the Castles and Fortresses of Love. His own books were intimate objects which he held easily in his hand; these were large as the kitchen table and thick as the wood of the door.

Back home he told his family of the wonders he had seen and Erich promised himself that, one day, he too would see them. On his eighteenth birthday he packed a few belongings, including five or six books that his father gave him as a parting gift, achingly taking them off the shelf; said goodbye to his parents and his brothers, and set off for Sankt-Katharienenthal. Since he was clever with his hands and had picked up much of his father's craft, he had no trouble obtaining a post as a man for odd jobs. As a token of thanks for the sturdy and elegant bookcases, the abbot

himself saw to it that Erich was lodged in a room that was well lit and free of damp. Here Erich read and reread the books his father had given him.

Handymen are not permitted into the library of an abbey where precious volumes might be soiled or damaged by fingers unaccustomed to handling vellum and paper. From time to time, Erich allowed himself to look into the spacious room when an errand took him past the library doors and a brother was coming in or out in studious concentration. The ceiling was painted with mythological scenes he thought he could identify from his father's Homer; the gilt mouldings glittered here and there through centuries of grime; the carved bookcases, including those made by his father, stood darkly solemn and yet voluptuous. But it was the hundreds of books in leather bindings, shelf after softly rippling shelf, that caught his eye. He longed to touch them. Many nights, under the warm eiderdown and in spite of the pastor's warnings, he had conjured up for himself the soft limbs of plump, naked women; the books had for him the voluptuousness of those intimate, desired limbs. On one occasion, the abbot saw him peering through the library doors and asked him what he wanted. Blushing, as if he had been caught in the midst of a sinful act, he stammered an apology and fled into the worksheds. He forbade himself from going near the library for several weeks.

One evening, when, unable to sleep, he was standing at the low door of his room watching the stars move slowly across the sky, he saw a light suddenly flicker in the library windows. He crossed the quadrangle that separated the workers' lodgings from the abbey proper, looked into the library through the rhomboid windowpanes, and discovered the brother librarian at work among his tomes. He watched for a long while until he saw him rise, take up the candle, and leave quietly along the vaulted corridor. He noticed that the brother librarian had neglected to lock the doors. He waited one seemingly endless moment and then crept in.

Because of the full moon, it was light enough to see inside the high vaulted

Opposite: Portrait of Laetitia Bird, a Métis woman, Red River Settlement, Manitoba, 1858.

library. The painted figures on the ceiling looked down blindly on him in their faded greys, the gilded volutes glimmered faintly here and there from the deep shadows, but the rows of books stood clearly out on the long shelves, offering their glistening backs and soft edges. He reached out and pulled one off the shelf and opened it gently. He touched the letters with the tips of his fingers. He read a few words and put it down. He opened another one and did the same.

He could not be sure of how long he spent going through the books in the library. He abandoned one shelf and started on another. Then he crossed the room and inspected another section. Sometimes a small volume, no larger than the palm of his hand, attracted his attention. Other times it was a huge tome, too big to handle on his own, so that he had to be content with trying to decipher the title on the spine.

When he reached the far end of the library, he noticed a medium-sized book standing open on the wings of the golden eagle of a lectern. It was too dark there to make out the writing; something like a great thirst overcame his caution; he struck a light and lit the lectern's candle. He read the open page, wonderfully illuminated in blue and crimson and gold. The book seemed to be an ancient description of the world. It listed animals and rocks, lakes, forests, and distant cities, the customs of strange peoples, and the names of the stars. Erich read on, page after marvellous page.

A noise, or what he imagined to be a noise, startled him. He turned and his hand knocked over the candle. Next to the lectern was a pile of old papers. Before he could stoop down to put out the flame, they had begun to burn. Uselessly, he tried to stop the fire from spreading but the flames were now climbing up the shelves, row after row. He grabbed the illuminated volume from the lectern and ran. The alarm gave him time to enter his room and throw his belongings into a bag. A few hours later it was dawn and he entered the village where Lord Selkirk's notice had been posted.

During the long crossing towards the New World, he spoke little. His upbringing told him that seeking salvation was now useless, but he still felt the need for atonement of some kind. Destroying a book, his father had often told him, was like killing a person, and he had condemned hundreds to the agony of the flames. The dead are kept alive through a monument to their memory; could not a book (he told himself) be kept alive by erecting such a monument in one's mind? In Von Morstein's *Martyrology* he had read that Saint Lawrence, on being asked by a widow how best to honour the memory of her husband, replied that she should care for the sick and the poor, since what was done to one soul affected all others. He never knew or barely recalled the titles of the books he had destroyed, because he had only leafed through a few of them. But he could honour their ashes by memorizing other books, the ones he carried with him, for instance, creating as it were a library in his mind that would, for as long as he lived, be the shadow of the books he had lost forever. On board the musty ship he memorized the *Martyrology*.

The Reverend Jones listened and then asked Erich how many books he had learnt by heart until now and, when he heard that Erich had almost come to the end of his last book (the rescued encyclopedia), he suggested that the final redemptory act might be to make concrete that which Erich had so painfully constructed in his mind. Long before reaching Kildonan, Jones had imagined that his new parish would require books. In the church and in the school, he and Mrs. Jones had promised themselves they would teach the settlers' children, and those of the Métis, Crees, and Chipewyans. But without the solidity of print, the words would certainly fade away, like water on water. The Reverend Jones had dreamt of a library.

At first Jones wanted the library to be in Kildonan, next to his church, his school, and his house, but under the quiet reasoning of Mrs. Jones, he quickly realized that such a choice would alienate the settlers of St. James, St. Charles, and St. John's, not to speak of the ones of farther places in the settlement, already jealous of the advantages of Kildonan as seat of the Anglican mission. He decided that the log house with Georgian doors and fanlights, built by Peter Fidler, the mapmaker who had died a few years earlier after laying out the river lots for the colony, would suit his purpose admirably. It stood overlooking the crossroads where both the

Assiniboine and the smaller Seine met the Red River flowing northwards into Lake Winnipeg, among several limestone houses in the Norman style of Lower Canada. Fidler had left his books to the colony, and they were sitting (Jones had found out) in the house of one of the colonels, waiting to be transferred to one of the schools or churches. Together with Erich's little lot, they would be the start of the colony's first library.

Over the next few months, Jones campaigned among the Catholic missionaries, the Scottish brethren, the old Swiss families, and among the Métis who, he suspected, not infrequently held a few books brought over many years ago from France or Québec. Jones even wrote to the Missionary Society in Manchester, begging his superiors to contribute to the shelves. Volumes began to pile up inside the cabin, to Jones's satisfaction and Erich's wonder. By Christmas of 1825, the library held an eclectic collection of some fifty or sixty titles and Mrs. Jones, after fulfilling her obligations to her classroom, compiled a catalogue of the treasures in her neat English copperplate hand which Erich read over many times. Occasionally a settler, nostalgic for the letters of his or her childhood, would enter the roomy, dark library and ask Mrs. Jones for a book, while Erich watched the transaction with a mixture of pride and jealousy.

The winter was long and heavy. Snow fell on the watersheds of the great rivers in banks taller than a man, and held throughout April and most of May. Several Métis and Indian families packed up and left to sit out the coming of spring in the higher ridges of Bird's Hill and Stony Mountain. A young Chipewyan who had helped Reverend Jones collect the donations of books now offered to move them east, to Silver Heights, but Jones told him not to worry: the mapmaker's house was high and sturdy, and would protect the books better than a makeshift Chipewyan tent.

One Friday in late May, while his wife went about her usual silent business, Erich entered the library to sit among the books. Mrs. Jones kept the doors locked, but in recognition of Erich's contribution, Reverend Jones had given him a key, which Erich never let out of sight. In the morning it had begun to rain, but an opening in the sky seemed to promise better weather, and even though it was late in the afternoon, there was enough light to read close to the window without a lamp. Erich opened his beloved encyclopedia and read (but he knew the words by heart) of the wonderful properties of a stone that is taken from the dragon's brain but does not harden into a gem unless the head is cut from the living beast, and of the seafaring kraken whom sailors mistake for an island and whose long black tentacles can envelop and sink a ship. All at once, the sky darkened, it grew wonderfully silent, and then the rain began to fall.

It fell in thick, deafening sheets, hiding everything from sight, blinding the windows. Inside the library, it occurred to Erich that in that impossible immensity of the downpour nothing else existed: not his fellow settlers, not his wife, not Reverend Jones and Mrs. Jones, not the ancient trees nor the rocks nor the long fields and the cattle, nothing except himself and the books.

It took him a long while to hear the frantic pounding on the doors and then to understand the Chipewyan in the roar of the water. Protecting the encyclopedia under his jacket, he allowed himself to be dragged outside into the storm and onto the tall two-wheeled cart where his wife and three or four other De Meurons were waiting. Then the horse struggled eastwards, away from the houses and into the trees, and up the side of the low ridge that they knew was there but which the water made invisible.

When they reached the top, the Chipewyan helped them down and then led them and the horse under a leather canopy that had been fastened over four dead trees. The Reverend Jones and his wife handed out a few blankets, too sodden for protection. In the back, someone had managed to light a fire and was boiling a large kettle.

Erich looked down towards the riverbanks that now, under the blinding rain, appeared impossibly higher than the horizon. Then the grey swell began to curve and rise, and finally, after what seemed like hours, the surface of the river broke with a deadened crash and the waters began to spread over the plain. Trees, rocks, the roofs

of the log houses were swept away and carried off. What looked like the head of a horse or a cow appeared above the water, and then went under as a tree, large as a church, thundered past. The waters reached the library.

With a shout, Erich began running down the streaming slope, falling over, picking himself up, unable to distinguish clearly between the waters above and the waters below. He came to the edge of the ridge, the flood bucking at his feet. Among the branches and bits of wood, and the thin corpse of a dog, in the sudden spark of a bolt of lightning, he thought he saw his precious books. There was his father's Homer, drowning. There was the beloved *Martyrology*. There was his Plutarch. There were his fellow countrymen, Heinrich von Wittenweiler and Johann Caspar Lavater. There were books that someone had brought from Brittany, from Ayrshire, from London, from York. The vague shapes swept along in the torrent, indistinguishable from the rest of the debris, their dear pages transformed now into wood, dead flesh, putrid water.

Many days later, after the rivers had almost subsided and the blackened carcasses of the houses had begun to rise from the evil-smelling mud, most of the settlers returned and started to rebuild their businesses and farms. Not, however, the

A Chipewyan boy, Churchill, Manitoba, 1926.

Swiss who had come from so far in search of a better place. Both the old soldiers and their families, and the young men recruited by Selkirk's agents knew they had had enough. The land had made it clear that it did not want them; now they did not want the land. They loaded the creaky Red River carts (the only gift they felt the land had given them) and headed south, to the Upper Mississippi valley. Erich's wife, who had managed to rescue a few things from the mud that had engulfed their house, including her grandfather's embroidered Belagula standard, was among them, but she did not say a word to her husband, either then or later, when they reached the place to which they were destined.

Roch Carrier

GOLD AND SAWDUST

When I was invited to write a short story on a historical subject,

I replied at once that I didn't have the time. They insisted: "Choose your favourite period." I explained that I had no time for writing.

I didn't do so out of self-importance. I really was busy. As head of the National Library of Canada, I'm responsible for twenty million books and other historical documents. There isn't enough room, the plumbing is old, the staff needs support, technology is making possible some exciting projects that will erase a great many inequities. Intensely involved in the present as I am then, I couldn't undertake a journey into the past. Why did the person on the telephone add: "You could write about the Klondike gold rush." Then and there I found some time.

The Klondike gold rush was an extraordinary human adventure involving men and women who pitted themselves against the most arduous difficulties on the planet. They became as strong or as spiteful as their desire for gold. Even the

A Klondike dancer, the Belgian Queen, Yukon, ca. 1900–1905.

adventurers who seemed normal were a little crazy. A certain madness was as real as the cold that bored through their clothes. And that's how the great human migrations are experienced.

But it wasn't my main reason for wanting to write this story. Let's go back more than fifty years. I'm a little boy learning to read. My mother is holding my hand. We're making our annual visit to the village cemetery. It's the biggest day of my life because I can finally read the inscriptions on the stones. Except for the one on a piece of wood standing crooked, with some letters worn away: Y . . . k . . . n. "That says Yukon," my mother tells me.

I don't remember what else she said. But there was a man who'd travelled very far, and mountains, cold, and gold in the rivers. Later, I was able to read accounts of that incredible epic that saw men and women risking their lives to arrive in the land of their dreams. It was an inexhaustible mine of adventures that I've never stopped reading about.

Later still, I travelled to the Yukon. And I went on reading about the gold rush.

Shall I confide to you that when it's really cold I pull on boots that I bought from some Newfoundlanders who'd emigrated to the Yukon? That when I exercise I still wear the sweatshirt I was given by some students in Whitehorse, with "Yukon" in yellow letters on the back?

Don't smile. I've never talked about all that to anyone, except to my closest friends and to them I talk about it all the time. But the young woman on the phone couldn't know that.

"Are you interested in the Yukon?"

"Yes."

And I began to write this story.

GOLD AND SAWDUST

WHILE FAR, FAR AWAY in Western Canada, in a territory called the Klondike, apparently you just have to pull out a little grass and you'll find gold nuggets the size of potatoes, here in the East, in Bellechasse County, our ploughs hit nothing but poor stones.

The newspaper says that in a tiny stream in the Klondike there's more gold than in all of California. Horses that drink in the river are liable to choke on the nuggets that roll in the water. Here in our streams we fish small trout. The great resources are elsewhere: tall pine trees, vast fields of wheat, fine land, fine game, big factories. Here the hard soil contains more rocks than earth. The spruce trees are scrawny. In winter the wood doesn't produce a warm fire. Here we have few dreams, few words.

Why didn't the good Lord plant his nuggets for good French-Canadian Roman Catholics? Why did the good Lord bequeath us stones instead? Like poor people, we don't expect answers to these questions.

And we drudge and we slave and we toil so hard that we grow old. But we go on working. And then when we're completely exhausted, we pass on responsibility for their future legacy to the children. And they manage things in their own way. It's obvious that they don't like the way their fathers did things. We watch them work. We smoke our pipes. We're sad because we're useless. We're unhappy because we can no longer work. We smoke. In silence. We listen to the distant murmur of the world. And we daydream about those mountains in the Klondike whose flanks are swollen with gold.

When we were young we could have done as others did and gone to California to seek our fortunes. What would have become of us if we hadn't stayed on the land in Bellechasse? A number of our people went there. We wanted to look after our old parents. Those who left never came back. California swallowed them up. Are they any happier at the ends of their lives? We smoke. We observe our sons. They've got heart, they do their best. We think about the future even if we're too old to have one. We think about the future of our children.

The girls are pretty and plump; they'll find husbands. The boys? Eustache is cut out for Bellechasse County. Jasmin is different. It's as if he was made for somewhere else. We thought the good Lord was calling on him to become a priest. We sent him to the seminary in the city of Québec. He was intelligent enough to get an education but he found not learning more enjoyable. He came back to the house.

Eustache and Jasmin took over the sawmill. We worried. One day, as the men of Bellechasse do, those two fine lads will start a family. The sawmill will never be able to feed two families. We smoke. We get even older. Finally, very apprehensive, we write our will and then we gently pass away, like a lamp going out. We'll be put into the soil of Bellechasse County where the gravedigger's shovel won't strike a vein of gold.

March 1897

Eustache, I've hopped onto moving trains. I've travelled on a ship; I was the one who threw the wood onto the fire that makes the big wheel at the back turn. I've rowed boats. I've gone overboard on a raft in the rapids. The Klondike's mountains of gold are still far away but I know I'm getting closer because sometimes there's a smell of gold on the wind. I hope the sawmill is doing well. I don't know when my letter will reach you, but when I've made my fortune, I'll be anxious to come home. We'll build the biggest sawmill in Bellechasse County.

Your brother, Jasmin

THAT'S THE FIRST LETTER received since he left. Has he written any others? Eustache counts: Jasmin left a good ten months ago. It was right after they buried their father. They were properly sad and then they dried their tears and divided up the inheritance. The sisters shared the modest savings. Eustache, the older son, got their father's house and the sawmill, to carry on the name. There was nothing left for Jasmin. It was no surprise. He'd already been given the finest inheritance: an education. The other children hadn't received that privilege. Jasmin was supposed to become a priest, but just after the death of his poor mother, he realized that he no longer felt like praying.

After the will was read the two brothers talked. Eustache offered to sell Jasmin the house and the sawmill. They could divide the sale price between them. No. That would have been an insult to their father's memory; he had built up this heritage with his own hands. The two brothers could go on working together . . . No, that wouldn't work. One day they would get married and the sawmill wouldn't be able to feed two families. No, they mustn't break up the inheritance.

"During Father's last days," said Jasmin, "I did some thinking. You're the oldest, you're inheriting the name, and you'll keep the sawmill going. And me, I'm going to the Klondike! I'll come back with gold, and you and me, we're ambitious, we'll build the biggest sawmill in Bellechasse County . . . And I'll ask Victoria to marry me."

"You're crazy, Jasmin . . ."

"The crazy people who go to the Klondike scoop up gold by the shovelful . . ."

The Klondike! People said that in the earth there, every stone was gold.

Adventurers came from all over, from Australia, China, Poland. That gold must exist for French Canadians too . . . Every week, the newspaper had a story about the Klondike and its gold.

And so Jasmin left with a new pair of good sturdy boots, blankets, a mackinaw, and some warm sweaters in his haversack. The Klondike is so far away that he's not there yet.

Eustache puts Jasmin's letter back in its envelope. Tonight he'll take it to show Victoria, who hasn't had a word from him since he left. He came to see her as she was watering the flowers in front of her parents' house.

"I'm going to the Klondike," Jasmin had announced. "When I come back I'll be richer than the bank. If you've had the patience to wait for me, I'll ask for your hand. And I'll have a fine gold ring for you."

She asked, "Aren't you afraid of being all alone so far away? There can't be many French Canadians over there."

"Foreign places don't scare me, Victoria. They attract me. That's how I'm made."

For the rest of her life, she'll remember this day.

That winter is very cold in Bellechasse County. Icicles hung from the horses' sides. Even though she doesn't like to go where all the men look at her as if they've never seen a young girl, Victoria comes to the sawmill for news about Jasmin. As the weeks go by she grows concerned. Once, she asks, "Is he still alive? The newspaper said some men froze to death in the Klondike."

"Where he is they haven't got a post office," Eustache explained. "There aren't even any houses. People can walk for months and not see a single human face."

Victoria imagines mountains that disappear into the clouds, snowy fields that stretch out to the horizon; she sees bears, wolves . . . Eustache lights his pipe and grows pensive too: no, a man can't survive the Klondike winter on his own. He thinks about the stories that he too has read in the newspaper. For a moment he forgets that Victoria is there, with a rabbit-fur hat framing her pretty face.

He'd like to take Victoria's hand, he'd like to squeeze her warm little hand in his own, but she belongs to Jasmin. . . Jasmin was attracted to the great open spaces. He's never really liked the sawmill. Or the good smell of wood. His head was forever in his books or in the clouds. Jasmin always wanted to go away and see what the world was like somewhere else. If he's still alive, he was right to go away. But Eustache has to get back to work. He shoves a raw log over to the saw that bites into the wood and sends up golden dust. It's not gold dust like in the Klondike.

In the middle of the summer, Victoria turns up at Eustache's sawmill in her pretty pink dress, all out of breath.

"Jasmin wrote!"

And Eustache reads the letter. Victoria reads along with him but she already knows every word by heart.

Dear Mademoiselle Victoria,

No man knows beforehand what he'll be able to do. I'm lonesome here, but if I'd stayed at home, I would never have known I could do what I've done. Be patient, Victoria. When you see a man at your parents' door who's a little bit thinner, who has a long beard and hair and a sack on his back, you'll know that it's me; and in my sack I'll have some Klondike gold. My brother and I will be the kings of lumber. And you, Victoria, you'll be my queen!

Your own Jasmin

AFTER READING THAT, Eustache can't work. He sits on a log, lights his pipe, and lets himself be swept away by daydreams as he watches the sun go down. He feels dazed, overwhelmed, his heart is upside down. He's ill at ease. Eustache has always known

his brother's thoughts. He wishes he'd never sent this letter to Victoria. After a moment's contemplation he says, "Could I have another look at Jasmin's letter?"

"You'd better light the lantern."

And then time passes the way that time passes in Bellechasse County: leaves appear, leaves fall, the snow comes, the snow goes away. And at the sawmill, logs roll in an avalanche, the circular saw slices them with shrieks that spread over the countryside. The boards pile up. But they're behind. Customers who are always in a hurry complain that they have to wait too long. Times are changing. No one is patient any more. The world seems to want to turn faster. It's because of all those new inventions.

Girl in the Klondike, ca. 1898–1910.

Eustache needs more up-to-date machinery, a bigger, more powerful saw. In its pre-sent state, the sawmill can only do small jobs. If Jasmin were to find gold, that would change . . . But there's more to life than the sawmill. He often dreams about Victoria. Too often. He would like to have Victoria, but she belongs to his brother, who is so far away . . . It's said that those who travel great distances forget. Could Jasmin have forgotten? If he hadn't, he would write to her . . . When you miss your sweetheart who's at the other end of Canada, you must want to write to her ten times a day. Eustache knows that *he* dreams about Victoria several times a day. Does she sense that Jasmin has forgotten her? Does she sense that *he* thinks about her all the time? Eustache would like to talk it all over with her. It isn't easy for a man to bring up such matters with a woman. Has she decided to spend the rest of her life hoping for Jasmin? Eustache would like to confess to her the thoughts that are in his heart. The time is not yet ripe for confidences.

October 1897

Eustache, men like you and me have one big flaw: the only thing we think about is work, hard work. It's all we know. Eustache, when we've got sacks of gold to stretch out on, that's when we'll learn how to rest. I'm earning a fair amount of money from boxing. Whenever I introduce myself somewhere, people already know about the French-Canadian Sledgehammer. That's English. It means "la Masse canadienne-française." When I go into a tavern I'll throw out a challenge to the best man there. People gather round. The fight doesn't start till there's enough money in the hat. I deliver punches, I take punches. Sometimes I'm a little bit stunned. But you mustn't stop hitting. By the end I'll have some blood on my face, a lump over my eye, a few scratches, a few cuts—but the hat gets turned over to the French-Canadian Sledgehammer. I haven't lost a single tooth yet. I know how to hit where it hurts. Besides, on account of my education I'm not as dumb as my opponents, who take up my challenge with fists like horses' hooves.

The Ukrainians are as hard as the stones in the fields. A few times they've laid me out on the floor. But when you come from Bellechasse County, you get back on your feet and deliver a right that's like a cannonball from Napoleon's cannon.

Your brother, Jasmin, Boxing Champion and Future Millionaire

DID EUSTACHE REALLY UNDERSTAND what he read? Can he truly believe it? Jasmin punching people? Sure, Jasmin can hit. As hard as he claims? No. Take punches? You need courage to put your face within range of a man's fists. Does Jasmin have that courage? The seminary made him soft. Nice manners, Latin, prayers: those things weaken a man. Before the seminary, Jasmin was a real young man from Bellechasse: all he had was his arms and his hands. In boxing, if your head's too big, you stand a better chance of getting pounded. Jasmin, a boxer? Eustache can't believe that. Jasmin's instinct would be more for flight than fighting.

Why does Jasmin have to fabricate an incredible story? He must be in trouble. His boasting must be concealing misery. He's showing off. Eustache has a foreboding that Jasmin is hiding something not very nice behind his fine story about being a champ. The French-Canadian Sledgehammer: that's not boxing. Boxing isn't part of his behaviour.

Will the beautiful Victoria have that impression too? Women are better at sensing such things. Eustache is convinced that Jasmin's no champion boxer. Either he's been roundly beaten or he's doing something he's not proud of. He's disguising the truth. Eustache brings it up candidly with Victoria. He knows that she doesn't like this opinion of his. Jasmin is telling lies, and a lie is a lie.

"Maybe he's not telling the whole truth but we know he's alive," she says. "The truth will always be the truth. He'll tell it one of these days, when he comes home."

St. Jean Baptiste Day 1898

Eustache, at the end of the month of May, as soon as the ice is drowned in the water of the Yukon, we saw a procession of rowboats, rafts, and canoes arrive. Imagine a rainstorm on the village, but every drop of rain is a hungry, thirsty man. They want to eat, they want to drink. And what they're mainly hungry and thirsty for is gold. A French Canadian from Lac Saint-Jean, who knows about business, was waiting for these twenty thousand gold diggers with a thousand pairs of leather boots. They sold like hotcakes. I helped him because I can talk English. Everyone brings provisions in his bag, but there's men who have killed for something to drink. There are no real taverns yet. If you want to start a business, you raise a tent, and when you can, you put up a false front made of wood. When a rumour spread that the Dominion Creek area was open for prospecting the town emptied out in an hour. I was among the first to arrive but the stakes had already been planted by people who'd been told in advance by friends of the government. Even in the Klondike there's no justice. I was disappointed. But the Yukon is big and if I can't dig here, I'll go find my gold somewhere else.

IT'S A LOVELY EVENING IN JULY in the county of Bellechasse. Victoria's parents and her ten brothers and sisters have listened as she read the letter Eustache brought to her. He's there with them. They all rock in their chairs on the veranda. After hearing those words that have come from so far away, no one dares to speak. Their lives feel so small. But instead of travelling so far to look for gold, wouldn't it be better to mow the good Lord's hay in the fields? Victoria says:

"Maybe we worry about Jasmin too much. His life is hard but he's still following his dream."

Christmas 1898

Dear Mademoiselle Victoria,

I've travelled across provinces, towns, villages, prairies, and mountains. I've seen the Rockies, I've seen the Pacific Ocean. Often I've regretted starting out on this journey. My bag was so heavy all I wanted to do was sleep. So I'd stop, I'd eat some beans, some bacon. Here it costs six shillings; they rob us. After I ate I picked up my bag again and continued on my way. Like the needle on the compass that points north, I'm heading for the Klondike.

  During the long journey I thought about you often, Mademoiselle Victoria. When I was walking in places where I felt all alone on the earth. When I was travelling in a train whose whistle blew in the night to drive moose off the tracks. When I was happy because I'd set off on this adventure. I thought about you when I felt sad in my exile.

  Once I've filled some bags with Klondike gold, here's what I'll do. First of all there'll be one for my good brother, Eustache, and his sawmill. The second bag of gold I'll have melted to make a beautiful necklace for you.

  You'll chide me for thinking about the Klondike gold too much. I know that far from where I am now, in Bellechasse County, there's a much more precious treasure for me, I hope.

               Sincerely, Jasmin

P.S. I don't dare to write with ink on paper the words that come to my mouth when I think about you, but I want you to know that I whisper them on my way to the gold veins of the Klondike.

VICTORIA REREAD THIS LETTER several times. Slowly. In a low voice, in her bedroom, she savoured each of the words. Her hands were trembling a little, her heart was racing. She'd like to press this letter against her just as she'd like to embrace Jasmin. Eustache is convinced that Jasmin isn't telling the truth. Is he walking behind his brother, in his footsteps, to know if he's telling the truth or not? On the other hand, Eustache knows his brother. Eustache is a good man. If he thinks that Jasmin is patching up the truth with lies, he ought to know. If Jasmin isn't telling the truth, why does he feel that he has to make up stories? Is it possible that the truth is something not very nice? Probably Jasmin is having fun embellishing his trip a little. If he's not really a boxing champion, it doesn't change much. All men like to brag a little . . . It's not the same as lying.

Victoria doesn't want Jasmin to be a liar. She wants to believe what Jasmin has written to her. She places the letter in her drawer, but she doesn't press it to her heart.

May 1898

The rain has been falling for three days now and turning to ice. It's also dripping through the roof of the cabin. I killed a man who tried to steal my boots while I was sleeping. Can you see me in the Klondike with bare feet? I whacked him with my shovel and I saved my boots. I hope he didn't have any mortal sins on his conscience. A while ago I travelled down some rivers that were stirred up like holy water with a devil thrashing around in it. The water was as cold as ice. One time we brought a singer from France on the raft with us. Her name was Emma. I took her on our raft because she didn't want to step in the mud with her fancy little shoes. The ground is soft and she'd have sunk up to her ankles. She brought seven suitcases. Descending rapids is like tumbling from heaven down to hell. I'm sick of eating beans and bacon three times a day. In a while I'll be having champagne from France. Now and then we see people coming back weighed down with gold.

You'll understand why I'm not signing this missive . . . (It was him or me, I didn't have any choice.)

P.S. I don't know if my letters are reaching you.

EUSTACHE FOLDS THE LETTER and slips it into his pocket. To relieve his impatience, he delivers a useless kick to a log. Jasmin is so far away . . . Does he still think about Victoria? Tonight, Eustache will show her the letter from his brother.

1898

Eustache, you've only seen the hills in the village so you can't imagine a mountain three thousand feet high. When you finally reach the top of the Chilkoot with your two hundred pounds of baggage on your back, the North West Mounted Police check to make sure you've got what you need to live for a year. Every man has to transport a ton of gear: tent, clothing, food, tools. You have to go down and up again. Fifteen, twenty times. Climb up, climb back down. Carrying everything on your back. Some of the men hire horses but the horses collapse. Others hire Indians but the Indians are no more honest than the whites. I ran out of money so I decided to sign up with the army. Rumour has it that the Order of the Midnight Sun is getting ready to invade the Klondike. We don't want to see those bandits loot our gold. We had to defend ourselves. When I got to the recruiter's cabin, he told me to take off my clothes for the examination. They examined my feet and my teeth. And when I went to get dressed again, my boots, my sack, and my clothes had all disappeared. I was stark naked on the road to the Klondike. Eustache, only gold, and plenty of it, can avenge me.

Jasmin

AS A YOUNG SEMINARIAN, his brother had rushed towards heaven with as much faith, Eustache thinks. Now he dreams about nothing but gold. Is there still a place in his thoughts for Victoria? He never mentions her name. He doesn't write to her. For his part Eustache has to admit that he desires Victoria the way that Jasmin desires the Klondike gold.

After his day at the sawmill, Eustache takes a wash with scented soap, he combs his hair, puts on a clean shirt, and takes Jasmin's letter to her. She reads it aloud, for everyone. When she has finished she says, "It looks to me like we've lost our Jasmin."

"He'll be back," Eustache assures her.

Does he really want his brother to come back and take Victoria?

"A man always comes back to his country," says her father. "But there's times it can take a good long while . . ."

At the end of the summer there's a lively wedding. Victoria wears the white gown that her mother had sewn and embroidered long before. The bride and groom parade through the village. Behind their buggy come the musicians and the family. Fiddle. Accordion. Mouth organ. The day is as sunny as a day in June. Everyone goes to bed late, drunk on music, on dancing and homemade whisky.

The next morning Eustache pulls on pants and a shirt that are as stiff as leather from spruce gum and goes to the sawmill as he does every day. A big logging camp will open soon along the river. Already loggers are going there to work. The sawmill stands between the camp and the railway. The future will be wonderful. There'll be plenty of logs to saw. And if Jasmin finds gold in the Klondike . . . They'll enlarge the sawmill, they'll buy one of those powerful machines that shake the building, they'll modernize . . . Dreaming of the future, Eustache pays no attention to the teasing: "For a newlywed, you were out of bed plenty early this morning. . . ."

"You've got a letter from the Klondike," announces one of the old men who come to the sawmill to remind themselves of the good old days when they used to cut down trees.

1899

My dear brother, we are building a passage for the train through the mountain. It would never have crossed my mind when I was studying Latin in the seminary that one day I'd be dangling in the air like a spider. They fasten a rope around us, then they drop us down the cliff face with our hammers and chisels. If that rope should break, we'd have a thousand feet to ask forgiveness for our sins before we crashed to the ground. The first thing we do is make a foothold. After that we drill holes and stuff them with dynamite. And when it all blows up there's an earthquake. The sky turns black with dust. For a hundred miles around, men and animals cough and their eyes smart. We feel dirty inside and out. Luckily though, when we go to the village there are plump, pretty girls who are glad to soap us in a bathtub. I'm not asking for your news, Eustache, because you can't get in touch with me. But I haven't forgotten my promise. You're going to have the biggest sawmill in Bellechasse County.

Jasmin

P.S. I think about Victoria every now and then. She's too good for a hungry wolf like me. Maybe gold will turn me into a man.

AT VICTORIA AND EUSTACHE'S HOUSE, time passes. Another winter. Another summer. A child. A second child. And then a third one in Victoria's rounded belly. Big lumber camps are operating near the American border. Every day, Eustache sees a train loaded with logs chug through the valley. It's farther away, in the north country, that the train will unload the wood to be squared, sawed, planed. Up there is a big, powerful sawmill. His is too small . . . He hopes that Jasmin will be lucky in the Klondike. . . It won't be hard to figure out what to do with his gold. Whenever the train whistle blows in the valley, Eustache feels as if someone is laughing at him. His

family is growing. There's enough to eat, but Eustache knows that his life is imitating his father's. There has to be a way to enlarge the sawmill. It's a good thing Jasmin has gone. The sawmill could never feed two families. Will Jasmin find the gold he talks about? That would take luck, and luck has never settled on this family. But if Jasmin does find gold, Eustache will buy modern equipment. The trains will stop outside his sawmill. All around there will be piles and piles of beams and planks. Will Jasmin's dream come true? And will he keep his promise? Is he even still alive? There's been no word from him for two years. Could he have got lost in the Klondike? People who go too far away sometimes get lost. The less they know about what he's doing, the more they think about him.

"Eustache! Eustache! There's a letter from the Klondike!"

A hockey game, Dawson, Yukon, ca. 1900.

November 14, 1902

Eustache, they're saying that an Australian gave a belt made of gold nuggets to one of the saloon girls, but I did something better. If you'd been in Dawson City yesterday, you wouldn't have seen a single girl in the saloons because they were all with me. I also rented all the carts and packed them full of girls. With their brightly coloured dresses they looked like a garden of pretty flowers. They were all wearing French perfume too. In every cart there was champagne — I'll give you a taste of that. It's a drink that comes from the land of our ancestors. Eustache, I struck a vein where the gold is as thick as peas in soup. Today I deposited a crate of nuggets at the bank. I'm not naked in the Klondike any more. I wear a millionaire's suit imported from London. You can write to me, Eustache, in care of the Dawson Bank, they're polite with me and very obliging. Now about the sawmill, you must buy the best machinery. I want your sawmill to be the biggest one in Bellechasse County and the biggest south of Québec City. Borrow what you need. I'll be your guarantor. I'll pay off your debt. I'm also officially ceding you all my shares and all my rights to the inheritance. You're my brother, Eustache, and I have a lot of gold. Finding gold is like being born. Tell our sisters that I won't forget them either. There will be gold for all their children — the nephews I'll soon come home and hug.

Jasmin

P.S. Please note an important change: my name is now J.J. Klondike, Esq.

EUSTACHE CAN'T TEAR HIMSELF away from what he can see. At the bottom of the hill the train whistle blows, it spits smoke, its bell tinkles as it moves along to unload its unhewn logs somewhere else. He watches it disappear. He feels confident now. Soon the log train will have to stop here. Eustache will enlarge his sawmill, reinforce his equipment. Thanks to Jasmin's gold, his sawmill will be the most powerful one south of the St. Lawrence River. Eustache knows exactly what he has to do. He's been preparing for this moment for so long. Before, it was just a dream. Now Jasmin has found gold. Eustache doesn't need to explain anything to Victoria. They take all the children and go to see the richest man in the village, the innkeeper. They have to be careful. Even though he's stuffed with money the way a mattress is with straw, he's a man who'll bend down to pick up a penny.

"With Jasmin's endorsement," Eustache tells him, "I've come to get a loan."

He shows the man Jasmin's letter. Three days later, Eustache has hired workers and begun to enlarge his sawmill. Victoria has already written the letters and filled out the forms to order a powerful motor, a bigger circular saw, and a conveyor that will bring the logs to the saw. Long ago they'd made all the necessary comparisons in the catalogues and chosen what they need to make their sawmill the biggest in Bellechasse County. Ah, that train won't refuse to stop here any more. Victoria and Eustache imagine their children jumping from one pile of boards to another, climbing the way Eustache and Jasmin did when they were children. Already they can hear the sound of the new circular saw. It's as beautiful as the sound of bells in the village air.

December 6, 1903

Can you believe it, Eustache, I'm in Rome! During the typhoid epidemic in Dawson, I made a fine donation to the hospital and I got an invitation to meet the pope. He's the good Lord on earth but he's also an ordinary man like you and me. Eustache, if you could see the girls in Italy! . . . I'll bring some back to Dawson. Those girls are better than gold. Don't worry! There's a bag in your name at the bank.

The good Lord loves me. When I was on my way to the Klondike, the government people in Edmonton urged me to follow the old Hudson's Bay Company route. If I'd taken their advice I might be dead now. A government inspector told me that two out of three travellers who tried to go that way had died. And here I am in paradise, alive!

J.J. Klondike, Esq.

VICTORIA IS CARRYING ANOTHER child. Down in the valley the train still goes by, but it doesn't stop, it keeps on going with its cargo of logs. For the small amount of wood the farmers bring to the sawmill they don't need the new motor or the gigantic new saw. They've got rid of the old one. Every morning, a nervous Eustache goes to the post office to see if there's a letter from the Klondike. He's already late with his loan payments: a day, a week, a month, a year. The innkeeper doesn't say a word. In debt now, having broken his word, concerned about the future, Eustache feels as if he's in the flames of hell.

One morning in February the innkeeper shows up at the mill.

"Eustache, I've treated you well. I think I've given your brother all the time he needs to send you his gold. In my opinion, you and me will never see a speck of dust from the Klondike. I'm taking the sawmill to recover the loan. You're a good man so I'll forget about the interest. I'm not going to ruin you. I'll sell you a little piece of land to clear. And I'll sell you a cow and some hens. And a horse. You'll pay for it a little at a time, when you can. You're a good worker. You don't drink. You don't curse. I won't charge you any interest."

I don't know what date it is today.

Eustache, I went to a saloon to warm up a little. Eustache, if you got the letters I wrote you, did you keep them? Eustache, I can't remember my story since I left Bellechasse County. I've done so much travelling I don't look like myself any more. The winds in the West here have changed my face. Today I borrowed a mirror from the Pole in the next tent because I wanted to trim my beard. If I hadn't been sure it was me, I wouldn't have recognized my own face. I try to remember how I got here but I can't. My story has got mixed up with all the stories I've heard. I no longer know which one is mine. I'm writing to you on a table in the saloon. The owner's got an eye on me and I can tell from the way he's watching that he's going to kick me out. So I'm writing non-stop because the cold outside bites your fingers and toes. A man's not respected here if he hasn't got a sack of gold in both hands.

Eustache, don't think I've got the fever. I'm tough. In the Klondike you have to be tough. Eustache, all I can remember is today. If I try to remember more, I can only see black. It's the same colour as if I'd never lived.

I have lived though . . . When I go back to Bellechasse County, me and you, we'll sit for a while on my sacks of gold and we'll reread my letters. We'll tell each other it was worthwhile putting up with a little misery. Eustache, your sawmill's going to be the biggest one south of Québec City.

The owner of the saloon just told me to finish this letter. While he was kicking me out he promised he'd mail it.

Your only brother, Jasmin

EUSTACHE CLEARS A CORNER of his new piece of land for Victoria's garden. There are more stones than earth. With no gold in it. The quack grass is tough. They cut firewood for the winter. Victoria, though she's pregnant again, is thin and very pale. Eustache works quickly to build a shed for the animals. He gets up before the sun. He goes to bed after the sun. Victoria washes sheets for the inn. Eustache has written several desperate letters to J.J. Klondike, Esq., to his address at the Dawson Bank. No reply. Where is his brother? Could it be that when you're shovelling up gold you don't have time to think about those who've stayed behind in the village? Eustache fells trees, he grubs, he digs up stones. He's dog-tired. Jasmin can't have forgotten him. Jasmin promised him gold. Eustache writes again. Jasmin will help him buy back the sawmill. Now that the sawmill belongs to the innkeeper, the new motor is crackling, the big saw shrieks its pleasure as it bites into the wood. Now the log trains stop at the biggest sawmill south of the St. Lawrence River. Eustache digs up stones. He grubs. He's worn out. Time passes as if it weren't passing. A child is born. And another. His children are pale like their mother. They cough. They have fevers. Misery has moved in with his family. Will they get better one day? Jasmin has forgotten them. Eustache suspects that poor Victoria often cries. So does he. When he's sure that no one can see him, he lets his tears flow, thinking about all that he has lost since Jasmin left to look for gold in the Klondike. Furious, he doesn't wipe them. The years go by. The children grow up. They don't dare mention the name of their Klondike uncle.

At suppertime one autumn evening there's a knock at the door of the humble dwelling. It's a beggar, hairy, bearded, old. Eustache, a good Christian, signals his wife to give the man a bowl of hot soup, a slice of brown bread.

"I've come home," says the beggar.

"Jasmin!" Eustache roars.

And like dry branches exploding into flame when a lighter touches them, Eustache knocks over his chair, pushes back the table, leaps onto the beggar, hammers him with his fists. The two brothers fall to the floor, writhing like animals as they bite each other; they get up, strike again, they bash down the door and roll outside. They can be heard groaning. Yelling. One curses. The other begs. The terrified children cry,

huddling around Victoria who says, "Forgive him for our poverty, Eustache, forgive him."

After the roaring, silence returns. Her husband comes inside, his shirt, his hands, and mouth all stained with blood.

"Jasmin isn't moving. He isn't moving at all. He'll never move again."

The sobs of Eustache and Victoria sound like those of the children who have never seen a man cry. Abruptly he goes outside. The children hear him moaning like a sick animal. The children gather close around their mother. It seems as if the sky is weighing on the roof of the cabin like a stone. He comes back and nervously shoves two blankets, some boots, a sweater, and a mackinaw into a burlap sack.

Defeated Klondikers at Chipewyan, Alberta, returning south, ca. 1897–1902.

25 December 1904

Dear Victoria, my good wife, you can't imagine how far away I am here. I've got to where forgetting begins. Here in the Klondike my name is Joe Green. I'd like them to write on Jasmin's tombstone that he died in the Klondike. I didn't want my two hands to do what they did. I'm in a river here where people have fished up a lot of gold. I swear to you, dear wife, I'll bring back enough gold so you and the children will forget all the unhappiness I've caused you.

Your husband

(Translated from the French by Sheila Fischman)

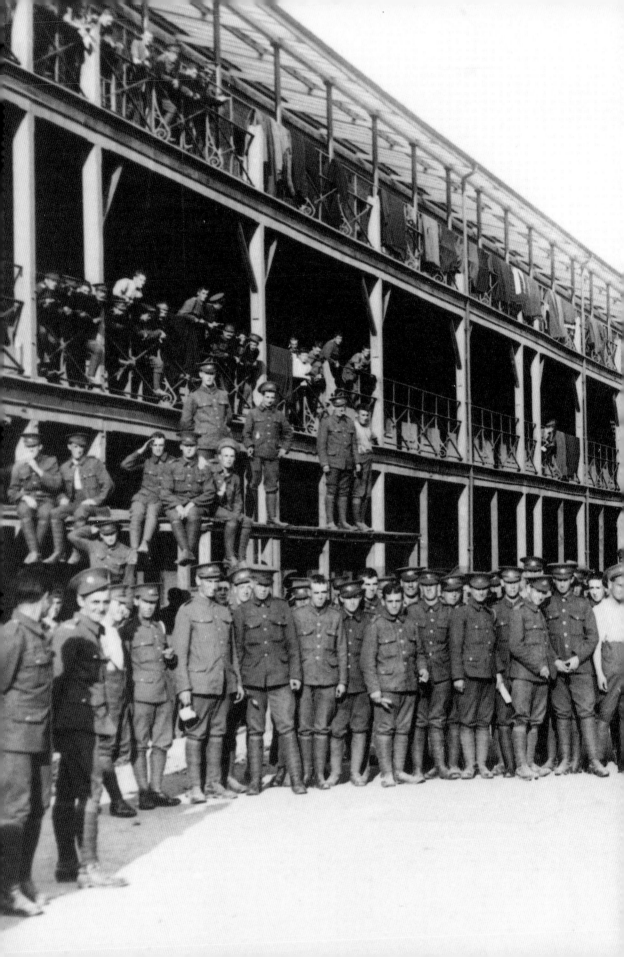

David Macfarlane

THE FIRST OF JULY

There can't be many days more conflicted than the first of July in Newfoundland.

Ever since 1916—when, near a French village called Beaumont-Hamel, the Newfoundland Regiment went over the top on the first day of the Battle of the Somme and was, within minutes, almost completely destroyed—July 1 has been Memorial Day, a time of solemn remembrance.

Newfoundland's losses in the First World War were staggering: two-thirds of the nearly fifty-five hundred men who enlisted were either killed or wounded—the largest proportion of casualties suffered by an overseas contingent of the imperial forces. There was scarcely a family on the island unaffected. From the end of the First World War until four years after the Second, the first of July was about as sad and as unconfused as an anniversary could be.

Above: Queen Elizabeth is dwarfed by a 30-foot-high birthday cake with decorations, Ottawa, July 1, 1967.
Previous: Newfoundland Regiment in Aldershot, England, just prior to sailing for Gallipoli, August 1915.

But things changed. In 1948, in a referendum that was as bitterly fought and as close as the more recent referenda in Québec, Newfoundlanders voted to join Canada as a province. Among the many transformations this brought was a change to how July 1 would be marked. For July 1 also happened to be Dominion Day—now Canada Day—the celebration of the anniversary of Canadian Confederation. This left slightly more than half the island's population remembering Beaumont-Hamel at church parades in the morning and lighting firecrackers for Canada in the afternoon. The other half remembered the opening minutes of the Battle of the Somme and, in the attendant gloom of that anniversary, mourned the loss of their country.

To make matters even more complex, the death of Newfoundland nationalism, such as it was, can be directly traced to the First World War and to what its fiercest nationalists consider one of Newfoundland's great achievements. Newfoundland raised its own regiment to fight in the Great War—a considerable feat for so tiny and so poor a population. To many Newfoundlanders, this signified something close to statehood.

But the war lasted far longer than anyone imagined. And Newfoundland's losses were far greater than anyone had feared. The extraordinary expense of maintaining its regiment—to say nothing of replenishing its manpower, and assisting those who were wounded or bereft—effectively crippled Newfoundland. The island carried an already insupportable debt into the Depression. It was virtually bankrupt by the 1930s, and by the end of the 1940s, fifty-one percent of its voting population came to the conclusion that joining Canada was the only viable option.

This has created in Newfoundland a typically Canadian ambivalence about July 1—so unlike the single-mindedness with which Newfoundlanders had marked the date before Confederation. And so unlike the uncomplicated patriotism with which our neighbours to the south celebrate the fourth. In Newfoundland, July 1 has become an extremely mixed-up anniversary. It remains a day of many meanings.

THE FIRST OF JULY

WE NEVER THOUGHT OF HER as Miss Allen. Or Miss Edna Allen. And certainly not Miss Edna Bellissima Constance Allen. We used to have another name for her. There had been a time when we thought of her as a witch.

The Bellissima and the Constance were discoveries I made in the summer of 1974. The names were on a nursing diploma I found in her study. That same muggy July I learned that she was from Newfoundland; I also found the revolver in her roll-top desk.

Her coming from Newfoundland was a surprise to me, but the gun, so I knew immediately, was one I had seen before. She had scared us to death with it once. It was a Webley Mark v with the patent date, 1914, stamped just above three letters—H.J.C. The faded, slightly blurred initials were stencilled onto the smooth grey metal behind the six-cartridge chamber and below the still-solid action of the hammer.

In 1974 I was eighteen years old, and I was in her house because my parents were trying to keep me busy. I had come home, back from university, to the town of Swan, Ontario, in order to complete a history course that I was in danger of failing. Generously ("altogether too generously, if you ask me," my father said), a professor had given me the summer to finish an overdue essay on the origins of the First World War. That year the rigours of my undergraduate social life had been such that the essay had somehow completely slipped my mind.

Completing a term paper is hardly a full-time job—as my parents, both of whom had full-time jobs, pointed out. So, along with painting the side of their house, cleaning out their basement, scooping maple keys from their eavestroughs, and sulkily cutting their hard, brown lawn, I was sent by my mother and father to Miss Allen's house a few weeks after she died to sort out her letters and diaries and photo albums. "Since," my father had said dryly at the breakfast when this new task was announced, "you are such a keen student of history."

My parents had kept an eye on Miss Allen in the last years of her life. According to my mother, she had been a bit of a grump. According to my father, she was an old woman who had been left behind by the modern age. My father had great respect for the modern age, although his notion of this triumph of political and social progress was so abstract it seemed to adhere to nothing that was actually modern. Me, for instance. That June and for the first part of July, I spent the hottest part of the afternoons sitting in my parents' den drinking Carlsberg and watching the daily instalments of Watergate on television. This seemed very modern activity to me, but I don't think it was what my father thought had left Miss Allen behind.

My parents said Miss Allen could be "a little difficult." But my parents, both of whom were teachers, were not the sort who would let a little difficulty put them off. Their chosen careers, to say nothing of their experience as my parents, pretty much attested to that. Both came from small towns in southwestern Ontario, and both believed that looking after one another was what neighbours did—however dyspeptic those neighbours might be.

In the last year of her life, Miss Allen had come to rely on my parents. They picked up her tiny requisitions of groceries, dropped off her little black shoes to be reheeled, took her spectacles in to be repaired, and stopped at her house every other afternoon to make sure she was all right. When it became clear that she had fallen finally ill, she had asked my mother to sort through her things when she was gone. She had meant to do it herself, she said. "Stupid of me to put things off at my age."

"Don't you worry about that," my mother told her.

But when the time came to fulfil this promise, my parents were too busy teaching their summer courses to have much to do with sorting Miss Allen's things. Enter the ne'er-do-well son. My mother thought that I might find the job interesting. My father could see another advantage. "At least you won't be sitting around here swilling beer and watching American news programs all day."

"It's history in the making," I said.

"Pull my other leg," he replied from behind his newspaper. "It's got bells on it."

Miss Allen had a niece in Boston to whom any papers of interest were to be sent. As stipulated in the will, everything else—the gloomy furniture, the lamps and brass candelabra and ancient kitchen utensils, the framed, dingy landscapes, the linens and the English wool blankets, and the deep-roofed, fieldstone-pillared house itself—were to be auctioned. The money raised would be donated to the veterans' wing of the Swan Township hospital by the late Miss Edna Allen.

But she had never been Miss Edna Allen to us. What she had always been to my friends and me when we were young—and what she had even been to my father one afternoon when some neighbourhood kids started a smoky, little fire in the old barn she owned that stood on an overgrown lot between the back of her property and the back of ours—was Old Lady Allen.

My father had always told her she should tear the barn down because one day it was going to burn to the ground and take the whole neighbourhood with it. The barn was a remnant of the days when the entire area had been the Allen family's farm. Her father's, we always thought. Or possibly her grandfather's. Of the original estate, only the house and the barn remained—both encircled now by the indignity of a bumptious middle-class neighbourhood. It was generally understood that the sale of so much acreage was the basis of Old Lady Allen's fortune.

The barn, while a picturesque addition to an otherwise ordinary block in the middle of an ordinary Ontario town, was without any practical purpose any more. Its access to the streets that now surrounded it had been cut off when the last few houses went in on the last few vacant lots in the 1950s. However, the two-storey, sway-backed, bat-infested structure was a good spot for boys to go and look at dirty magazines and pass around cigarettes.

More than the threat of fire, it may have been the building's encouragement to delinquency that upset my father. As far as I could tell, the barn was too far from any other structure to pose a threat to anything except itself and a few mildewy copies of *Playboy* were it to go up in smoke. But my father was prudent about uncontrollable things—such as fires. Such as children.

It wasn't the first time he had looked up from his Saturday garden chores to see smoke curling out the back of the grey, weather-beaten old place. He had a temper, my father. He marched into our kitchen that day, still holding his rake for some reason, and called the fire department. He was the assistant principal in one of the two high schools in Swan, and he could speak into a telephone as if it were a PA system. "Get yourselves round to Old Lady Allen's barn," I heard him say. "Now."

I'd never heard him say "Old Lady Allen" before, and I never heard him say it again. I must have been eight or nine. I was sitting at the kitchen table at the time, flipping through the coloured comic section of the Swan *Sentinel-Dispatch*. I grinned up at him. A grin he did not return. There was nothing about what he always called "the entire matter" of the barn that he thought was funny. There was nothing about very much of anything that he thought was funny, now that I think of it. Still, it was a revelation for me to hear him call her Old Lady Allen. It was as if he had suddenly popped some bubblegum into his mouth or had suggested we go throw rocks at squirrels for a while. Until that moment, I had thought that she was only Old Lady Allen to the kids on the street—at whom she banged the rattling glass of her living-room window when we cut through her privet hedge or slid on the ice that formed on her unused driveway.

I had a friend at that time named Gilmour McCullough, and the two of us were close to being convinced that she was a witch. This may have had its origins in a certain tension that surrounded "the entire matter" of the barn during several years of my childhood. My father grumbled about it from time to time from behind his newspaper as he sipped his Nescafé after dinner. The issue was eventually resolved some years later when another adjoining neighbour, a doctor, bought the lot from Miss Allen. He did indeed tear down the barn, but then installed a swimming pool there. The splashing, the yelling, the constant ka-thwanging of the diving board, the loud teenage music on the radio, the exotic laughter of nighttime pool parties, and the twenty-four-hour-a-day hum of the filter system all but dared my father to admit that he missed the peace and quiet of an overgrown lot and an empty, derelict old building.

But during my childhood, my father could get quite testy about the barn. I imagined that a feud existed between our family and Old Lady Allen. It was hardly that. But a sense that she was somehow set against us may have been the reason why, one night, I saw the witches.

I had awakened. Or so I thought. I sat up in bed and looked out my window towards the line of cherry trees at the back of our garden and the dark silhouette of the barn beyond. This was a familiar view. My father was as ardent a Canadian nationalist as he was an anti-monarchist, and he refused to have anything to do with May 24—Victoria Day. For our family, Firecracker Day was always the anniversary of Canadian Confederation. And when I was little, too young to stay up late on July 1 and too unpredictable a toddler to be allowed near T-shirt-igniting Catherine wheels, hair-blazing Roman candles, and eye-poking sparklers, my mother and I watched the Dominion Day fireworks through my bedroom window, from the perch of my bed. My father set them off at the end of our dark garden while my two older sisters danced around his solemn, fire-marshall-like silhouette.

The night I woke and saw the witches, Old Lady Allen was standing on the ground in front of the carriage doors of the barn. I could see that she was not dressed as a witch. She was in her ordinary old-lady clothes, but it was obvious that she was present in a supervisory capacity. Like a signaller on the deck of an aircraft carrier, she was somehow orchestrating the witches' departure. They were flying into the night in single file, witch after witch, from the barn's upper window. There were hundreds of them.

The next day I told Gilmour what I had seen. I wasn't at all surprised when he told me that he, too, had been up in the middle of the night, and that he, too, had seen witches flying around in the sky. This was typical of Gilmour.

I knew he was lying, of course. In large part because I suspected that I was. Gilmour had a weakness for supporting a lie with another lie in order to ingratiate himself with whoever had started the lying. It was a bad habit—a weakness that seemed to come from a mysterious source of loneliness in his wiry, nervous body. He was a bright kid with darting brown eyes. He was a math whiz at school and an adventurously advanced reader. A few years later he became the first among us to grow his hair long and to throw himself headlong into the jeans, the water pipes, the stacks of records, the capsules and pills, and the carefully cultivated weirdness of the day. He dropped out before finishing high school, and eventually hitchhiked out west. He was still seventeen when, in a hippy flat in Vancouver, he probably lied to the other idiot in the room with him. He probably said that sure, he'd shot up lots of times. And that, yes, the amount of yellow-white powder tipped into the spoon from the neatly folded little envelope looked about right. The police said that it was pretty obvious that neither of them had a clue what they were doing.

I knew my witches had been a dream. Or, at least, I thought they had to be. No other explanation made sense. But the reason I was not entirely willing to discount the story that I had told to Gilmour and that he had so predictably but, cross his heart, so earnestly corroborated was that I had never before had a dream that was nearly so vivid or so complete. Everything about it seemed real. I sat on the edge of my bed and stared from the open window. I could smell the mowed lawn and the watered garden of the muggy July night. The black shapes of the trees moved ever so slightly in what little breeze there was. I could almost taste the fusty iron of the window screen. Across the dark lawn, and through the trees, I could see Old Lady Allen's face as if in a spotlight shone from the moon. I could hear the neighbours' air

conditioners and, far away, the night bus changing gears on the steep part of Haig Avenue. I could even hear the flapping of the witches' tattered black clothes as they flew from the upper window of the barn and disappeared beyond the rooftops, over the wooded hill where the flocks of raucous crows always gathered. I remember my heart pounding; I was terrified that Old Lady Allen would turn and see me watching her from my bedroom window.

Over the years I could never quite explain to myself the unsettling clarity of this vision. Its non-dreamlike quality became the strangest thing about it for me—far stranger, as time passed, than the possibility that I had seen a coven of witches fly out

Centennial celebrations, Montreal, July 1, 1967.

the window of a barn. As I grew older, it just sat there in my memory, as fully real-ized as a film clip, but entirely impossible. Obviously. Just as obviously impossible, I thought, and just as vividly real to me as the time when Gilmour McCullough and I were standing on Old Lady Allen's front veranda and she came running at us with a revolver.

I remember this clearly—her shriek, her face twisted in anger, the clatter of her black shoes on the veranda floor, the surprisingly long barrel of the gun in her tiny pale hand—and yet, as the years passed, this came to seem as unlikely a scenario as the night-flight of witches. By the summer my parents sent me round to go through Old Lady Allen's things, I wasn't at all sure whether this strange memory was a moment from my childhood that had been dreamed or witnessed. It would have been nice to ask Gilmour about it. But he was never entirely reliable about these things, and anyway, he was dead.

By July 1974, with Richard Nixon locked in futile battle with the special prosecutor, Leon Jaworski, over the release of the White House tapes, it was apparent that the Watergate investigations were moving steadily towards their conclusion. The same could not be said of my history essay.

It was a particularly hot and sticky July. The humidity in Swan was often like soup in the summertime, and to make matters worse, my father had always disap-proved of air conditioners. I was the youngest of three children. My bedroom was on the second floor, above the kitchen, at the back of my parents' house, and it was, as it had always been throughout my childhood, the stuffiest room in the summer, just as it was the coldest room in the winter.

The house was silent all day. My sisters were away; they had summer jobs as waitresses at the Banff Springs Hotel. Both my parents were teaching summer school in order to cover the cost of having three children at university—a sacrifice of holi-days that made my lacklustre academic record and my loafing presence in their house almost too ironic even for me. My regular trips to the beer store and my occasional

foray to the back of the garden to smoke a joint were occupations that didn't interfere much with Watergate watching, house painting, basement clearing, or eaves-
trough cleaning. They did ensure that as soon as I sat down at the little desk in my
bedroom to work on the origins of the First World War, I began to yawn.

I could hear the droning rise and fall of the cicadas in the trees. The air in
the house was still and thick. Usually, I had stayed up until one or two the night
before watching movies or news recaps or talk shows on television. My university
library books and history notes were stacked in readiness on my desk. But as I recall,
I had only to see the words Triple Alliance, Austro-Hungary, Archduke Franz
Ferdinand, or the Schlieffen Plan, and I'd think that perhaps it would be a good idea
if I rallied my mental energies with a little nap before getting down to work.

All this made my assignment at the Allen house a relief. Not that I let my
parents know that I was anything other than further burdened by this additional duty.
Secretly, I was pleased. If nothing else, it would be a change of scenery. I was also
curious about a house that had figured so largely in the mythology of my childhood.
I wondered what I would find.

"Of course," my father said on his way to work on the first day I was going
to go to Miss Allen's, "if the police come round while you're in there, we'll deny
knowing who you are." I wasn't sure, but I thought this might have been a rare
attempt at topical humour.

"Sirica won't buy it," I replied. "You'll have to let Dean take the fall."

My father gave me a blank look.

"Have a nice time, dear," my mother said to me as she put the papers she'd
been marking at breakfast into her briefcase.

I'd always liked summer mornings in Swan, the time before the day got too
hot. I'd always liked the cherry trees at the back of my parents' garden, and the soft
blue of the sky over the shingled roof of their house. Then, I set out for my new job.
Walking around the block to Miss Allen's house, I encircled the land that had once
been the Allen farm. It was familiar territory for me—every tree, and hedge, and

lawn were from the landscape of my childhood. I knew the block intimately—from all our games of guns, and hide-and-seek, and tag. The flower gardens, the stone borders, the clumps of bridal wreath, even the cracks and buckles in the sidewalk had hardly changed at all over the years, and I had to admit that I found it unnerving to be walking through my past on my way to Old Lady Allen's. Her house was much older than all the others in the neighbourhood—darker, more overgrown, definitely spookier. As I approached, I half expected to see her white face at the front window and to hear the angry rap of her knuckles on the glass. She still loomed large in my imagination; large enough, I realized, to make me nervous about the task at hand. I decided that smoking the joint in the back garden before leaving my parents' may not have been the smartest move.

I got quite jumpy as I turned the key to her front door. "Psycho" came to mind, naturally. But then things settled down, as things do.

The house was furnished more sparsely and more modestly than I had imagined. Somehow I had not rid myself of the ludicrous way I had imagined the interior when I was a kid: exotic animal-skin rugs, vaguely decadent silk-shaded lamps, dripping candles, cavernous fireplaces, and enormous, heavily framed portraits of the Allen ancestry. This notion had more to do with horror movies than anything else, I suppose. In reality, the inside of the house was dated, but otherwise ordinary. The furniture, mostly oak, was plain and unimpressive. The drapery, utilitarian—even to my eye. Beyond a few small oil paintings and some porcelain figurines there was little in the way of decoration.

The place was dark, that much I had got right. The long overhang of the shingled roof acted as a sunshade, and the ground floor—the only floor Miss Allen occupied—was murky and surprisingly cool.

All the rooms, with the exception of one, had a slightly empty quality—as if the life that had passed through them had been provisional. The anonymity made me feel almost as if I had been expected, as if Miss Allen had known all along that some unlikely stranger would end up snooping around in her absence. Even her spartan bedroom seemed prepared for public viewing. Only the one room—the one at the east end of the ground floor—made me feel as if I were intruding. As if, in the era of covert operations and dirty tricks, I were a burglar.

The picture-hung, book-lined, folder-piled study was, clearly, where Miss Allen spent most of her time. It was also where, for the better part of two weeks that summer, I spent most of mine. For the first few days, I opened the drawers and sifted through the files as quietly as I could. It was as if I were afraid that somebody in the house might hear me.

The papers, letters, documents, articles, and photographs that I was to sort out on behalf of the Boston niece were all crammed into this one small room. I felt uncomfortable at first; the archive was so obviously private. Still, there was something about piecing together the story that it told that I found fascinating. I got, as we used to say in those days, very into it. This was a happy coincidence—one of the few occasions that I can recall when what my parents wanted me to do coincided with what I was interested in doing.

As it turned out, I had been wrong about almost everything to do with Old Lady Allen. To begin with, she had not always been an old lady—something that I had not quite apprehended. In fact, she had once been a striking beauty—slender, athletic-looking, with a face not unlike Deborah Kerr's and full, done-up tresses of what must have been either darkish blonde or soft-auburn hair. Even peering at sixty-year-old pictures I found myself captivated by her dark, sparkling eyes. Her posture seemed always to have a kind of mischievous tilt.

There were several framed photographs of her as a young woman, dated 1913. She was standing on a rocky beach in a full white skirt with a cinched waist. She was beside a handsome, tweed-capped and wool-vested, young man who, by the end of my first day in the study, I had come to recognize as Harold Jeffrey Cooper. Her beau.

She was from Newfoundland. As was he. They both grew up in Harbour Grace, but on opposite sides of the bay that divides the town. They had never met, it seems, until 1913. That spring she was hired as a maid by the Coopers, a merchant family.

Harry, the Coopers' only son, returned from Victoria College in Toronto for the summer holidays that year. His parents must have been extremely thick not to have anticipated what was bound to happen. Belle, as Harry always called her, was a very beautiful girl. Harry, at twenty, was an intense and fiery-looking young man.

That September, a completely smitten Harry Cooper returned to Victoria College to continue his studies in history, economics, and political science. She had fallen no less deeply in love with him. I discovered their correspondence in a pretty lacquered box on the study's bookshelf. It was hard to tell from the letters whether their engagement was public knowledge or a secret that only they shared. Their references to it were usually too passionate and flowery and sentimental to reveal very many of the practical aspects of their plans. But by the autumn of 1913 they may well have announced their intentions, for the difference in their stations was not as great as I had first assumed.

In Newfoundland, in those days, a maid was no improbable luxury for anyone even slightly more affluent than the average fisherman. The Coopers were not particularly well off. Or so I gathered (not without a pang of guilt) from Harry's frequent references to the sacrifices his parents were making to send him away to school. He often told Belle how hard he was working at his studies in order to do them proud. More than a few times he mentioned that his eyes were still sore from being up studying so late, and by such dim and unsatisfactory light, the night before.

Belle's letters were often highly poetic—observations of sea and sky and meadow, and entwined with these, the thoughts of love that occurred to her as she made her way back, after work, from the Coopers' to her parents' home. I was surprised by how quickly the image of the radiant young woman I was just getting to know supplanted that of the angry old lady I'd known all my life.

Belle commented intelligently on books Harry had left her to read— *Leviathan*, *The Prince*, Hume's *Treatise on Human Nature*. She would have been a good scholar, as Harry observed. And apparently she shared Harry's passionate love and ambitious dreams for Newfoundland. "Someday greatness will be bestowed on our fair island as generously as beauty has," she wrote to him.

She also seemed to enjoy the occasional wicked shock. The words "kiss," "corset," and "breasts" appear in her letters. Always in innocent context, but—winking up from her stationery at her fiancé—there all the same. I wondered how and when and by whom her own letters had been returned to her. I wondered if there had been anyone other than Harry and Belle—and now me—who had ever read them.

Harry's letters to Belle were almost plaintive in their beginnings: he missed her so; he longed desperately to hold her once again; he could, staring at her portrait on his desk, almost feel the weight of her lustrous hair as he remembered playing it through his trembling fingers. But by page two or three he was on to his own ambitions, and he poured his heart out to his girl. He was going to be—and the term came up again and again in his letters without any hint of embarrassment—a statesman. He was going to study, and work, and strive until, in some not-entirely-clear elected capacity, he would lead Newfoundland out of the shadow of the British Empire, away from the waiting, opportunistic jaws of the Canadian wolf, and establish a new and independent nation. The country of Newfoundland. And why not? he asked. The island had the richest fishery in the world. It had timber. It had mines. It's geographic situation was pivotal to the great international shipping routes. It stood as the gateway to Europe and as the entry point to North America. Its vast and uncharted interior would doubtless reveal a treasure trove of natural resources. And its people were honest, decent, God-fearing, hard-working. Its traditions were democratic and it would, by God, become an independent state soon enough if somebody had the gumption to push it towards its destiny.

Such a future was, he felt, within his grasp. Just as it was within his beloved island's. It would take hard work. It would take persistence. It would take earnest endeavour. And some day, he was certain, there would stretch from the Caribbean to the North Atlantic a commonwealth of island nations that would look to

Newfoundland as a beacon of prosperity, and industry, and freedom. "Oh my dearest Belle, these rambling dreams come to you with all my love. Yours most sincerely, Harry."

In the summer of 1914, Harry returned again to Harbour Grace from Toronto. His holiday must have been a kind of idyll for the two of them—until the news of war.

It appears that Harry was uncertain what to do: the hostilities, so everyone believed, would be brief, over by Christmas likely, and he had only one more year of studies before completing his M.A. His thesis, still in progress, was going to be entitled "A North Atlantic State: The Realities and Myths of an Independent Newfoundland."

Private C. Ballam, Newfoundland soldier
of the First World War

He returned to Toronto, but by October he had changed his mind. He came back to Harbour Grace and, after a visit of a few days, continued on to St. John's. He enlisted there with the Newfoundland Regiment. His leather identification medallion, which I came across in a drawer in the study, says: "H. J. Cooper, Nfld. Meth. 983." By the time he was overseas, under canvas and in training on Salisbury Plain, he was an infantry captain—"An occupation and a rank," so he noted wryly on a penny postcard to Belle, "that only a few short months ago I could not have imagined possessing."

At this point, Harry's letters to Belle become vague, uninformative, and dull—shortcomings that he recognized and for which he apologized. "The vigilance of the military censors does not allow me to tell you very much about where we are or what we are doing. As well, the knowledge that someone other than you will be reading these words inhibits any attempt I might undertake to communicate my tenderest affections for you. As you can see—that last sentence will suffice as example—this tends to turn my prose to stone."

It appeared that Belle's wartime letters to Harry had been lost, although it was clear from Harry's to Belle that sometime in 1915 she left Newfoundland—for the first and last time as it turned out—to train as a nurse in Toronto. Her intention was eventually to serve overseas—an ambition that Harry found alarming but admirable, and entirely in keeping with the character of the girl he loved so very much. Several of his letters to her, addressed to the Royal Nursing Residence in Toronto, begin: "My dearest Nightingale."

From his letters it was impossible to guess where he was stationed or where he and his men would soon be going. But he could be reasonably forthright about the ports of call they had already made. His itinerary—training in England, encamped in Egypt, plagued by flies in Gallipoli, disembarked in Marseilles, and finally, by spring 1916, heading northward, up the line, towards the front in France—could also be followed along one wall of Miss Allen's study. There were perhaps a dozen framed photographs there of the handsome Captain H. J. Cooper.

He had dark hair and round, buttonish eyes that had a hint of sad intelligence to them. He had fine, strong features, and a way of squinting a self-conscious smile that somehow made it clear that he was looking at a camera in the present and not at whoever it was in the future who might consider his photograph. He had a bulky, woollen uniform that by its ill fit emphasized his youth and that seemed held together by his Sam Browne. His boots were heavy and well worn, and he usually wore his peaked cap a little back on his head in a roguish, unmilitary fashion.

By April 1916, his letters, from somewhere in France, continued to be unrevealing. If I was hoping for graphic descriptions of the horrors of the First World War, I wasn't going to find them here. It was hard to guess how much Harry was holding back—holding back from the censors and holding back for the peace of mind of his worried girl at home. His understatement was impressive.

Egypt had been "a sweatbox." Gallipoli, "a bit of a hellhole." And now he and his men "are in fine fettle, all things considered." He wondered if Belle could see her way to send him some good woollen socks, "as the rain has been the devil and mine have fallen to shreds in the mud."

If he had heard rumours of a coming big push, the only indication was that in May and June his letters become more frequent and more openly heartfelt. "I can always keep my spirits up," he wrote on June 28, 1916, "by reminding myself how much I have to anticipate. The future is very bright. How can it be otherwise when I know that the day I take you once again in my arms will be, without doubt, the happiest of my life?"

No other letters from H. J. Cooper exist—although it took me the longest time that summer to admit what this meant. I'd come to like him and was disinclined to accept the obvious. The story of Belle and Harry had so taken hold of me I almost believed that its outcome could be changed by more thorough research on my part. Somehow—for close to a week, I think—I hunted through the papers and folders and albums of the study, imagining that I would find another pretty lacquered box, and another pile of letters tied with the same black satin ribbon.

It was during this period of foolish hopefulness—flipping through files, reading diaries, opening various cartons of correspondence—that I discovered that Edna Allen had graduated as a nurse a few months before the war ended. She never went overseas. Her diploma, made out to Edna Bellissima Constance Allen was dated June 17, 1918. In several of the typed and carbon-copied essays that she called "An Autobiographical Sketch," and that she seemed to begin every so often and eventually abandon, she explained that Bellissima and Constance were both the names of fishing schooners that had gone down—one near the Grand Banks, the other returning from Labrador—each with one of her mother's brothers on board.

I also confirmed what was already clear: that neither her father nor grandfather had owned the property on which she eventually lived—as we, in the neighbourhood, had always imagined. Shortly after her graduation she took a position nursing an ailing uncle at his fieldstone-pillared farmhouse on what was then the outskirts of the little town of Swan, Ontario. It appeared that both her parents died of tuberculosis in Harbour Grace in the mid-1920s. Unwilling to risk her own health perhaps, or possibly unable to leave her enfeebled uncle, she did not return to Newfoundland for their funerals.

Nor was there any vast and fabulous fortune. According to her diaries, her uncle—kindly, childless, a widower—was the victim of a slippery Toronto stockbroker. Before the war, he had made several catastrophic investments in American cotton and South African diamonds. After the armistice, what money her uncle made selling off his land covered his debts and the legal fees that resulted from a tangle of suits and countersuits that carried on late into the twenties. The Crash finished him off. When he died he bequeathed "to my beloved niece"—a niece I was, by then, falling a little in love with, myself—his remaining funds, the fieldstone-pillared house, and the old barn. "The nest egg," she wrote, "was about the size of something a starved sparrow might have left behind." I had never imagined her working, but I learned that she was employed as a nurse at the Swan Township hospital until her retirement in 1956—the same hospital and the same year in which I was born.

Among her papers, there was some correspondence between Miss Allen and the registrar of Victoria College. She had tried to track down any versions of Harry's incomplete M.A. thesis that he might have left with professors or fellow students. At first I thought she had succeeded in this quest, but eventually I realized that the various typewritten and carbon-copied drafts of "A North Atlantic State" that I was reading were her attempts to duplicate his lost essay—mostly from memory. They were a little ornate in their prose, a little flowery in their discursiveness, and it was obvious that she didn't have the resources of a university library at hand. The drafts were all incomplete—a failure with which I had more than a little sympathy. My unfinished essay was sitting, ignored, on the desk in my bedroom in my parents' house. But her excuses were better than mine. Anyone's would be. Her duties to her uncle consumed her time, and later—so the brief and hasty entries in her diaries made clear— the demands of the veterans' wards at the Swan Hospital left her with little energy for anything else.

She continued to write when she could, and eventually her efforts to replicate Harry's thesis were replaced by what appeared to be an essay of her own. I could see this taking shape in the handwritten notes she made in her journals, in her carefully catalogued clipping files, and in her voluminous correspondence with several professors of history at several universities.

She was an extremely finicky writer. There must have been a dozen drafts of an article that was eventually published in 1954 in a pamphlet put out by the Swan Amateur Historical Society. Almost buried in its own statistics, the essay was called "The Death of a Dream." It argued that it was the accumulated effect of Newfoundland's First World War debt, compounded by the disaster of the Depression, that led to the colony's near-bankruptcy, its abnegation of democratic rule, its abandonment by Great Britain, and finally to what she called "a trumped-up, predetermined referendum" and "the annexation of a once-proud island" by Canada in 1949.

Her bitterness was thinly disguised. Her language, extravagant. It was the oddest essay—part earnest treatise, part sorrowful elegy. And as I read I realized that she was often not writing about Newfoundland at all. Her subject was something else entirely—something she disguised with her statistics, and her footnotes, and her carefully documented evidence. She was writing about what she had lost to mistakes, and to blunders, and to meaningless sacrifice. History, from her point of view, had unravelled in error and in tragedy. Nothing had turned out as it should have. Her heart had been broken. I had the impression that when she wrote the word "province," she willed her typewriter to spit out the eight offending letters.

She also contributed regularly to the Letters to the Editor page of the Swan *Sentinel-Dispatch*. These letters were carefully clipped, dated, pasted on small panels of cardboard, and stored in the bottom drawer of a filing cabinet—the drawer in which I found the key to her rolltop desk, the only part of the study that, by my second week in Miss Allen's house, I had not yet explored.

By the 1960s, her published letters dealt with a single recurring subject. In the newspaper they always appeared in June, and were almost always headed "Lest We Forget." Their tone, long-departed from the gentle, poetic flights of the young Belle, had taken on the crankiness of the crabby old woman who rapped at her living-room window when neighbourhood children cut through her privet or slid on her driveway. "In Newfoundland," she wrote in a letter to the *Sentinel-Dispatch*, published on June 28, 1966, "July 1 is Memorial Day—a time of grave solemnity and heartfelt remembrance. This year this is particularly so, for it was fifty years ago, on July 1, 1916, that so many of her sons fell so bravely on the field of a terrible battle. It is contemptible that this sacred hour, by an unhappy coincidence of dates, is now pushed aside in popular imagination by the noisome firecrackers and the frivolous celebrations of Canada's birthday."

The appearance of this complaint must have been something of an annual event for readers of the *Sentinel-Dispatch*. "Oh, look," people must have said, snapping back the editorial page. "Miss Edna Allen has written one of her letters to the newspaper again. The old girl certainly has a one-track mind." They must have sipped their after-dinner instant coffees, and there, from the perspective of the modern age, chuckled at her angry and old-fashioned choice of words.

IT WAS THE SUMMER of 1966 when Gilmour came up with the idea. We were both ten years old at the time.

I wasn't sure about it myself. I'd never heard of anyone going from door to door to sing the national anthem on Dominion Day. But there was already a lot of talk in the newspapers and on the radio and television about the approaching Centennial Year, and Gilmour thought we could capitalize on the growing excitement.

"Like carollers," he said. "Or trick-or-treat. We'll ring their doorbell and sing 'O Canada.' Then they'll give us money and we'll go to the next house."

"Why would anyone give us any money?"

"Because it's such a patriotic gesture," said Gilmour, who had an excellent vocabulary.

So I went along with the plan. I'm not sure I was convinced it would work. Nor was I at all certain that the two of us could successfully carry a tune. But the fact was that neither Gilmour's family nor mine ever went away anywhere for the holidays, and probably, even as early in the summer as July 1, we were bored. At least it would give us something to do.

I can't imagine why we chose to begin on Old Lady Allen's veranda. We were both afraid of her. We both shared some suspicions about her supernatural powers. Did we dare one another to climb up those steps? Perhaps. Or perhaps, in a moment of bravado, I lied to Gilmour and told him that she didn't scare me one bit, and perhaps he lied back. I can't now recall. But somehow, against what must have surely been our better judgement, we ended up starting our rounds on her veranda. We thought a little after nine in the morning would be late enough. We rang the doorbell and with quavering, off-key voices began to sing "O Canada."

I think now that she only opened that desk once a year. Once I realized what the key was for, and once I rolled back the desk's rounded top, I was surprised by how regimented and exclusive its contents were. I expected to see the little wooden cubicles crammed with pens, and stamps, and paper clips, and stationery. I was still, even then, hopeful that I would find another sheaf of letters from Harry Cooper. But in fact, except for three objects laid out in a perfectly neat row on the writing surface, the desk was entirely empty.

In a small, velvet case there was a single medal: the Military Cross. In a varnished wooden box, there was a revolver: a Webley Mark V with the patent date, 1914, stamped just above three stencilled letters—H.J.C. And in the kind of cardboard container that typing paper might have come in, there was a stack of articles clipped from magazines, and newspapers, and military journals. The cardboard had been neatly covered with black lining fabric and bore a typewritten label: "The Battle of Beaumont-Hamel, July 1, 1916."

There was something so unused about the inside of the desk, and yet something so established in its purpose, I guessed immediately that it was the place of an annual ritual. I think that on the morning of every July 1 Miss Allen must have opened that desk and sat there in silence: staring at the medal; holding the heavy, grey weight of the gun, perhaps the last object that Harry Cooper ever touched; reading over and over the accounts of that awful day, as if by peering closer and closer at those printed words and examining those reproduced maps and blurry old photographs she could see exactly what happened to him and know precisely the hour that he fell.

She would have known the story very well. How, just after midnight on July 1, at the Twenty-ninth Division's front and not far from the French village of Beaumont-Hamel, the Newfoundlanders had moved into a trench called Tipperary Avenue. They were ordered forward. Two hours later they were huddled against the front wall of a support trench called St. John's Road. This would be their jumping-off point, and they spent the night there while the British artillery screamed in the darkness over their heads.

The Germans were only a little more than five hundred yards away. Their elevation gave them excellent firing position. They had an unobstructed view of the Allied trenches, of the loops of barbed wire, and of no man's land. The British commander, General Sir Douglas Haig, thought that the artillery fire would shake the enemy from this advantage, but it did no such thing. They were too well dug in. The steadily increasing bombardment had only one effect: it alerted the Germans to the

Battle of the Somme: General view of the battlefield looking towards Contalmaison, July 1916.

fact that Haig's long-suspected advance—the opening of the Battle of the Somme—was imminent.

As I read the accounts of the battle, I was interested to see that Miss Allen had underlined a quote from an officer of the South Wales Borderers, the regiment that occupied the two trenches in front of the Newfoundlanders: "Just before dawn the salvos along the line had increased to a point where the artillery fire no longer sounded like punctuated noises, but more like a steadily growing rush in the darkness above us—an uninterrupted stream of sound and invisible flight, rather like the terrifying sensation of a thousand bats flying out the window of a barn at night. We couldn't have given the Bosh better warning that we were coming." Beside this, in turquoise fountain pen, Miss Allen had written, "Haig was an idiot."

Just after seven-thirty in the morning, the South Wales Borderers went over. The Newfoundlanders crouched, waiting, and although they couldn't see what was going on, they could tell from the shouts, and the screams, and by the blanketing rattle of German machine guns that the artillery bombardment had been useless. They must have all realized what was going to happen.

They all knew that they would have to advance unprotected and unsupported, across an open field, into a blizzard of bullets. And just after nine, on the morning of July 1, 1916, that was what they were ordered to do.

I don't think that Old Lady Allen meant to frighten us as much as she did. I imagine that she was just sitting at her desk, in her study, as she sat at that time on the morning of every July 1, staring into the years—now more than twice as many as he had ever lived—trying to picture the moment when the young officer had stood and had somehow found his voice within his own frightened jabs of breath and pounding heart. "All right, lads. Buck up. This is it."

She must have wished so much that she could see clearly what she had tried so often to imagine. Through the smoke, through the bursts of mud and flesh, through the ever-darkening and inexplicable past: to his last few steps, to his shouts of encouragement, to the revolver in his hand with which he waved his men forward.

The doorbell and then the sound of two little boys singing "O Canada" would have been the last things she would have expected or would have wanted to hear at that moment. It would have been like waking from a vivid dream. She would have stopped. She would have stood slowly in her study, listening, bewildered at first. Then she would have hurried on her thin, frail legs to the front door. She would have opened it abruptly. She would have shouted at us and clattered forward to shoo us away. She would have been furious, of course. But not as furious as we thought she was. She was dressed in black, and she came out of the darkness, flapping at us angrily. We were scared to death. She must have forgotten what she was holding in her pale, tiny hand.

Michael Turner

THE DEATH OF
ALBERT "GINGER" GOODWIN
(*As Told by a Very Old Man*
Who Wishes to Remain Anonymous)

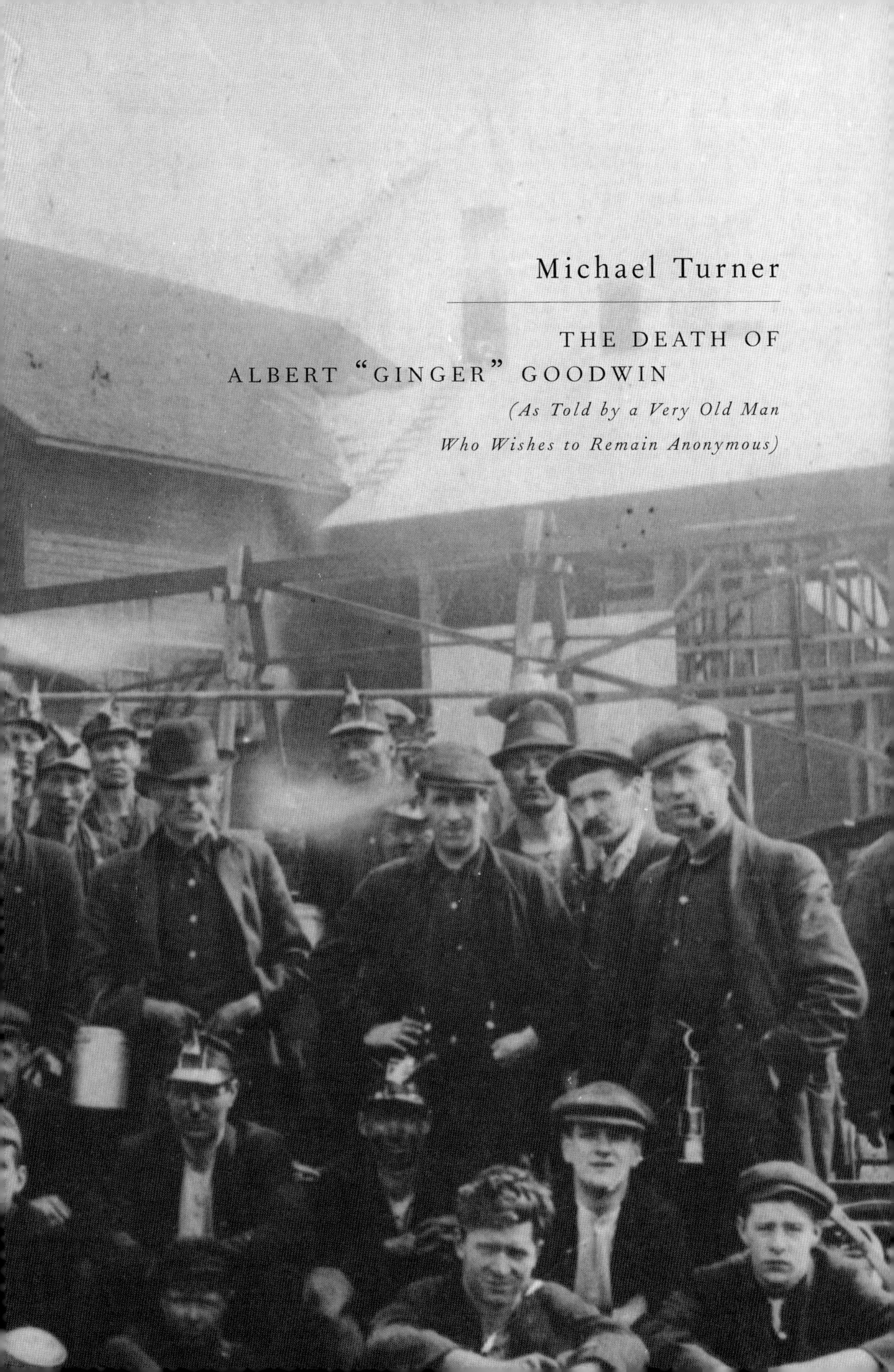

The history of any country can be told through the human labour it takes to maintain that country.

Afterall, who would know a country better than the builders of its canals and railways, its factories and homes? Problem is, "official" histories are usually the stories of those in control of their nation's wealth: employers, not employees; members of Parliament, not members of the rank and file. Certainly, this is true of Canada.

One reason labour is underrepresented in Canadian history is because a labour-based party has never formed a federal government. Another reason can be found in our age-old obsssession with spectacular individual achievement, from the mythic exploits of Greek and Roman gods to Madonna's latest "look." But perhaps the biggest impediment to labour's place in "official" history is best explained by our ambivalence to that which most of us do every day—and that's work.

At the turn of the twentieth century, Albert "Ginger" Goodwin came to

Above: The headstone of a working man, Albert "Ginger" Goodwin.
Previous: #5 Mine Crew, Cumberland, British Columbia, ca. 1910.

Canada in search of work. His specialty was coal mining, and he was good at it. Like many young workers, he was lured here by the prospect of big money and broad horizons; it also promised to be a lot better than the squalor he and others were leaving behind, be it a feudal Asia or a class-bound Western Europe. Canada seemed undefined (many would argue it still is), and perhaps Goodwin and his fellow workers felt that what they didn't know couldn't hurt them. Perhaps they might even contribute towards its distinction, leave their mark, make history.

But Goodwin learned all too quickly that what was happening in his native England was happening in Canada as well. Men and women continued to toil under abysmal conditions, for less than adequate wages. Didn't matter whether it was the Maritimes, Central Canada, the Prairies, the Territories or British Columbia—by the time Goodwin arrived in the coal mining town of Cumberland, B.C., he had seen it all. And Cumberland would prove no different.

Not much is known about Ginger Goodwin. Had he been born into the Dunsmuir family, the family who owned the mine where he worked, we might know more. But because his life belongs to the labour movement, and because labour history is only an upper-level undergraduate course as opposed to a shiny coffee-table book, Goodwin remains more mystery than biography. Hopefully my fiction will change that; hopefully by the end of my tale you will see the importance of Ginger Goodwin's murder and how it helped spark what I consider to be a Great Canadian Event: Canada's first general strike.

But before I begin I would like to say a few words about why my entry looks the way it does. This has to do with yet another reason why labour history is underrepresented: and that's because labour histories, like local and folk histories, are primarily oral—and very often unreliable, eccentric, and impolite. As everyone knows, "getting it in writing" is always better than "what you thought you heard." This bias extends to the idea that literature is what appears in a book, not what's said in a nightclub or a sweat lodge.

In researching this story there were a number of occasions when I wished I could have spoken with someone who knew Ginger Goodwin. Unfortunately, that was not possible, because all those who knew him are now dead.

But what if? What if there was someone who remembered him? What would they have to say about a man whose importance to the Canadian labour movement cannot be overstated?

THE DEATH OF
ALBERT "GINGER" GOODWIN

(As Told by a Very Old Man Who Wishes to Remain Anonymous)

THIS INTERVIEW TOOK PLACE during the last week of August 2000, at the informant's West Vancouver home. We met in the den, a fir-panelled room where the informant was wheeled in by his granddaughter and positioned before a roaring fire. I was shocked when I saw him. Until then I had only seen photographs, all of them taken during a 1935 log-chopping competition at the Pacific National Exhibition. He was a big man in those days—and by big I mean broad-shouldered and muscular, dressed in a T-shirt and dark pants. Only now he was a twig in comparison; his canary-yellow track suit two sizes too large, the left side of his face a cancerous scab, his brown eyes dried paint. Yet despite his physical condition he remained sharp and energetic. Each session was held in the presence of his granddaughter, a middle-aged woman who spent most of her time at the window, rapt in the latest Shields.

MONDAY

Nowadays, when we talk of something great, we think of something good. That's how much language has changed. When I was young, the First World War was the Great War. It took the invention of the Second World War to turn the Great War into World War One. When I asked my granddaughter—a lawyer—if I should accept your offer of an interview regarding my brush with Ginger Goodwin, she said it was a good idea. Great, I told her, let's do it. That's why she's with me today. Not only is she in charge of my oxygen but she's also going to make sure you don't ask me anything stupid, get me into trouble. For all I know, the Dominion Society is just another branch of Revenue Canada. Not that I don't pay my taxes.

What do I know about Ginger Goodwin? Very little. Truth is, nobody knows that much about him. In that respect I'm not alone. But I can tell you this: he was a great man. And history has been easier on him than that idiot, the kaiser. Not that I could appreciate Goodwin's greatness when I saw him running through the woods that day; that would come later. We're talking July 26, 1918. I was a kid then, a teenager. Fifteen years old I was. In those days, a fifteen-year-old was considered a man, although today we're supposed to call them "young adults," even though they don't know the first thing about responsibility on account of all that dope they grow in their cars . . . [inaudible]

He was a great man, Ginger Goodwin. But he was just a man, you know. Nothing special. A little guy. Scrawny. Red hair, brown teeth. I saw him speak once, in public, and he was good. Not the best, mind you, but good. Coughed a lot, but that was the silicosis talking. What else? Rumour had it he came from Yorkshire, where he started in the pits at fifteen. You were a man then, at fifteen. And if you didn't have property, and you weren't the oldest son, then you went into the church or the military, or you went off to work in somebody's hole. Which might explain how he ended up here, in Canada. That or he was on the lam. Or maybe he was just curious. *Who knows?*

My grandfather worked in the mines. But my father—he never worked in the mines. Too smart for that. Which isn't to say he was stuck-up. More on that later. My father had a barbershop, in Cumberland; it was on Dunsmuir Avenue between the Waverely and New England hotels. He did well by it, and we were never without. This despite all those free shaves he gave to retired miners. There were rough patches, of course. Not many people know this but there was a depression at the turn of the century. I only know about it because my mother kept its memory alive as an

excuse to get me to eat my kale. Thank God for the depression: if I hadn't eaten all that kale, I never would have lived to see that asshole Muldoon get bounced from office. Who the hell does that guy think he is . . . [inaudible]

Of course, there's a reason for a depression; they don't just happen. Nothing *just* happens. That's the problem with free markets—big peaks, huge valleys. Just like Cumberland itself. Not that there's anything natural about capitalism.

Ginger Goodwin, 1917.

[Informant sips water.]

The kind of society Ginger Goodwin was hollering for when he wasn't demanding better wages and a shorter workday was a socialist society, a society where everybody would have just enough. No big bank accounts, no lawn greener than your neighbours'. And no wars to fight. Everybody would get looked after; nobody would be without. Pretty idealistic if you ask me. Then again, I spent the better part of my life working towards those very goals. And for most of my life I thought we were going to get them, too! You have to believe in something. If you don't, you might as well go to Paris and read Camus. Ginger Goodwin got people fired up. He'd have you think your ass was on fire if you let him. That's what a good talker can do.

It's impossible to know how great Goodwin was without knowing what else was going on in the world at the time, and how that affected what was going on in Cumberland. I mentioned the depression. I also mentioned that nothing *just* happens. This is important. Depressions are a product of capitalism, and capitalism was the language of the Industrial Revolution, which as you know began in Western Europe in the eighteenth century. It was the Industrial Revolution that led to massive displacement, the Enclosures Act, people getting kicked off the land so the landlords could use it more profitably. Eventually these landlords brought in machines to do the work of people. These machines led to a smaller workforce. A smaller workforce and an increasing population meant rising unemployment. But with all these people out of work, who can afford the product? So what you had was this huge rift between those with money and those without. Sure, there was a so-called middle class—but those idiots wanted to swim with the rich, not the poor. The middle classes are the scourge of the earth as far as I'm concerned; they wreck everything. But they're important historically, as everything's important. Like I said, nothing *just* happens.

[Informant takes oxygen.]

Another thing that's worth mentioning is the rise of the nation-state. European countries, by now the richest in the world, were getting very competitive with one another. In order to better compete, they began looting the rest of the world for raw materials and labour. Imperialism—a.k.a. colonialism. So now what you had were all these European countries sailing off to Africa and Asia and South America, planting flags and shooting anyone who didn't like their colours. Of course, this had been going on for centuries. Columbus, Magellan, Cortez—those guys were pricks! Even your Captain Vancouver—he planted flags all up and down the B.C. coast. At one point Cumberland was known as the farthest corner of the British Empire: a mile up the road, nothing but trees. Shadows all the way to the bloody North Pole! It was enough to scare the shit out of you. You get lost in those woods and your only hope was Saint Nick putting you back in your stocking at Christmas.

Nothing excites an economy like war. Because when you have war, you have emergency measures. You've heard of rationing? Well, governments all of a sudden start dictating what you can and can't eat. That's just the beginning. Pretty soon they tell you when you can and can't go to the crapper. You have no idea how much money this saves a government. It's called a command economy. [Informant becomes agitated.] So where does all the money go? Into the war, of course. And how are wars paid for? The spoils of war! This is all figured out in advance, through treaties and alliances. [Informant stops. As if on cue, his granddaughter steps towards him, applies eyedrops. They run down his cheeks like tears.] What a waste of human life. [Five seconds of silence.] When that faggot Trudeau announced the War Measures Act, he justified his actions because of what was happening in Québec! But if that's the case, how come the RCMP were busting hippies and trade unionists in British Columbia? How come . . . [inaudible, expletive, coughing]

[Fifteen seconds of silence.]

But what if you don't want to go to war? Well, Ginger Goodwin didn't want to go to war. Didn't believe in it. In fact, ninety-five per cent of the men conscripted during the Great War applied for exemptions. But like most of the men conscripted he showed up for his physical anyway. Course he didn't pass. Not with those teeth. They took one look at those teeth and said phooey. You know why they don't let you into the army with bad teeth? Well, I'm asking you—*Do you know why?* [No.] Ever tried holding a gun to your cheek when your gums are swollen, every tooth in your mouth a potential stick of dynamite? [silent] *Well?* [No.] Try it sometime. I guarantee you won't pull the trigger for fear your whole face will explode.

[Informant has a coughing fit. I am told by his granddaughter to come back Wednesday.]

WEDNESDAY

Granddaughter says you want me to spend more time on Goodwin's death and less on the rhetoric. Well fuck you! [agitated] How can you talk about the importance of somebody's death without the life that came before it? What's more, how can you talk about a life without the lives going on around it, the conditions in which those lives are lived, and what comes next, et cetera? You want me to talk about Ginger Goodwin because I was the last one to see him before his killer—*which is exactly what I'm trying to do!* As for your so-called rhetoric, you don't know what the hell you're talking about! Where do you think I get it from—*books?* Everything I learned I learned in the lock-up. That and experience—which I'll get to later. You asked me to talk about Goodwin. Good. So why don't you shut up and let me.

[Informant takes oxygen.]

Before he started proselytizing, Goodwin used to go into the woods and practise. That's how I came to know him: I was just some kid sneaking off for a pull. [Informant smiles for the first time.] Now what do you make of that, huh? The story of a young man's urges and how that set him on the path to class politics. Why don't you write about that? [Informant's granddaughter winces, shakes her head.] Oh, you thought guys my age just passed the day sucking government oxygen, did you? Well, think again!

[Informant sips water.]

I believe I left off with Goodwin being excused from military service. Let me take that back: he wasn't excused, he was declared unfit. Lots of men were declared unfit. Category D, they called it. Only some of these men were later reclassified A—A for overseas duty. Goodwin was one of these men. We're talking May 1917. The Military Services Act—or conscription—had just passed vote; all part of what I was getting at earlier: emergency measures. Anyway, Goodman was in Trail two years after getting blacklisted in Cumberland. Did I mention that—Goodwin getting blacklisted? [No.] Well he was—in 1915. He was blacklisted for organizing the coal workers—him, Joe Naylor, and a good many more. The Big Strike, we called it.

After Cumberland he went to work in Merritt, then the Crow's Nest Pass, then the Trail smelter, where he became a big shot with the union. It was around that time Goodwin was mysteriously reclassified. He tried to appeal, but the powers that be wouldn't have it. The British needed cannon fodder, and our man Borden was only too happy to oblige. But even more than that: reclassification provided this country with an excuse to get rid of its critics. Goodwin could see the writing on the wall, and that's why he took flight, eventually returning to Cumberland, where he and some others hid out in the woods.

[Informant stops, turns his head towards the window.]

Where was I? [agitated] Aw, now you've got me flustered; I don't know where I am! [thinking] Let me back up, let me tell you how Goodwin got black-listed—

—Why don't you tell me what happened in the woods that day?

—No, this is important.

—Yeah, but I already told you, I'm not interested in that stuff. I'm—

—That stuff?

—I mean his labour activities.

—That stuff?

—Okay, how'd he get blacklisted?

—Forget it! If you know so much—*you tell me*!

—Okay, you're right. It's important.

—Too late.

—Pardon me?

—*Too late.* Now get the fuck out of my house!

Michael TURNER

FRIDAY

I appreciate your letter—your apology—and I thank you for the [courier] package. I'm already familiar with the Mayse book—by far the best book on the topic—even though she never spoke to me when she wrote it. The Bowen book is good, too. Nice lady—smart. Not sure what I make of the [Hanebury] book because I don't generally go in for fiction. But I like what I've read so far; the kid has a feel for the times—rare for a man his age. I'll get to the [Bowering and Leier] books later.

[Informant sips water.]

You seem to know quite a bit about the labour movement. I'm impressed. I suppose what concerns me, though, is that I'm not sure of your intentions. You say you're writing a fictional account of Goodwin's last minutes, but what you expect to say in all that is beyond me. I've never heard of those other stories you mentioned [Beirce's "Incident at Owl Creek Bridge" and Golding's *Pincher Martin*], but if they're as good as you say they are, then I don't know why you're copying them when there's so many other things you could be writing about, like Joe Naylor or the greedy Dunsmuirs—or me, for that matter! [laughs] Just my opinion.

That said, I suppose I owe you an apology. Granddaughter reminded me you were straight-up from the beginning, and that you were only interested in what I saw in the woods that day. And I guess I got excited because I wanted to tell my own story, see? Don't know if I would've agreed to this interview had I remembered that. [laughs] Not too late to change my mind, is it? [laughs] Suppose I owe her an apology, too. [aside] Sorry, dear. [Informant's granddaughter looks up from her book, shakes her head.]

[Five seconds of silence.]

So let's start over. Let's start with what I did that day. I'll start at the beginning, because that way it'll help me remember exactly what happened when I came upon Goodwin.

[Informant takes oxygen.]

July 26, 1918. A Saturday. I woke up early—earlier than usual—after a particularly vivid dream concerning myself, Lotte Gerber, and a spongy patch of moss. It was not unusual to have a dream like that, because it was all I could think about in those days. Gals. If it wasn't Lotte Gerber, well, it was probably Missie Parks or Biddy McKay, or some drawing I'd seen in my mother's Hudson's Bay catalogue. Point is, I got up early, my heart set on a walk. Couldn't do much with my brothers snoring beside me. Or pretending to, that is. There was an unspoken rule amongst us brothers: no you-know-what in the bed.

We lived in the back of my father's shop. There were three bedrooms in our house: my sisters in one room, the boys across the hall, and my parents in the room upstairs. The path from our room to the back door led directly through the kitchen. Usually when I got up my mother and sisters would be baking bread, plucking chickens, making antipasto, whatever. They worked hard, those gals. I remember thinking it must be pretty early in the morning because the kitchen was pitch-black. I lit a match and held it to the clock: 3:27 A.M.

The back door made a terrible racket. Took me a full five minutes to open and close it. Of course, as soon as I closed it I realized I wouldn't need my coat, because it had been hotter than hell that summer. Even at three-thirty in the morning it was way too hot for cotton. Thought about leaving it on the stoop, but there were drunks in the alley, and I knew if I left it there, somebody might come along and scoff it. That or they'd use it to wipe off their shoes. My mother paid good money for that coat; it was the first piece of clothing I owned that wasn't purchased from the boys' wear department of Campbell's, so I wasn't going to take any chances. I tied it around my waist instead.

At the far end of the alley, a fat man in a singlet was playing a squeeze box while the guy beside him sang along. I reckoned it was them that woke me. Every time the singer came upon the word "Siobhan" he'd let rip with the most blood-curdling scream I have ever heard in my life. If I close my eyes, I can still hear it. [closing his eyes, then demonstrating] Sio-bhaaaaan! [coughing] And that guy with the squeeze box—he cracked up every time that happened. [coughing, then laughing]

[Informant sips water.]

Everybody was out that night. I mentioned the drunks, but there were also couples on their porches, fanning themselves with cedar shingles, their faces ghoulish in the candlelight. I remember Mrs. Drummond in her rocking chair. Poor woman. Her husband and sons were killed a couple of years before in a cave-in at Mine Five—which, incidentally, is where Goodwin once worked as a pony man. Oh yes, I remember her well: she was wearing her husband's housecoat, and it was open in such a way that you could see her flesh from neck to belly. From where I stood it looked as though she was crying. That or she was grimacing. Either way, she had reason to be upset: Lord Dunsmuir never gave two shits about the men in his mine, and a lot of good women were widowed on account of that fact. I wanted to say hello but lost my nerve. I thought maybe she didn't want anyone to see her like that, but I also knew she could bend your ear for hours if you let her, so I kept on.

As I approached the end of Dunsmuir I saw a huddle of men near the playing field. I'd been around long enough to know what that shape meant, and that was a fist fight. These were loud affairs, and usually you'd hear one before you actually saw it. But I had never seen a fight in the middle of the night before, so I suppose that accounts for how come it was quiet. There was a space between Toe Wong and his cousin Clark, so I peeked in. But instead of a fight, what should I see but a militiaman, maybe nineteen years old, on his hands and knees, blood pouring out of his mouth.

Awful. Crouched next to him was a stranger, a well-dressed man, middle-aged, hold-ing a small lantern beside the kid's face. He was asking, in a very hard whisper [imi-tatively]: "What did you tell them?" and "What did they say they were gonna do?" The militiaman responded with a spit tooth. The stranger patted him on the back, told him it was okay, told him he did his best. I asked Clark what was going on but he ignored me. Like everyone else, he was only interested in the militiaman. I stepped back and that's when I bumped into Vito.

Vito Oliva worked for my father on Saturdays. He was an old guy, quiet, and relatively new to the area. Nobody knew much about him, but what we did know was that he came from Alberta and that he spent his weekdays building a house at Comox Lake. A lot of families had taken up residence at the lake that summer, on account of the hot spell. I would've asked him what was going on but he beat me to it.

"What are you doing out?" he demanded, as if to accuse me of something.

I told him I couldn't sleep. "The heat," I said, which should have been good enough for anyone, given the temperatures.

Vito looked over his shoulder. "Do you know any of these men?" he asked me.

I lied, told him no. I don't know why I lied but I did.

"Okay," he said. "I'm going to need your help."

Now I wished I'd told the truth.

I followed Vito across the playing field, towards the woods. The grass had just been cut, and the smell was so hot and thick it was like leaning over a pot of cabbage. At one point I thought I saw a man and woman kissing, but as we drew close they turned into a couple of gunny sacks, both of them overflowing with clothes.

"Grab those sacks," said Vito, not stopping. He was a sliver in the distance by the time I knew what I was doing with those sacks.

I entered the woods exhausted. There was no way I was going any farther, not with those sacks. Must have weighed a hundred pounds those sacks. I sat down, rubbed my shoulder, and waited. And waited. Waited for what must have been a half-hour. Just as the sky was changing from black to dark blue I heard a horse snort, then the punch of hooves.

Three pit ponies, Vito in the middle holding the reins.

"Bring me those sacks," he whispered; and his whisper was hard, like that man with the lantern.

We tied the sacks to the ponies.

"You know how to ride?" he asked me, stepping into his stirrup.

I did.

"Who are the sacks for?" I asked.

"Who do you think?" he replied.

I knew they were for the resisters, but I didn't say. I didn't say because I was afraid he might ask me how I knew—because I wasn't sure how I knew, I just did. People talk, you put it together. That's what really scared me—not being out on my own but having to answer for something I didn't have an answer for. I didn't know why I knew the clothes were for the resisters, and the reason I didn't know was because nobody told me. Up until then, that's how I came to know everything—somebody told me. It was only later that I knew what I was doing. But even then somebody had to tell me. Once I learned how to think for myself I was off to the races.

Vito turned his pony around, gave it a kick. I jumped on mine and did the same.

[Informant sips water.]

I'm not sure how long we rode for, or what route we took, but the sun was coming up as we made our descent on Comox Lake. I could hear children splashing, their mothers calling out, the sound of axes splitting wood. Vito told me he wouldn't be very long. He tied the ponies to a tree and ambled down a trail, only to return a

moment later, all smiles. He held up a canvas mailbag and announced he'd just bought lunch.

     I had no idea what was going on. And I was nervous. Nervous because my mother was up by then and she was probably out of her mind with concern. What would I tell her? It was then that I suggested we go back to Cumberland; not because I was worried about my absence but because Vito was supposed to be working for my father. You can imagine how surprised I was when he told me that everything had

Families at Lake Comox, British Columbia, 1914.

been taken care of. Vito had arranged in advance that he wouldn't be going into work that day, and that news of my whereabouts had already been passed on to my father. Even more surprising was that word had travelled back! Apparently he was proud I was supporting the cause. Funny thing—up until that day I had never talked to my father about anything other than school or sports, and now, all of a sudden, he was proud?

My assignment was to take a very small envelope to Arthur Boothman, one of the men hiding out with Goodwin. In the top right-hand corner of the envelope was a tiny map. I was told that if I was confronted by Mounties or militiamen, then I was to tear off the corner and swallow it. The place I was to take this letter was what's known today as Forbidden Plateau. From now on, I would be on my own.

The walk probably took an hour, and a lot passed through my head. I always look back on that walk as a significant time in my life, where everything I'd seen and heard and felt fit together to form a whole. For example, it was impossible to avoid the consequences of the Big Strike, all those men out of work, their children losing weight before your very eyes, the slow erosion of hope as, one by one, families left town in the dead of night, in advance of the company reallocating their house—or worse, ashamed to let their neighbours know they couldn't take it any more; just as it was impossible to ignore the fact that Cumberland was a coal-mining town perched on the edge of the so-called Commonwealth, how the aristocratic Dunsmuirs came from Her Majesty's Britain and we—the Indian, the English, the Italian, Scottish, Irish, Welsh, Chinese, Japanese, Slavic, Scandinavian, all those who provided muscle to make coal happen—how we made up their working class.

You couldn't walk down Dunsmuir without seeing some physical evidence of how dangerous it was to work in those mines, be it some old man coughing his lungs out in front of the Bucket of Blood, or some youngster hobbling along on one leg, the weight of that lost leg tugging at his best attempt at a brave face. Same goes for Mrs. Drummond: it was impossible to look at that woman without seeing the horror in her eyes, the memory of her husband and sons lying there dead in a hole. All that came together on my walk. Because now it was the face of Lord Dunsmuir I would see whenever I thought about how bad things could get—and the face of Ginger Goodwin when I realized how much better we could make it.

[Informant sips water.]

I found the rendezvous point no problem, a huge cedar beside a running stream. I sat down and made myself visible. Then I shut my eyes and thought of Lotte Gerber. Something snapped. I looked around—nothing. Heard it again: a branch breaking, then another. Footsteps. They were moving quickly. I stood up. Coming down the slope was Goodwin. His eyes were huge and he kept looking behind him. He was breathing heavily, and you could hear each breath as loud as you could his footsteps. Passed no more than six feet in front of me. Not that he saw me— too caught up in what was coming. He disappeared behind a stump, his feet splashing as he made his way across the stream. That was the last I heard of him.

Fearing the worst, I took out the envelope and tore off the corner. I put it in my mouth and chewed until it was soft enough to swallow. Then I took the envelope and shoved it down a hole at the base of the cedar. I was sweating and my stomach was in knots. I knew I had to collect myself, so I sat down on a rock, pulled out my penknife, and started to whittle. Then I laughed—how ridiculous! Whoever was chasing Goodwin would be on me in a second. They knew I would have seen him. And besides, what was I doing miles from home, sitting in the forest whittling? It wouldn't add up. So I put the penknife in my pocket, opened my trousers, and uri-nated. Seconds later a voice called out. "You there—halt!"

Coming down the slope were five militiamen, armed to the teats. The guy in front, leading the pack, was forthright.

"You seen a man pass by—short, red hair, in a light-blue shirt?"

Course I did, you stupid pig. Only I didn't say that. We didn't call cops pigs in those days; that was a word we used for the Dunsmuirs. Yet another example of how much language has changed.

No, I wasn't sure how I might respond. I'd already told my lie that day—and look what it got me! That's when I realized there was no other answer but the truth. Which is what I told him—the truth. Not that I opened my mouth to say so—no way. I just looked him in the eye and pointed. That's all I did—pointed. And off they ran like a pack of dogs. No sooner did they disappear behind the stump when a shot rang out. Then another. Then another after that.

We still don't know whether it was the militia or [Dominion Constable] Dan Campbell who gunned down [Ginger] Goodwin, but it hardly seemed to matter at the time. That bullet was all I needed to start running. Didn't even stop to pick up my coat. I ran and I ran and I ran. And in many ways I haven't stopped since. Not until today, that is.

—So you killed Ginger Goodwin.

[Informant's granddaughter advises informant not to answer the question. Informant waves her away.]

—Market forces killed Ginger Goodwin.

—Okay, so you *helped* kill Ginger Goodwin.

[Informant's granddaughter advises informant not to answer this question either. Once again he waves her away. This time she leaves the room.]

—I've helped a lot of people in my life.

[Informant sips water.]

I've helped a lot of people in my life, yes I have. [Informant pauses, looks out the window.] Because from that day forward not only did I know what I wanted in life but I knew the means to achieve it. But when I say *means* I'm not suggesting anything as horrific as what happened in the woods that day; not because I have avoided situations like that—I would have done it again had the opportunity arisen—but because those situations come but once in a lifetime. And when they do, not only do you have to act but you have to live with the consequences as well. Of course, what's good for the cause can also be very bad for your heart. So yes, in a way, I did my bit to kill him.

[Four seconds of silence.]

—I don't know what to say.

—Don't say anything.

[Eight seconds of silence.]

Coffee-table historians will have you believe that the Great War began when a young Serb named Gavrillo Princip, a member of a secret society called the Black Hand, pulled a pistol from his coat pocket and shooting two holes into the chest of that fatso, the archduke. Interesting how that action kicked off the very war Ginger Goodwin was protesting, the war that provided our government the justification it needed to kill him.

Princip's bullet was not so much a beginning as an ending. Sure it marked the beginning of the Great War, but it would be a mistake to think it was the sole cause of that war. Why? Because nothing *just* happens. All those European countries fighting over stolen land, all those paranoid alliances, big business . . . Princip's bullet was just the tip of the iceberg. Why it's all placed on him is the product of a history that's only concerned with distancing us from that which really matters: and that's the whole rotten system. It's much easier to remember a name and a date than it is to understand how capital works—or organized labour, for that matter.

If Princip is a villain, Goodwin's a martyr. The Canadian labour movement needed a martyr, and Goodwin was perfect. Would he have agreed with me? You're damn right—he was a very intelligent man. But would he have volunteered? Not on your life. This guy had an ego the size of the sun. And guys with swollen heads don't go down easy in Cumberland. Did you know the whole time he was hiding out he would sneak into town for dances? A real charmer, that Goodwin. A great man.

—Thank you for your time.

—Don't thank me yet.

[Informant takes oxygen.]

Six days after Goodwin's death, Vito and I arrived in Vancouver and took part in this country's first general strike. August 2, 1918. The strike couldn't have happened had it not been for the outrage over Goodwin's murder, because Campbell, who took credit for the killing, claimed Goodwin pointed a .22 at his head, which may or may not have been the case. Not that it matters. When he was acquitted, everybody went nuts. Which is why I went to Vancouver with Vito: in this case, to defend the Metal Trades office from returning servicemen, all those shell-shocked veterans pissed off not only with our protest but our anti-conscription stance as well. Although it was the servicemen who destroyed the office, it was us who went to jail.

It was in lock-up that I met the people who would ignite my passion for organized labour, a passion I turned into a profession until my retirement in 1968. These were just everyday people, like Vito, but they taught me more in one week than I could learn in a lifetime. It was them that taught me the importance of workers like

Joe Hill and that tiny little woman who visited Cumberland during the Big Strike—Mother Jones. You've heard of Joe Hill and Mother Jones, haven't you? [Yes.] Joe Hill became a song. And Mother Jones—she became a magazine. Had a subscription until it went liberal.

But these people also taught me something else: they taught me that history is a business, and like any good business you have to manage it properly. Me, I like to think of it as a bank. In order to attract customers, you have to offer a good rate of

Ginger Goodwin's funeral procession, August 2, 1918.

return. And the best way to do that is through poster boys like Goodwin. As I said earlier, he was good at raising interest; but he was even better at it once he was dead. Because once you're dead you're perfect. And if you're lucky, you get to live on in people's imaginations. The sense of purpose his death generated was like money in the bank for organized labour. And that's basically what I did all those years— managed people's imaginations.

Once you understand how history works, then you can make it work for you. It's as simple as that. But that's not why I pointed out Goodwin that day; that was just a feeling. It was only later that I learned to put it all together, make it bigger. Which is why, despite your best intentions, I can never really tell you what happened in the woods that day. Some things are better left unsaid. [Informant smiles.] As for what's left, you'll just have to use your imagination.

—Are you finished?

—No. But you can go.

Timothy Findley

THE BANKS OF THE WABASH

There is some current and reliable scientific evidence

that if we do not bring about our own demise, nature will do it for us. As a species, we are particularly vulnerable to viral infections which can and do take a terrible toll—first there, then here, then somewhere else. And because we have developed such a sophisticated system of intercontinental travel, one human being on returning from a journey abroad can become the carrier of a virus that can decimate a whole community. One man, one woman, one child can unwittingly become a walking plague centre.

This, in effect, is what happened at first in Europe and then in North America at the end of the so-called Great War. Soldiers returning to their homes in 1918 and 1919 spread the deadly virus that came to be known as the Spanish Flu. The result was catastrophic. The epidemic reached continental and then intercontinental dimensions, leaving the shores of Europe and North America to claim more victims elsewhere. By the time it had run its course, it was responsible for more deaths than

AIDS day ceremony.

all the weapons and armies of the Great War combined. The flu killed twenty-two million.

Twenty-two million.

In my own family, the victim was my mother's brother, whose death was both tragic and ironic. Because of his age, he had been spared induction and this way had managed—just—to avoid death on the battlefield. But, as the war wound down to its close, the virus killed him in the very moment when the whole of his life lay before him.

While I myself was growing up, I heard the story of his death many times, and of the death of my father's brother from war wounds. This way, the Spanish Flu and the Great War became the stuff of family legends. The images of one uncle's downed plane in no man's land and of the other's battle to survive in an iron lung became the twin symbols of how utterly powerless we are—in spite of all our brave accomplishments—in the face of death.

I am one of that generation whose witness of the twentieth century has been no less than staggering. The scars of the Great War and the Spanish Flu were writ large in the world into which I was born, followed in all too rapid succession by the Great Depression, the Spanish Civil War, the Second World War, the dawning of the Atomic Age, a myriad of local wars, the advent of AIDS, and the all too real prospect of universal disaster brought about by global warming. And all of these but two—the Spanish Flu and AIDS—were the result of human folly.

Is there a lesson here?

Yes.

The viral wars provide all the enemies we need to satisfy our apparently unquenchable thirst for violence.

Could someone please wake up to this?

Could we not all wake up?

Why not.

And that is not a question.

THE BANKS OF THE WABASH

1. Morning, Wednesday, May 1, 1918

Far off, at the back of the house, a child with a sweet untutored voice was singing.

> *Oh, the moonlight's fair tonight along the Wabash,*
> *From the fields there comes the smell of new-mown hay;*
> *Through the sycamores the candlelights are gleaming,*
> *On the banks of the Wabash, far away . . .*

A young man in uniform stood in the middle of the front hall, with bright sunlit rooms on either side of him. He used a cane to support himself.

Closing his eyes, he almost sang the song—the one his mother had used as a lullaby for each of her children—but remained silent. Silence is life, he had learned in the war. If you are silent, no one can find you.

In the vestibule behind him, a red setter sprawled on the tiles between two Chinese urns filled with dark-green ferns. It was hot—especially for May. It could have been July.

In the kitchen, someone dropped something metal, laughed, and closed a wooden drawer. There was then the clatter of dinner plates being stacked, the bright sound of women's voices and the slamming of a screen door.

The young man waited—stilled. He did not want to move. He wanted to lock all this in place forever. For the first time in three years, he felt safe.

2. Evening, Monday, July 27, 1914

"There cannot and there will not be a war," Ned Hart had said, one July evening in 1914. "I don't care who says there's going to be—there won't be."

"Yes, Papa." That was one of the twins, Edith.

"What's a war?" Midge had asked. She was the youngest.

"Hell on earth, that's what," Ned had said—Ned, who had never been there, but who knew a separate personal hell he never talked about. Except to Phoebe. Don't foist your own hell on other people and never, never, never on your children had been the rule.

Phoebe Hart—Ned's Indiana wife—was a beautiful, smallish woman with mischievous eyes and a generous mouth. Nonetheless, she was ruthless. There would be no failure in her brood. Failure and pain were all in the past—buried with her diseased parents and dead children. Two sons had died—but the rest had lived: Tom and Edith, twins; Graeme next and Midge last. No more. And no more deaths, she had vowed in 1914.

Nineteen Fourteen—and another world entirely. One they could all attempt to recapture—now that Tom was safely home and the war, so it seemed, was winding down.

3. Morning, Monday, June 10, 1918

He set up his machine gun at the bottom of the garden. This way, he could see each one of his victims as they brought their morning tea and coffee onto the porch.

It was another beautiful day. Cloudless, windless—scented with early peonies and late freesia. Hunter lay in the shade of two tall sycamores, his belly full of pork fat and cold porridge. The machine gun glinted, but no one saw it. The one who would fire it sat completely hidden behind a screen of cedar boughs. One by one, the others would come into view. And they did.

Edith. Tom and their mother. Midge. Their father . . .

Marian was the last. Mernie. Their father's sister. The nurse who had brought Tom back from the war.

Would he take Aggie, too? And Winona the parlourmaid and Trevor the gardener-chauffeur?

No. He would need them to help in cleaning up the mess—destroying the evidence, disposing of the bodies.

One-two-three-four-five.

Six.

Everybody.

"I WONDER WHERE GRAEME IS," Phoebe said on the porch.

"Probably sleeping in," said Ned. "Can't blame him. School takes it out of you. It's good to have him home for the summer. Company for Midge."

"No," said Midge. "I won't be keeping company with Gray any more. He bores me—and he scares me. He's a bully."

Tom shifted in his chair and set his coffee cup aside. He closed his eyes. His shirt was clean. It smelled clean. It felt clean. It still amazed him. Clean. *No more mud—no more blood*, he thought. *It rhymes.*

"I'm afraid it's true about the boy," Ned said. "I had a letter from the headmaster, saying that Graeme's behaviour was troubling. He said the parents of various other boys had lodged complaints."

"You didn't tell me that," said Phoebe. "Why didn't you tell me that? Who complained? *Who?* Anyone we know?"

"Some. The Richardsons, the Temples."

"Surely not the Temples," Phoebe said. "Their boy is only nine years old. Do you mean that Graeme is bullying boys who are that much younger?"

"Apparently."

"But he's sixteen years old, for heaven's sake! Are you saying he *harms* them?"

"In his way—perhaps. Maybe."

Tom sat back. He tried to relax his hands. *Don't listen.* Edith watched him.

Midge looked at Hunter. "He kicked the dog, once," she said.

"Don't tell tales," said Phoebe.

"Well, he did. I saw him."

"Keep it to yourself. I will not have bad things said about your brother."

"Mother," said Ned, and touched her hand. "It is best to know the bad things. We have to deal with them."

Phoebe said nothing. She looked aside.

Where is he? Damn him.

THERE THEY ALL WERE.

Graeme opened fire.

In his mind, they fell—one by one.

In his mind, he killed them all.

In his mind, he stood up, wiped his hands, and said: It's done.

In reality, he took his mock-up and hid it in the pony's straw. If Trevor found it, so be it. When he walked across the lawn, he stuck his toe in Hunter's flank and said, "Get up, you lazy bastard. Next time, I'll kill you, too."

Hunter did not stir.

He knew better.

Graeme came to the screen door. He had an odd expression on his face which no one understood.

"I'm not going back," he said without inflection. "I'm not going back to school. I won't. I can't. They don't want me. I'm not going back."

He opened the door and walked into the house, looking at no one. They saw and heard him pass, and looked away.

Finally, Phoebe said, "Just as well. It's his decision, now. We don't have to tell him."

She drank her tea—lighted another cigarette—looked out upon the lawn, and said, "What a lovely day. And here we all are together. Aren't we lucky?"

No one replied.

Twenty minutes later, Phoebe retreated to the conservatory with a tumbler of whisky in her hand. There, she sat amongst the dangling begonias and pondered the lives of her remaining children. *Tom is home—and so is Graeme. But at least I knew where Tom's war was taking place. Where is Graeme's—and what can it be about?* She reached up, touching one of the flowers. *Everything's a mystery*, she thought. *Everything and everyone. Even your own blood . . .*

4. Night, Tuesday, June 11, 1918

"Are you awake?"

"Yes."

"Can I come in?"

"You're already here. Since when do you ask?"

"I want to sleep with you."

"You're too old to sleep with me. *I'm* too old."

"I'm afraid."

"What of? The dark?"

"No. I don't like being alone."

"I'd've thought, after all that time at school, you couldn't wait to get away. I never could."

Graeme shifted expectantly. Tom said nothing more. Graeme touched the bedpost.

"So," he said. "Can I?"

"If you must—but it's hot. There's only one sheet."

"That's okay. I'm not cold."

There was moonlight. The bed creaked as Graeme climbed on. The window was open. A dog barked, down the block. The night choir sang—the crickets, frogs, and peepers.

"You're naked," said Graeme.

"I always sleep naked, now that I can."

"Should I take off my pyjamas?"

"Suit yourself."

Graeme skinned down. They lay there.

"Can I touch you?"

"Jesus, Gray—why would you want to touch me? I'm your brother."

"I just want to touch your wounds."

"Oh, for God's sake . . ."

Tom sat up against the pillows, reached for a cigarette, and lighted it.

Graeme, leaning on his elbow, pulled back the sheet, and looked at Tom's thigh—his knee—his shin.

"Do they hurt?"

"Of course they hurt. What sort of fool question is that?"

"I just wondered."

Graeme reached out with his fingers and ran them down the side of Tom's leg.

"They're like potholes in the road."

"What would you know about potholes?"

"Everything. I almost wrecked the car because of them."

"When in hell did you drive the car? Pa doesn't let you drive. He said so in a letter."

"I went out with Trevor and Trevor let me. Last December." There was a pause. The fingers wandered. "They are, you know—just like potholes. What did it feel like when it happened?"

"Nothing."

"Oh, come on! A shell exploded."

"You don't feel anything at first. I tried to stand up so I could run and I couldn't even get to my feet. That's when you feel the pain. That's when you panic."

Sharing a light, a wounded Canadian and a wounded German in the mud at Passchendaele, November 1917.

"What happened then?"

"Everyone else was dead."

Tom drew a deep draught of smoke and let it out into the moonlight. He waved his hand.

"Bombardments are like that. They take out whole companies of men. Even divisions. I was left for dead—along with all the others. A Frenchman found me. I ended up in a French field hospital. That's why they said I'd gone missing. Nobody could locate the corpse." He grinned and looked at his brother. "Then Mernie came and identified me. Thank God. She'd been serving in a nursing station down the line. I'll never forget looking up and seeing her standing there. Good old Mernie and that smile . . ."

Graeme rested his hand, palm down, on Tom's stomach.

"You kill anyone?" he asked.

"Of course I did. What a stupid question. What the hell's the matter with you?"

He removed Graeme's hand and looked out the window.

"What's it feel like—killing someone?"

Tom did not answer. He considered Graeme, wondering what had happened to him. Who was this boy—this stranger, who lay beside him the way they had at the cottage up at Jackson's Point before the war.

Where had he gone, that child—the one who had been such a wonderful companion? All the games, pretending to be Indians—hiding in the woods, learning how to walk on dead leaves without making a sound, paddling the canoe—with penalties for every stroke that broke the silence. Swimming off the dock with Hunter, games of tennis on the neighbours' lawn. All gone. But where? Into this strange, unhappy, troublesome boy with his odd obsessions—weapons, wars, his brother's tormented flesh—God knew what else. At dinner, all he had talked about was guns.

The dog barked yet again.

Tom stubbed his cigarette. "I'm going to sleep," he said.

He rearranged his pillow and rolled onto his stomach—sighed—and was gone.

Graeme turned and looked at him, thinking, *He has everything. I have nothing. Not even wounds.*

In his mind, he sang:

Through the sycamores the candlelights are gleaming,
On the banks of the Wabash, far away . . .

GRAEME REMEMBERED HIS MOTHER singing it to him and later to Midge, when they were small.

At last, he began to drift.

In their own backyard there were sycamore trees. Maybe, one night, he would set out a dozen candles on the screened-in porch so he could watch them through the leaves. Then all he would need was a river and some moonlight. Already he had decided that anything he made up was better than what was. The trees could be his fortress. He could sleep up there with the machine gun and his self-inflicted wounds.

Yes. He would do that, too. Tomorrow. He could carve some potholes in his leg. And maybe one or two on his arms.

I must have something . . .

Something.

Then, he slept.

5. Evening, Saturday, July 27, 1918

Over one hundred people.

"Who would have thought we had so many friends!" Phoebe sighed.

"I would," said Ned, and put his arm around her shoulder. "Congratulations, Mother," he added. "You've created a triumph."

They were standing on the stairs and every room was filled with flowers, with men and women—young and old—and everyone had turned in their direction. *Even the roses*, Phoebe thought, and smiled.

This was the announcement of a marriage, though, like any mother, she had wanted the first to be Edith's. Still, how could it matter? They were both the eldest. Twins.

Tom was going to marry Georgia Carling. Ned had just proclaimed it. He had even called it "a proclamation." Everyone had laughed, everyone had cheered. They drank champagne—or what passed for champagne, a concoction known as Bubbly, got from a source Phoebe was not privy to. Somewhere in Montréal. But no one talks about it. Once you talk about it, the source dries up.

Graeme had got his wish. The screened-in porch was candlelit, and the candles ensconced in glass chimneys. Not a single flame wavered.

After the toasts, after the congratulations, Tom and Georgia retired to the stable. A band was playing—or what they called a band. A violinist, pianist, cellist, and a man who played the flute. The music was oddly charming. Even the neighbours liked it.

There was a waltz.

"It's called 'Maytime,'" said Georgia.

"But it's *July*!" said Tom, and they laughed. "My dancing's kind of rusty," he added.

"Never mind. I love you."

They danced in Clara's straw.

The pony watched.

"Are you happy?" Tom said.

He was smiling.

"Yes," said Georgia. "More than I'll ever deserve. Oh God, my darling"—

she embraced him—"what if you hadn't come back?"

Tom said nothing.

He held her.

The smell of her hair was almost strong enough to drown in. No flower—nothing—compared to it. She was tiny—in white—but not the least bit delicate. She had won him just before his enlistment, at a ball which, given her age, she should not have attended. But her parents had brought her, nonetheless, at her mother's insistence.

"All the men are disappearing," Mrs. Carling had said. Her meaning was all too clear. If not Tom Hart, then Graeme.

Tom had needed no prodding. Nor had Georgia.

It was the old, old story with the oldest dialogue in the world, told and retold in every war since the Greeks set sail for Troy.

Will you wait? he had asked.

Yes, I will, she had answered.

And here they were.

6. Evening, Friday, September 13, 1918

When Ned came home from the factory one Friday afternoon, he did something he had never done before. He went to the dining room, where Winona was setting the table for dinner, took down a cut-glass tumbler, and poured himself three fingers of brandy.

Turning, he saw that Winona had paused to watch him, her left hand clutching half a dozen spoons.

"You didn't see this," he said, and left the room.

"No, sir," Winona muttered, but Ned was already gone.

He then retreated to the stable, passing the McLaughlin Buick parked in the drive, giving it a gentle pat with his right hand. "Good boy," he muttered, having no idea what he meant.

Clara greeted him with a soft whinny. Trevor was about to feed her. He was up in the loft relieving another bale of its binder twine.

"Hello, old girl," said Ned and gave her nose a rub. "It's coming, it's coming. Be patient." He sat on the step and drank. Trevor would have to climb down over him. He was not going to budge.

When at last Trevor did appear, having forked half the bale through the trap, he swung out, using the banister, and stepped over Ned's knees, the fork still in hand.

When he had done with the hay, Trevor carried a pail to the tap, filled it, and took it into the box stall. Only then did he speak.

"You told them yet?" he asked.

"No."

"Will you?"

"Of course. I have to. Better me than a rumour. Better me than the papers."

"Yes, sir. I guess."

Then Ned said, "Twenty-two dead already. Over a hundred, in the States. And it's only just begun. I'm not afraid of telling my sister. Mernie's a nurse—she will cope. It's Mrs. Hart I'm concerned for. There's been enough danger—been enough sickness—too many losses, as it is."

"Yes, sir."

"We always have a drink before our dinner. I'll tell her then, when we're alone. Then I will tell the others."

"Will you tell the kitchen, sir? Aggie? Winona?"

"Yes. It's my household, and my responsibility." Ned drank again. "Thank you for being so calm about it."

"It's for all of us to get through together," said Trevor. "That's what I've been thinking, sir. Like the war. We must all get through it together."

THEY SAT IN NED'S LIBRARY. He brought two glasses, a bottle of whisky, ice cubes, a box of Phoebe's cigarettes, and a single rose, cut from the garden and set in a silver bud vase.

"What is this?" said Phoebe, when he had shut the door.

"This is news," said Ned. He tried to smile, succeeding to some extent— enough to make her smile in return.

"The War? They know it's nearly over and you've been directed to . . ."

"No. Something completely different."

Phoebe sat down. The chairs were not congenial—unskirted leather, totally male and utterly unattractive. She came so seldom to the room that she winced every time she entered. Bad memories, also. It was here she had found Ned when she had to tell him Andrew had died, seven years before—the second son. The beauty. Aged nine. Of peritonitis. An unexpected death.

She watched as Ned poured some whisky into a glass.

Why such a large glass?

Ned lifted a piece of ice.

"You seem to like this," he said. "The American way." He smiled.

"Yes. I like it. I started out American. Three pieces, please."

Twenty-two dead already. Over a hundred, in the States. And it's only just begun.

Phoebe said, "Is something wrong?"

Ned handed her the glass and went to the window.

The world he saw—its trees, its grass, its flowers, its sky—seemed utterly, utterly normal. Blooming—blossoming—vibrant—alive with birds and the neighbours' cats, the scent of Clara's manure, and the sound of "that dog down the street."

"Something has happened . . ." he said. "Begun to happen . . ."

Phoebe waited, tilting the shards of ice in her glass. She said nothing.

He has a good back, she thought. *Shoulders. Beautiful skin . . . When was that? We lay somewhere in the grass—and there were children playing. Now . . .*

"We must prepare ourselves to deal with a new plague."

Whisky is bitter. It burns.

"There have been deaths already. Many of them . . ."

"Of?"

"It's called the Spanish Flu," he told her. "Three of the workers have caught it. Three—and one of their children. A wife has died."

He turned and looked at her.

Phoebe set her half-emptied glass to one side. The right side. On a table.

"Yes?" she said, not looking at him. "And?"

"And we are in danger . . . Everyone. All of us."

Ned waited. Watching.

At first, nothing happened.

Phoebe reached for her glass and toyed with its stem.

And then she laughed. Laughed so quietly that, as he watched her, he was

At a casualty clearing station a nurse is presented with a dog by a group of wounded Canadians.

They brought the dog out with them from the trenches, October 1916.

not quite certain it was laughter.

Then it broke free of her.

He went and knelt at her feet.

"Don't," he said. "Don't."

Extracting herself, she stood.

The laughter continued.

Then it stopped.

Looking down at him, she spoke in a dead voice.

"Have we a gun?" she asked. "I want a gun. With six bullets."

"No," he said. "We are going to survive this. There will be no guns."

"I want a gun," she whispered.

Ned stood up and held both her wrists. "Don't," he said. "Don't."

She began to weep, clinging to him as if he was life itself.

"Do you want Winona to bring your dinner here? Upstairs? To the porch?"

Slowly, she wound down and the weeping came to an end. She pushed him gently away and fished a handkerchief from her sleeve. "I just can't bear the thought of waiting for someone else to die."

"We'll survive."

"You've said that before—when Andrew died. And Newton."

"Well, I can hardly say *we're all going to perish*, my darling." He tilted her head and smiled at her. "Can I, eh? I can hardly say that."

Phoebe tried to smile back. "No," she said. And then she said, "You're a wonder. Thank God."

"And so are you."

"I'll try. Yes. I will. I'll try."

"All right. Sit down. We'll both sit down and finish our drinks before we go in."

"Dinner will be stone cold," Phoebe said, and sat.

"It's already stone cold," Ned grinned. "I happen to know about the potato salad, the sliced tomatoes, and the cold ham."

He gave them each another splash of whisky. "And the chocolate ice cream Tom and Edith made this afternoon. Trevor told me all about it on the way home."

"It was meant to be a surprise. Don't tell them you know."

"No, of course not."

There was a pause. Phoebe turned in her chair and looked at the mantel-piece. There they all were—the living and the dead in silver frames. She turned back and sipped her drink.

"All the ice has melted," she said.

"Yes. It does that."

She reached out and took his hand, inadvertently burning him with her cigarette.

"I'm sorry."

"Don't be. These things happen."

"Yes." She looked at him. "Yes," she said, and touched his hair. "These things happen . . ."

7. Nighttime, Monday, September 30, 1918

"Mernie?"

Silence, but for breathing.

"Mernie?"

"Yes . . ." She woke. Phoebe was standing in the open doorway, lit from behind by the night light in the hall. "Yes?"

"I'm sorry to wake you, but there's something wrong with Graeme . . ."

"Yes. I'll be right there."

Marian was used to being roused in the night. In France it had almost seemed a mandatory occurrence. Most nights, she had slept in her uniform—otherwise, in her underclothes. Now, she shuffled into her slippers, dragged on a robe, and followed Phoebe down the hall.

Graeme was lying on his back, with the covers pushed aside. On entering the room, Marian could feel the heat emanating from his body. His pyjamas were soaking wet.

The bedside lamp was on. She lifted Graeme's wrist and felt his pulse.

"Bring me the thermometer," she said to Phoebe. "And the alcohol."

Phoebe hurried off to the bathroom.

Edith came to the doorway and asked what was happening.

"Graeme is ill. Find another pair of pyjamas for him."

Edith began to rummage in the highboy.

"Oh, my God . . ." she said hoarsely.

"What?"

"There's a gun."

Marian hurried across the room, picked up the revolver, and placed it in her pocket.

"Say nothing," she said. "Tell no one. *No one.* I will deal with it."

"But a *gun* . . . Graeme . . ."

"Be quiet," Marian hissed. "Bring the pyjamas. Close the drawer."

Edith did so, unfolding the pyjamas as she came towards the bed.

"Give them to me. Go to the linen closet. Bring new sheets and pillowcases. Bring some towels. Hurry."

"Yes."

Edith left as Phoebe entered with the thermometer and alcohol.

"We must get him out of these pyjamas and dry him off as best we can."

They stood on either side of the bed, pulled the sheets entirely away, and threw them on the floor. Then they stripped Graeme and laid him on his side. His eyes were wide open but clearly he could see nothing. Nothing of them, at any rate.

Marian shook the thermometer, dipped it in the alcohol, shook it again, and put it under Graeme's tongue.

"Is it the flu?"

"Yes. That's why you heard him. It infects the lungs."

"When I woke up, I thought it must have been Hunter having a bad dream . . ."

Edith arrived with the towels and sheets.

"Should I wake the others?" she asked.

"Your father's already awake. He's gone to the kitchen to make some tea. Leave Tom and Midge. The fewer the better." All this from Phoebe.

Edith departed.

Marian began to dry, as best she could, the perspiration on Graeme's body. His flesh was freezing cold and yet he seemed entirely bathed in heat.

She removed the thermometer from Graeme's mouth and held it under the lamp.

"Well?"

"A hundred and six," said Mernie, and began to shake the tube back to normal. "Put it in alcohol." She handed it to Phoebe and laid down her towel. "He's as dry as I can make him, now. We'll get him into the new pyjamas and make the bed. Then we'll telephone Doctor Cooper-Cole."

Graeme was now an unconscious dead weight, and the pyjamas did not co-operate. It was almost as if they protested. But the women struggled with them and won. Then they sat Graeme in a chair and began to remake the bed.

DOCTOR COOPER-COLE ARRIVED at four-thirty, made his diagnosis, tried to reassure Phoebe, and then—in Marian's presence only—offered what he called "our sole defence against this bloody, merciless thing." Then: "It isn't much. It isn't adequate, but it's all we have."

"Yes, Doctor."

"I want everyone in this house to wear a mask. And I want you all to get as much fresh air out of doors as you can. And, as long as it's not too cold, keep Graeme's windows open. All this nonsense about hermetically sealing the patient in an airless room—that's what kills. Yes. And the first sign in anyone else in this household, you're to get in touch with me immediately."

"Yes, sir."

"Marian—Mernie. You and I are years beyond sir and Doctor . . . years beyond Nurse. You know my name."

"Yes, sir. But that's not professional. I prefer to call you Doctor."

"Very well. I will see you before noon."

As he struggled into his coat and accepted his hat and bag, he said, "This is my ninth case in three days, Marian. Thank God you're here. I will have to sleep when I get home, but of course you can call me if there's an immediate crisis. My wife will know where to reach me if I'm treating somebody else."

He left.

Marian closed the door.

His name was Robert.

IN HER BEDROOM, having checked on Graeme and Phoebe, who had fallen asleep in the chair, Marian sat by her open window and took the gun from her robe. *It must be Tom's*, she thought. *But why does Graeme have it?*

There was daylight. A crow called, a robin sang—that dog barked.

How strange we are, was all she could think. *The way we give birth and kill— the way we search for answers and refuse to hear them—the way we remember we're alive and the way we forget. The way we strive and the way we give up. And the way . . . the way . . . the way . . .*

She brushed the revolver with her fingers. A Colt. Six chambers.

And the way we lose our way.

8. Afternoon, Tuesday, November 19, 1918

The war was over. No one rejoiced.

Yes, they all went into the streets. The bells rang. Everyone sang. There were fireworks. People climbed to their roofs and sat there, waving flags. A loud, long cheer went up. But no one rejoiced. On the third day of peace, there was silence. Another war had begun. A war for survival.

There were now well over a thousand dead of the Spanish Flu in the East—plus a growing number of victims, station by station, town by town, and city by city, as the plague moved west across the continent.

Mostly, it moved on troop trains, coming home with soldiers returning from France. In Europe, there were already fifty thousand dead. There was nothing a person could do. Or medicine. Every answer had been applied and not one worked. If you lived, you lived because your immune system had a built-in defence against this particular virus—whatever this virus was. No one knew.

Graeme had lived. He had just begun to come downstairs and was allowed to sit at the dining-room table in his bathrobe. So long as he is clean. And neat.

He treated his survival as a foregone conclusion: a right. He thanked no one. He scanned the daily lists of the dead in the *Mail and Empire* and was heard, from time to time, to snort or giggle when someone he had not enjoyed had died. *Mrs. Gibbon! Hah! The old hag . . . Martin Colegate, that prick*, he said privately to Tom. *Serves them all right. Who needed them?*

The others turned away. They had watched and prayed for him, ministered to him—got him through a month and more of darkness. Yet he said nothing. His door was always closed—often locked. Only Marian and Edith knew he would be wondering, worrying about the gun. *Which of them had it?* Nothing was said. Marian had it beneath her mattress. It was not a secret she wanted to keep, but she knew she must and kept her counsel. Graeme retreated into a world of fantasy and vicious masturbation. Sometimes he bled. Always, he wept.

Midge came home from school. It was thought unwise to keep her there. Three of her classmates had died.

On the afternoon of November 19, a Tuesday, she came and stood at the foot of her mother's bed. Beyond the windows, there was a heavy mist through which the trees held up their arms and the neighbours' houses seemed to have been set adrift.

"Mama?"

Phoebe turned from her side beneath her afghan and stared as if her daughter might be a stranger.

"Yes . . . ? Yes . . . ? What time is it?"

"Three-thirty," said Midge. "I got Mernie first, but I think you ought to come."

"What is it?" Phoebe sat up.

"It's Tom."

A victory parade in Calgary, Alberta, during the influenza epidemic with revellers forced to wear masks, November 11, 1918.

HE LAY ON HIS BED as if it was another battlefield—another Ypres, another Somme, another Passchendaele.

His arms were flung aside like discarded clothing. He wore one shoe and not the other. His tie, unknotted, had not been removed. His hair was matted, eyes half-closed, his mouth open—gaping, gasping, ugly—a seeming confirmation of death.

Seeing him from the doorway, Phoebe waited, closed her eyes, and whispered, "Don't."

Marian busied herself with what already seemed a corpse, stripping away its soaking shroud of clothes and laying towels on its nakedness.

Phoebe approached the bed, said nothing—and ran her hand along his damaged leg.

After a moment—looking at Tom, not Marian—she said, "How long?"

"In the night," Mernie said. "Unless . . ."

"Unless?"

"We could try an iron lung. This is far beyond the effect it had on Graeme, but there are experiences—so I've heard—where an iron lung can get them through."

"Who do we call? Get one. *Now*."

"I will telephone Robert," Marian said. As she left the room, she turned and said, "Dry him, if you can."

Phoebe took each piece of clothing, folded it, laid it aside. When at last she was finished, she began to press the towels, one by one, against his flesh. He has no skin—only flesh, she thought.

She had given birth to this flesh. When? Twenty-something years ago. Five. Twenty-five. *Two packages—neatly delivered, end to end. Should one sign for these?* she remembered thinking. Five pounds each—Tom and Edith. Standard fare. And standard agony. The pain had been, until their final arrival, unimaginable—though afterwards—*why?*—she could not remember it. There they were.

Now this.

Marian returned.

"Tonight," she said, referring to the arrival of the iron lung.

Together, they manoeuvred Tom beneath the top sheet and stripped the bed of its other covers.

Midge, who had been joined by Hunter, waited at the windowsill, seated with her feet crossed and one strand of hair in her mouth, while her fingers stroked Hunter's ears and the mist beyond the window intensified.

THE LUNG ARRIVED AT MIDNIGHT.

Doctor Cooper-Cole arrived with it.

Four men carried it into Ned's study. Two of them brought Tom's dead weight down the stairs. Doctor Cooper-Cole supervised the placement of the body in the machine, after which it was activated.

"It makes such a ghastly noise," said Midge, who stood with Hunter by the door.

"Go to bed," said Marian. "Now."

"Yes, ma'am."

"One of you must sit with him every minute," the doctor said.

"Can't I sit with him?" Midge asked from the doorway.

"Tomorrow."

"Yes, sir. Tomorrow."

She walked away to her room, but Hunter did not follow. He crept into the study and lay beneath the bed.

9. Morning, Wednesday, November 20, 1918

Tom drifted.

Where was he now?

On the ground somewhere, unable to move. His arms were trapped in the mud. He could not feel his legs. They might not even be there, for all he could tell. He could barely breathe. Something alive was lying on his chest. Who was it? What?

He wondered if one of the horses had fallen on him. Such things happened. He had seen it once—a fallen horse lying dead on top of a man who was drowning in the mud, unable to rise. Nothing could be done to save him. Nothing. The machine-gun fire had been relentless.

"Tom?"

Someone was calling him.

"Tom—can you hear me?"

It sounded like his mother, but that was impossible. She was in Canada, thousands of miles from the battle. How could she have got here?

"Tom—I have Georgia with me. She's come to see you."

"Hello, my darling. I'm breaking all the rules of quarantine, but I couldn't bear not being with you."

Somebody dried his forehead with a handkerchief.

You'll get it all muddy, Tom wanted to say. And then: "What are you doing here? I don't understand."

He must have lain there for hours, and now these women. Where were the Germans? Why weren't they firing?

And what was that noise? It sounded like a tank. Or perhaps a train.

"You can't even hold his hand," someone said.

He heard weeping.

"You can't even hold his hand!"

"Don't. Don't, my dear. Come away."

There was movement somewhere beyond the top of his head—somewhere behind him.

Whoever had been there was gone.

He tried to turn his head. He was soaking wet. He could not even cough.

His shoulders might have been a board nailed to the ground and the ground, cement . . . And yet, he was sinking in mud.

I'm a ship, he thought. Titanic, Lusitania . . . *Something has sunk me. Into a sea of mustard gas, of chlorine gas, of . . .*

Gas.

Blue—then green—then yellow. Silent, at first. Not a sound—just a mist descending—just a mist, the way it used to rise from the lake at Jackson's Point—late evenings, early mornings, last and first sunlight—swimming with Hunter,

If only I could reach the lake . . .

Hear the loons. See the moon. Sleep with Hunter against my back . . .

A gas canister landed beside his ear.

Don't.

The canister began to hiss.

To whisper . . .

Now . . . now . . . now . . .

Come over . . .

No. I don't want to. Please don't make me. Please.

But it's time, now.

No. I'm not finished.

I haven't even begun!

He sank into darkness . . . into silence . . . into . . . Nothing.

"MARIAN! QUICKLY!"

"What?"

"It's happening. It's happening. Make it stop . . ."

"Stand back. Stand away." And then: "Tom? Tom?"

"Ned! Ned! Edith! Come at once!"

Hunter crawled from beneath the bed.

Ned and Edith crowded into the room. Midge lingered in the doorway, afraid. She had never seen a death.

Graeme did not come, but Aggie did. And Winona.

"Tom! Tom!"

Marian sounded like a sergeant major issuing commands as she tried to revive him. "Tom! Tom! Tom!"

Midge turned away and sat in the hall.

The sun shone.

It was crazy.

As she listened, Midge heard the voices in the room beside her, but did not go back.

Georgia came from wherever she had been and went in to join the others, caressing Midge's face as she passed.

All at once, there was silence.

Total.

The iron lung had been shut off.

It gave a final sigh and was gone. Oddly, Midge waited for a door to close—as if it might have risen from its place and left the house.

Edith came and took Midge's hand.

"Come now," she said, her voice hushed. "You must see him. He looks so peaceful. Don't be afraid."

They went back in and stood beside the bed.

No one spoke.

Indeed, it was true. He was at peace.

It was over.

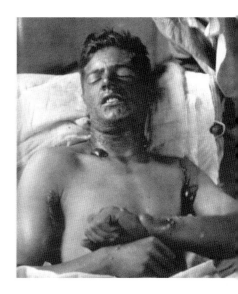

Victim of a gas attack. Ypres, April 1915.

11. Afternoon, Wednesday, November 20, 1918

Marian had completed the preparation of Tom's body. She had dressed him in his uniform, having kept his ribbons as a memento. His medals were already ensconced on Phoebe's bedside table in an open mahogany box not unlike a miniature coffin.

Don't say coffin. Don't even think of it. They would come for him soon enough and the lid would descend.

Robert Cooper-Cole and Ned together had had to pull every string available to them to secure a casket. They were at a premium, given the number of deaths the city had endured in recent weeks. It was said that in Europe the dead were being lowered into their graves in simple shrouds, because there was nothing else in which to bury them.

When she was done, she went into the living room to find Phoebe and bring her to the library. Phoebe was sitting near a window, staring out at the bare trees.

"Now?" she asked.

"Yes," said Marian and held out her hand.

Phoebe set her glass aside and rose without further comment.

Even the clock, so it seemed, fell silent. The two women stood on either side of Tom and watched as the light began to fade around them. The books on their shelves lost their gilded titles, one by one. On the mantel, the photographs in their silver frames also began to go out like lights, until the only source of illumination came from the electric chandelier in the hall beyond the open door.

Finally, after twenty minutes, Phoebe leaned down and kissed her son's forehead. She then turned away and left the room. She had not said a word. All the words for this had been used and were now discarded. Watching her depart, Marian saw a rigid back, a spill of careless, greying hair, and an unbowed head.

Slowly, Marian followed her and closed the door. Within five minutes, she was back. The Colt revolver was in her hand. She fitted it into the holster she had deliberately suspended from Tom's wide belt, and closed the leather eye with its brass pip. Done. It would go where it belonged—to the grave.

Leaving the second time, she switched on one lamp. Somehow, it did not seem right to leave Tom in the dark.

IN THE KITCHEN, Aggie said, "Are they in there now?"

"Yes," said Winona. "All except Gray. I can take him up a tray, if you think I should."

"No," said Aggie. "We've got to force him down."

"You want me to serve tonight?" Trevor asked.

"Yes," said Aggie. "I think that would be just right. Guess is, they're not much interested in food."

Graeme did not come.

Nor did Midge. At first.

She went down the hall to the piano—Hunter trailing after, tail down, ears flat, tongue extruded. He had aged a decade.

There was little light, but Midge knew the fingering by heart. And the words.

Everyone heard her. Everyone listened. Halfway between the kitchen and the dining room, Trevor hovered, not wanting to set the tray on the sideboard until the song was over. Aggie and Winona came to the open door and, holding hands, joined in the stillness.

> *Oh, the moonlight's fair tonight along the Wabash,*
> *From the fields there comes the smell of new-mown hay;*
> *Through the sycamores the candlelights are gleaming,*
> *On the banks of the Wabash, far away . . .*

Any minute now, the future would begin.

John Ralston Saul

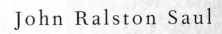

D-DAY

Perhaps the oddest thing about D-Day was how long so many soldiers had to wait to die so fast.

Most had been in Britain two, three, even four years, leading a strange, unreal yet real life of waiting.

Of course they trained while they waited. They prepared. And they were together in a way adults never are in civilian life. Doubly so. After all, they were in a foreign/not-foreign land as participants and yet observers of a great social drama. And they were in regiments that were usually miniature reconstitutions of their hometowns and regions.

Above: Soldiers of the Royal Winnipeg Rifles awaiting embarkation for the invasion of France. June 1, 1944.

Previous: Lieutenant William Saul photographed in Winnipeg just before going overseas with the Winnipeg Rifles.

There were several regiments to pick from in Winnipeg. The volunteers all chose in the hope of getting overseas quickly. The lucky ones, it turned out, were the unluckiest, because they chose the Winnipeg Grenadiers and found themselves in Hong Kong. And then the survivors found themselves in Japanese camps.

My father, with many of his friends, went into the Royal Winnipeg Rifles, an old regiment that had been at Fish Creek and Batoche—that short tragedy of internal Canadian war—and in South Africa and through the worst of the First World War. The Little Black Devils was what they were called, and still are, after a Sioux witness at Fish Creek had been surprised to see soldiers in dark-green uniforms, not bright red, and had asked who those little black devils were. The Winnipeg Rifles were among the regiments that trained and waited and trained as the 1940s wore on.

Of course, Canadians who were in the air force and navy were permanently part of an ongoing battle. And along the way, the army itself suffered a major catastrophe at Dieppe, raising the question of that classic division between the efforts, sacrifice and courage of the men and officers on the ground versus what you might call "bad generalling." The inadequate generals and admirals in the case of Dieppe were British, a strangely reassuring factor.

There were also unexpected interludes over those years. In 1942, some officers—my father among them—were transferred temporarily to British regiments fighting in North Africa. They were sent to get battlefield experience. Those who were chosen to go considered themselves lucky. Lucky? Well, what do words mean in war? Since volunteering, the central desire of all these men had been not to wait but to fight. Whatever that might eventually mean. And so, in North Africa, they stopped waiting for a few months.

And then, a few months later, thousands of others, including my father's postwar regiment—the Princess Patricias—were thrown into the impossible Italian campaign. Starting from the southern tip of Sicily, they were required to fight their way from one end to the other, over a few plains and a lot of hills, mountains and rivers. With time, that strategy has come to seem increasingly odd.

It was a long and questionably generalled ordeal, which, in the First World War manner, killed many for each little bit of progress. But the soldiers and field officers did what was asked of them and stubbornly fought their way north.

All that, you'll say, is far from D-Day. Well, what's the rush? We know the story. The grand, swashbuckling story that still crowds our imaginations. The great armada. The five beaches. Juno. The Canadian task somehow reminding us of Vimy. The men rushing through the water, across the sand, through minefields, around obstacles. Breaking through.

And then our imaginations, as if in a miracle, fly over Normandy. Paris is taken. And we liberate Dieppe—revenge for the earlier disaster. Then Hitler is dead in his bunker and it's all over and the citizen soldiers mysteriously are reabsorbed back into their families, farms and desk jobs across the ocean.

So it goes. Or so the grand story of history goes.

BUT WHAT ABOUT THOSE INDIVIDUALS from Winnipeg? What did they do, experience, suffer, accomplish? Would their lives be reality or myth?

Memory of war is such a delicate thing. To remember is not to boast. And not necessarily even to talk about. I grew up surrounded by these men because my father stayed in the army. And I never heard them tell a war story, except perhaps as a joke.

They were each other's memories, for better and worse. How hard it must have been for the majority—the other soldiers—who went back to their civilian lives. They went back to people who didn't know. Who couldn't know.

I thought the other day, walking through the streets of Ottawa, behind the coffin of the Unknown Soldier, that that was the full message of the day. That the thousands of veterans marching behind us were, in their own way, also the unknown. They have never wished to explain what they know, only expected that the others will accept their silence as a form of memory that could only be lessened with explanation.

So I feel no rush to retell historic tales. Instead, I think of Colonel Meldram, who commanded the Winnipeg Rifles from the landing on D-Day to October. I knew him only through photos in our family album. "A gentleman," people always said. Strange, old-fashioned words like gallant would come out when he was mentioned. A palpable sense of affection.

Or Lockie Fulton. My father's best man. I should explain that Captain Saul had met the daughter of a British army officer during those years in Britain. Beryl Ralston. In fact her father, Major Ralston, had died young, from the effects of being gassed in the First World War. And her only brother, John—pilot of a fighter bomber—had been shot down and killed over Germany early in the war, his body never recovered.

But back to Lockie Fulton, the man who took over the regiment from Colonel Meldram. He had commanded D Company on D-Day and had gone on to become a great regimental hero. He went through terrible battle after terrible battle without a scratch.

Luck, Napoleon always said, was a great quality in a leader. And he was a wonderful leader of men. I remember the wartime photos of Fulton. A dashing look, a great smile with an elegant moustache that followed the smile. The aura of a natural leader. He came from a big farm near Winnipeg, led his regiment with great courage and talent, and then, like Cincinnatus, went back to his farm. I hope he'll forgive me the compliments.

And there was Major Hodge. He commanded A Company which, during the terrible battle of Putot-en-Bessin two days after the landing, would be dug in next to C Company, where my father was second-in-command. Hodge's company would be virtually annihilated. As the regimental history put it: "Major Hodge's boys acquitted

Major Lockie Fulton two months after the battle of Putot-en-Bessin
and before taking command of the Winnipeg Rifles.

themselves like Napoleon's Guard at Waterloo." That is, they stood their ground until most were dead.

Before writing this, I phoned my mother to ask if she remembered Hodge from those years when the regiment was in England, more than half a century ago ago. She said yes, she thought he was a big man with hair that tended to stand straight up. Is that accurate? Have I said how fragile memories are? Each of us who knows carries tiny fragments with us. A large man caught with his men in an impossible situation, fighting on until everything has run out. He and a few survivors were captured, apparently by Kurt Meyer's SS, unsuccessfully interrogated, then taken out into a forest and executed.

That's another photo that haunted my childhood. It represented evil. Evil in a personal way. Hitler was a planetary figure, at once the devil and grotesquely comic. Meyer was the evil we knew. The other day I read a remarkable diary by a minor German aristocrat—Friedrich Reck-Malleczewen—who had hated the Nazis from their very beginnings. He was eventually deported to Dachau and executed in 1945. He saw Hitler for the second time on August 11, 1936:

> I got the impression of basic stupidity . . . the kind of stupidity which equates statesmanship with cheating at a horse trade . . . The fact remains that he was, and is, without the slightest self-awareness and pleasure in himself, that he basically hates himself, and that his opportunism, his immeasurable need for recognition, and his now apocalyptic vanity, are all based on one thing—a consuming drive to drown out the pain of his psyche, the trauma of a monstrosity.

The point being made is that respectable and responsible Germans, and by extension the leadership of other Western countries, were responsible for not recognizing the maniacal stupidity of the man and so preventing it from getting out of hand.

But General Kurt Meyer had nothing comic about him. He was that unusual combination of a talented professional soldier and an absolute disciple of Hitler

and of Hitler's mania. In the photo—because he was the subject—you sense a perfectly hard human being. There is a strange unidentifiable energy in the way he is
striding into his own postwar trial for war crimes. He is quite undecipherable by any
standards we might know in a normal, middle-class democracy.

It was he, we were told, who had murdered my father's fellow soldiers. His
friends. Men in his own company and others. Directly or indirectly, Meyer had had
them executed when taken prisoner. None of that was ever really explained to us. It
was one of those things we children talked about among ourselves; one of those
things that children somehow knew all about.

It was a photo we stared at carefully whenever the album was opened: I'm
sure that image—a copy of that exact image—exists in hundreds, perhaps several
thousand photo albums across Canada—a man striding into a courtroom, an officer
from the Winnipeg Rifles leading him on either side. There is such a curious expression on his face; so hard to measure.

But let me go back to the beginning. The Winnipeg Rifles landed on Juno
beach at Courseulles-sur-Mer, B and D companies in the first wave of landing craft,
A and C not long behind. C Company of the Canadian Scottish landed on their right;
the Regina Rifles on their left.

The sea was very rough. Most of these men from the Prairies were horribly
seasick. Reality has little to do with the romantic view of any heroic moment. Most
of the Rifles vomited their way to the beach. By a fluke of family genes, the Sauls
don't seem to get seasick. There is no particular reason. It's just one of those things.
That was the only thing my father ever told me about the landing—he wasn't seasick.

The artillery barrage from the navy had missed the German defences on
Courseulles-sur-Mer and so the first two companies landed cold to full enemy fire and
heavy losses. Some craft were caught on reefs, forcing the men to come out into deep
water with their heavy equipment. There were five concrete casements and fifteen
machine guns waiting for them. When the next two companies landed, the beach was
still in full battle.

Lockie Fulton's men in D Company poured through the minefield with astonishing determination and headed inland. They were on the beach at 0749 and off it by 0900. B Company cleared three of the casements and twelve machine-gun nests. Only Captain Gower and 26 men came off the beach unscathed.

Periodically I run into a veteran who was part of the regiment during the landing, perhaps even of C Company. One said to me a few years ago: "I was crouched near your father on the edge of the beach. There was a radio between us. It was blown up and neither of us were touched." These are the strange fragments of memory.

By the end of the day the regiment was well inland at Creully. They had liberated various villages along the way—Ste-Croix-sur-Mer and Banville, where C and D companies met solid resistance.

Total casualties for the day? One hundred and thirty. What does a number

Winnipeg Rifles heading for the beach in the first wave of D-Day. The figure in the top left is Lance Sergeant Laurence Chartrand of A Company who would be one of those executed by the SS at 3 p.m. on June 8, 1944.

mean? What are 130 lives in a world that delights in big numbers? One hundred and thirty friends, companions, people you knew, went to school with, lived in close quarters with for three and a half years. Numbers are such unsatisfactory memories.

The next day, June 7, they pushed on with relative ease to their D-Day objective. The Winnipeg Rifles and the Reginas were the first Allied units to reach their goal, which was along the Caen-Bayeux highway. Just on the other side lay the village of Putot and beyond that a sunken railway track. There, near the tracks, the four companies dug in from east to west—A in front of a railway overpass, B and my father's company, C, with D on the extreme west. Colonel Meldram's headquarters was just behind them in Putot.

And there they waited for instructions from above while the overall front was being consolidated. Three technical points should be added. After their heavy losses on the beach, the companies were badly understrength, some badly short-handed. And, to the east of Gower's A Company, the front was to be held by a British unit which was not yet in place. So there was a hole. Finally, having reached their objective first, their position was effectively a small, exposed salient, blocking both railway and road.

But there the classic D-Day story ends. There the Hollywood movie reel runs out. What follows is taken for granted—the nitty-gritty of mopping up, and liberation.

FOR THE CANADIANS IN GENERAL and the Winnipeg Rifles in particular, it was there that the consequences of D-Day really began. During the 40th anniversary of the landing, my brother, Alastair, and I were in Normandy. Our father had died suddenly, seventeen years before, of a cerebral hemorrhage while still a serving officer. Forty-nine years old. A colonel. The two of us went looking for the Winnipeg Rifles contingent. We found the group and, as we had a car, offered to take two of them to Putot—Colonel Fulton, the regimental leader and hero, along with Tiny Thompson, a large man who, as a heavy machine-gun battalion officer, had been attached to the regiment.

Neither Fulton nor Thompson had been back since the battle, forty years before. It seemed that little had changed. The highway, the village, the railway track were still there. It was still a mixed-farming area. It was still bucolic, unthreatening, with that soft Norman charm.

We walked around while the two of them tried to reconstruct what had happened. Tiny had been badly wounded. Lockie had come through it unscratched. The fates. The luck of war.

ON THE NIGHT OF THE SEVENTH, the Germans had begun feeling out the front. A few tanks and elements of the Hitler SS Youth Corps had advanced and been driven back; then a Mark III, some infantry and armoured cars. With the morning, mortars began, and shells, which burst in the air, spreading shrapnel.

At about 7 a.m., the SS began a major counterattack, which involved almost two battalions and some sort of armoured vehicle. War and battle, once it starts, is such disorder. Men who were there are still arguing about what they saw. In any case, the Winnipeg Rifles had no armoured vehicles, few anti-tank weapons and were heavily outnumbered. The battle went on all day until eventually the SS got between the companies, and so were able to cut off A, B and C companies from behind and then pour into Putot. Colonel Meldram had to move his headquarters westward into D Company with Captain Fulton. They managed to repulse the attack.

But the other three companies were somewhere out there on their own. What followed was one of those terrible fights in which the best you can hope for is to hold on. All accounts have the SS forces swirling around the spread-out companies and platoons, swirling around the Canadian slit trenches, isolating them one from the other.

The three companies were virtually destroyed. There were no reinforcements. The men gradually ran out of ammunition and those who survived fell back on the village as best they could. My father never spoke of the battle, but according to others in C Company, he ended up in command and tried to break out by sending a platoon forward across the railway line. When this proved impossible, the company was faced with capture and—although they didn't know it—probably execution. He then organized them into a fighting patrol and indeed they fought their way back through the SS to their own reformed line.

The whole business, along with what happened to the Regina Rifles, the North Nova Scotia Highlanders, and the Sherbrooke Fusiliers, was a small version of the first gas attack at Ypres in the previous war. The situation had been terrible, but they had held on. The Germans had not been able to exploit their advantage and break through. Had they done so, anything might have happened. The beaches were badly secured. At the end of the day, the Canadian Scottish, supported by tanks, were brought up and mounted an aggressive counterattack that solidified the line.

The count? More than 300 casualties. The bodies of Major Hodge and 18 soldiers were discovered the next day. They had been taken prisoner and then executed. Gradually it became clear that other casualties were also executions. The Regiment now calculates the number at 58. Altogether the Rifles had lost more than half their fighting strength. In the two and a half days since landing on Courseulles beach, they had had 450 casualties. Their line companies had been effectively wiped out; much of what had been slowly constructed over those years in Britain.

Putot was the first hint of what lay ahead on the way to Caen and Falaise. Battle after battle seemed to revolve around heavy casualties and unclear, impossible situations. It isn't often mentioned, but Canadian casualties throughout the Normandy campaign matched the levels of the First World War.

We have such trouble focusing on how much of war is not a victorious romp, but slogging and holding on and doing your best, while generals somewhere above you try to figure out how to do it differently or better. In a war each death is left behind as a regiment moves on. Reinforcements arrive, the line changes, another battle is fought, and what seemed so stable during those years in Britain takes on a new shape, with new faces and personalities.

Some, like Lockie Fulton, come through from end to end and are with us today as witnesses of the regiment's life at war. As I said, he went back to farm his land on the Prairies. Others went back to jobs or built new lives.

Some adjusted well, finding a way to deal with their new reality—one in which those who were now around them could never really know. Little could be accomplished by explaining. That would just accentuate the distance. And besides, to explain would be to suggest that such things were explicable.

So instead they told a few jokes from time to time, about army food and curious habits or happenings. Others buried themselves in work. Others couldn't adjust at all. They shut the experience in and it ate them up. There was alcohol. There were more suicides than we like to talk about.

It made so little sense, that personal experience, when you came back across the Atlantic to a place that had experienced none of it. The more I think of it, the more it makes sense to think of the Unknown Soldier as an image of the survivors as much as of the dead.

LET ME ADD A FINAL THOUGHT and then two curious stories. The thought is quite simple. I was brought up surrounded by the men who had landed on D-Day, had fought in Normandy, or in the air, or on ships.

Whatever their personal drama, there was a certain public self-confidence about them. They knew who they were, what they'd done, what place they came from. Whatever their ideas, they seemed able to think of themselves as coming from a real place that wasn't dependent on references to other, more powerful places.

It wasn't really what you'd call nationalism. It was a sense of self. Something that can't really be handed on. All the same, I'm always surprised today to find men and women in positions of great responsibility who clearly don't know who they are or where they come from. And so they desperately reach out in a frightened way for larger, more powerful models elsewhere.

What of the curious stories? Well, the first was told to me as one of those funny anecdotes that stand in for the impossibility of explaining the rest. At that same

40th-anniversary celebration in Normandy, I fell into conversation with James Renwick, who was then an MPP in the Ontario Legislature. He had been a junior officer in the armoured corps during the Normandy campaign. In one of those endless, difficult battles around the Falaise Gap, his tank had been knocked out and he was captured.

Covered in the grease and filth that comes with escaping from a tank which has been hit, he was marched back behind German lines until a large open staff car drew up and stopped. Beside the driver was a general in a leather jacket. There were two big dogs sitting behind. It was half-light by then and so he couldn't quite make out the features of the general who was cross-examining the guards. Abruptly Renwick was ordered to climb up into the back seat.

It was only then, in the falling light, that he realized it was Kurt Meyer. In the aftermath of the 19 executions at Putot, and then 39 more, and then others in other regiments, the Canadian soldiers had talked of little else. They had focused on Meyer as the general-cum-devil who lay just out of sight on the other side of the front. He was their personal devil—a personalized devil for Canadians.

How often can it be said—war is extremely odd. Thousands had already been killed in battle. But that was war, victory, defeat, courage and all the rest. Those 58 executed soldiers, they belonged to another category, something quite different from the idea that these soldiers had of war.

You may say, "What difference?" You may argue that it's all about killing and death. And I won't even bother to reply with words like honour. The point is that in order to fight, the soldier must give himself an idea of how and why. That you, the reader, may today agree or disagree is neither here nor there. Meyer was their devil. He executed soldiers.

And so Captain Renwick looked at the neck of evil, catching glimpses of his profile from time to time as Meyer asked questions. There was an astonishing toughness about the face. This man had been through every battle since the beginning. He was a very different beast to anything a young Canadian might have met over the preceding years. And all Renwick could think of was the 58 executed soldiers.

When they arrived at Meyer's tent, the questioning continued. The general was obviously dissatisfied with the results. It was night. Meyer said he had finished with the prisoner and turned away while Renwick was led out.

The guard pushed him down a path through some woods to a small river. In the darkness, alone, walking away from the camp, he realized he was going to be shot.

Still, he managed to walk on. When they got to the river the guard told him to bend over. When he hesitated, the soldier insisted. Finally he demonstrated that the prisoner should wash himself. After all, he was filthy—the sort of state you might expect when your tank has been knocked out in a battle.

He began to wash and only slowly realized that he was not going to die.

WHAT OF THE SECOND STORY? Well, it is more of a conundrum than a story. A complex conundrum. The end of war brought access to very precise military documentation. It turned out that Kurt Meyer had not been responsible for the executions. Not those executions. He hadn't even been in the same sector. He had commanded a part of the 12th SS, one sector to the left facing the other half of the 9th Canadian Infantry Brigade. And there his soldiers had captured men from the Sherbrooke Fusiliers and the North Nova Scotia Highlanders. Eighteen of them were interrogated, then executed.

Meyer was captured in 1945 and tried. Although he had been involved in other murders, the centre of the prosecution's case was the clear evidence surrounding the fate of the eighteen. He was sentenced to death. But then, amid great controversy, a Canadian general commuted the death penalty to life imprisonment. He was by then in Dorchester prison in New Brunswick. Later that sentence in turn was shortened, he was sent back to Germany to serve it out and was then released. Meyer went on to a relatively successful career in the beer business and remained an unapologetic Nazi. His funeral produced a great showing of ex-SS.

These rather peculiar events were only the beginning of the conundrum. Despite the precise nature of his trial, Canadians tended to go on believing that he was the one who had executed the 58 Winnipeg Rifles. One factor might have been that his two guards during the trial, the officers visible in the famous photograph, were from the Rifles. Perhaps it was also because his role had been built from the very

beginning into the story of Putot, the decimation of the Regiment and the executions. He had become part of the explanation and of the grieving process for families and fellow soldiers. Such profound emotion is difficult to reverse. It isn't really any longer about documentation. Certainly I went on believing the original story. It somehow hovered about us all. In fact, when I look at that picture of him striding in to the court, I still believe it at an emotional level. The accompanying fact was that of his trial and conviction.

There is no question here of innocence or guilt, only of which soldiers he murdered and whether there is an identifiable figure to take responsibility for the death of the others.

The answer is that there is and there isn't. Across the line from the Winnipeg Rifles was another part of the 12th SS, commanded by Colonel Wilhelm Möhnke. He was the one responsible for the counterattack and then for the fifty-eight executions. But he was never brought to trial and for reasons which have all the strangeness of a world collapsing inwards. In fact, here the tragedy of those executed men—a small

General Kurt Meyer on trial in Aurich, Germany, for the execution of Canadian soldiers.
December 10, 1945.

number by world war casualty standards—joins up with the grand, swashbuckling story which films love to tell—the great D-Day landing, Paris liberated, Berlin taken, Hitler dead in his bunker.

Wilhelm Möhnke, by then a general, was commanding that bunker when he was captured by the Soviets on May 5, 1945. The rest is less clear. He remained a Russian prisoner for some time. British requests to have him turned over for trial were ignored and with time dropped. He was released and apparently lived out his life in East Germany—a Nazi war criminal protected inadvertently or consciously behind the Iron Curtain. But then many others found their way into protective obscurity in each of the Allied countries, including Canada, and often with surprising sorts of help.

The point is that his obscure existence provided no concrete focus for the memory of what happened at Putot. And the battle, small though it was, remained, and remains, a fulcrum of unresolvable questions. For a start, it was not the battle the young Canadians expected when they trained over the years in England—a battle of desperate confusion and carefully carried-out executions, with so many of their child-hood friends dead in the first 48 hours after the landing; a battle to be admired because they held on just enough that neither Möhnke nor Meyer could convincingly break through at a time when the whole Allied line was fragile.

Lockie Fulton, after his return to Putot during the 40th anniversary, began to rethink what had happened. It became a key illustration in an annual lecture he was asked to give on battlefield tactics at the Canadian Army Staff College. Another Winnipeg Rifle, Cliff Chadderton, set about collecting first-hand information from all sources. He became a great expert on the events and made a film on the battle and the executions.

As for those who survived, after Putot came the incredible hard slog, first to Caen, then Falaise, then across coastal France and Belgium to the opened dykes of Holland and battles in the flooded fields. But somehow that first encounter at Putot remained a defining moment. After all, the deaths on the beach were in a sense counterbalanced by the great success of the landing and breakthrough. And after Putot, the campaign was at times impossible, but it did seem to lead towards eventual victory. Putot was the line between the two—the line between the astonishing energy of the landing and the long, hard, but successful campaign. Perhaps the SS had grown used to interrogation/executions on the Eastern Front, where the normal conventions of war didn't really exist. But for the Winnipeggers and the other regiments it was another matter. In clichéd terms, Putot was the end of innocence. It was the beginning of another life for those who survived.

The fragility of memory is a terrifying thing, yet it carries men through wars and through life after war, as it carries all of us. Why fragile? Because it is never quite what it appears to be. It may be about fact or fact may not be what we need. We may focus our fears and energies onto the name of a general never seen, who may later turn out never to have been there. Memory can help us, betray us, spin us in and out of complexity.

Then historians, good and bad, will begin their work. Analysts will comment at first on reality, but then on each other's comments. The debate will slip into reflections upon reflections of reality. It will all spin farther and farther away from the young men vomiting in their landing crafts, dying or not on the beach, rushing across bucolic fields towards their first objective and then holding on, as best they can, by a railway track near an obscure village, of which few would later hear the name.

NOTES

John Ralston Saul quoted from *Little Black Devils: A History of the Royal Winnipeg Rifles*, by Bruce Tascona and Eric Wells (Winnipeg: Frye Publishing, 1983), and *Diary of a Man in Despair*, by Freidrich Reck-Malleczwen (London: Duck Editions, 2000). Information on the battle at Putot was provided by Colonel Lockie Fulton and Cliff Chadderton.

Dionne Brand

ONE DOWN

On Friday, November 8, 1946, Viola Desmond was bodily thrown out of the Roseland Theatre

in New Glasgow, Nova Scotia, because she sat in the white section of the movie house and refused to move when ordered to do so. She was jailed overnight and convicted the next day of defrauding the Province of Nova Scotia of one cent tax. Though no signs were posted, there was in Nova Scotia and Canada at the time de facto segregation in some public places like bars and movie theatres. In many bars, from British Columbia to Nova Scotia, blacks were not served. In movie theatres, whites were sold tickets to the house and blacks to the balcony exclusively. At the Roseland, tickets to the white

Viola Desmond following her high school graduation, June 1930.

section carried a one-cent-extra tax. Ms. Desmond had requested a ticket to the house but was refused and was sold instead a ticket to the balcony. When she insisted on sitting in the house the police were called to remove her. At her trial, racism was never mentioned. Her conviction was couched in the legalese of taxes. Church leaders, the Nova Scotia Association for the Advancement of Coloured People, and the black-owned newspaper *The Clarion* rallied to Ms. Desmond's defence. All appeals failed however and the conviction stood.

ONE DOWN

THERE'S A PICTURE OF YOU at the Hi-Hat Club in Boston in 1955. There's a curl on the left side of your forehead, you have hanging earrings, pearls perhaps, and a black ribbon with a diamanté around your small neck. Your eyes. What to make of your eyes? They are bright, direct, slightly sad because of the way your head tilts to the left. You are smiling. There is a tall glass on the table in front of you. The woman next to you dressed in a dark evening dress is your sister Wanda. She too has pearl earrings, her clutch purse rests on the table, she seems younger. She too is smiling. The man to your left is her husband. He is handsome, his hair is a slick lye perm, a cigarette dangles between the index and middle finger of his right hand. Milton has a beautiful smile—a Nat King Cole smile. All three of you seem cool sitting at the Hi-Hat Club in Boston. There must be music there. Dexter Gordon's band is playing "Don't Worry About Me." Your dress, your dress is two-toned. Was it beige lace and brown taffeta? Your shoes must be stiletto. Your feet are tapping to Dexter Gordon.

The Hi-Hat is packed with suave ebony men and beautiful women. Perfumes thicken the air. A chic well-being pervades. The band is swinging and you feel like dancing. You've been sitting there half the night talking, catching up on the news from Halifax. Talking louder than the music sometimes or dropping your voice behind Carl Perkins's piano solo. You're remembering Gottingen Street and all the young women who would crowd into the beauty parlour on a Saturday, their chatter and laughter and you telling them, "Ladies, ladies, please. We are ladies here." That pretty tilt of your head and the smile which makes you look wistful even at the Hi-Hat Club in Boston in 1955, did you always look that way? Is it the memory of Vi's Studio of Beauty Culture on Gottingen Street that brings it on?

Dexter Gordon's "Rhythm Mad" takes you back to Halifax. That 1940s Dodge sedan of yours—a clunker. When you just bought it, it seemed a slick ride. You were proud of it, you being a woman of moderate means, a woman with a future and plans. That Dodge sedan was your prize, wasn't it? For all the hard work, all the building of yourself you'd done. "Such ambition in a small woman," they must have said at the Cornwallis Street Baptist Church and anywhere else you went. You didn't expect to be in New Glasgow but the Dodge began to give out. Several times you'd stopped, started the engine up again, finally just praying to make it to a garage.

It broke down in New Glasgow on a good day in November 1946. A Friday, light snow fell in the morning but the wind from the sea took it right out. A day with a blue sky, brisk wind. One of those days you loved, crisp, bright. A good day for driving to Sydney. Had to see a man about a new venture. Vi's would be branching out. There were ladies in Sydney who needed their hair done and had nowhere to go. The white beauty salons wouldn't have them. A good opportunity for an ambitious woman like you. And there were young women who could be taught how to do hair, to press and curl and give a permanent, there was a market in Sydney for your hair product line—so it was a good November day. A clean sweet day to drive there— maybe stay over until the Saturday and drive back in time to go to Sunday service at Cornwallis Street Baptist as usual. What Dexter Gordon's saxophone can do! Sweep you back to Cornwallis Street Baptist Church—imagine that.

When you first bought the Dodge, the interior smelled as rich as the life you had in mind. A smooth life. You would work your way through the obstacles. They were just a way of God testing you. But if you had faith and kept your head up, life would open up. It wasn't so bad, if you had faith in God and yourself. The little prejudices would not hold you back. Things weren't always said, mind you, but it was there all the time—the colour bar. But if you put your head down and mind how you went, things would sometimes turn out well. Like the 1940 Dodge sedan smelling new and full of promise. The interior was plaid, green and brown.

Remembering when you bought it—you planned to carry the supplies you ordered from Montréal and, later on, the products from Madame C. J. Walker's of New York. If you had to, you could drive the sedan all the way down to New York City to visit Madame C. J. Walker herself.

The Hi-Hat feels suddenly hot. The band is in the middle of "Rhythm Mad." From the table behind you there is loud laughter. All around you there is quick movement and fast talk. Leroy Vinnegar is on bass. He is doing impossible things with his fingers. The strings on his bass lead to every sinew in the room. Your smile is more wistful, your eyes are brighter, you can see the road into New Glasgow that crisp day. The bass thrums that tensile memory stark. If someone had told you it would turn out the way it did, you wouldn't have believed them. Even though on waking up every day you anticipated trouble, you still wouldn't have believed them. Why a day that started out so simply would end that way.

The Dodge gave a final sputter and you were happy perhaps because at least it wasn't far to the repair shop. You knew how to see the good part of any setback. Maybe it was a small problem and you could get it fixed and be on your way again. At least you weren't stranded on a deserted road between New Glasgow and Sydney. You wouldn't complain. The Dodge was a good car though you'd been overcharged for it. You took the car dealer, Phillip Kane was his name, you took him to court for overcharging you. After all, there was a Wartime Prices Order and whatever his prejudices he didn't have the right to do that. That man didn't know who he was fooling with, Jack said. Jack used to tease you, he did. Said you were too proud. Said you wouldn't pick a stray penny up from the street if you were dying.

That face of yours with its sweet smile, its demure eyes. That face doesn't tell the half of it. There was iron in you. The man at the garage in New Glasgow said it would take time, might take till the next day. He had to put in a new part. He was backed up as it was, he said. Tomorrow for sure. Well, what could you do? No other way to get to Sydney or to get back to Halifax, and besides, you didn't want to leave the Dodge there, that would mean coming back tomorrow anyway.

Jack would be worried so you must've called him at the barbershop to say you'd be staying over. "The King of Gottingen Street," they called him. An easy man with people, friends. Being one of eight children had taught him to get along, smooth things over. A man people seemed to give their trust or love to easily. That was what took you about him. A man with an upward look and faithful, too. He'd travel all the way to Montréal to court you when you were in training at the Field Beauty Cultural School. A dear man. You must've called him. That time of day on a Friday, Jack would be waiting for the onslaught. Men coming out of ships at the dockyard, men preparing for Friday night at the Brown Derby—a cut or a lye slick—men sitting with lye burning their hair straight, having moustaches pruned and tweaked. The talk would be all about music and uplift and where a man could find work in this town— and why after the war and after they served in the army, why was it the same as before they went to fight Hitler. Men from Preston and Tracadie and Truro working day labour would haul their tired legs into Jack's if not to get a cut and shave then just to hear talk, just to meet with other men like them. Knocking the dust off their shoes, willing their rough hands to turn soft on the back of some fine woman that Friday night. They came to Jack's to talk themselves up, to give themselves a bit of courage for the coming week. A shave and a cut would transform them from men with scarcely a penny in their pockets to jazz musicians and athletes—men who could use the raw power of being to make something. "Man, did you hear about that Benny Carter? Said he can hold a note, I tell you. Gon' get me a horn myself someday . . ." "Seen young Joe Louis fight. No better man . . ." Every morning that week in November most of them had stood in the early cold of the docks, stamping their feet warm, hitting the numbness out of their bodies, waiting to be picked for a day of lifting and throwing load or cutting fish. It had been a good week and they had extra in their pockets to get a shave, to slip into Jack's chair with a warm towel around their face.

Jack is not with you now, he is not in that photograph at the Hi-Hat Club on Columbus Avenue in Boston. Good as he was, a distance opened between you that Friday in November 1946 when the Dodge broke down. Not right away, but little by little. When you called he must've said, "Do you want me to come out there, baby?" You must've told him that you were fine, no sense in two of you being stranded here and losing business. "Might as well make the best of it," you said. You thought you'd make an evening of it. You knew some folk to stay with overnight. No sense trying a hotel, no sense putting yourself out. No telling the way you'd be treated. So you decided on a movie. You'd packed yourself something to eat for the trip to Sydney. That was supper, and then you would go to the seven o'clock at the Roseland Theatre. This could turn out to be pleasant, after all, you thought, leaving the Dodge at the garage. Tomorrow would be a busy day at Vi's Beauty Parlour. You would have your hands full.

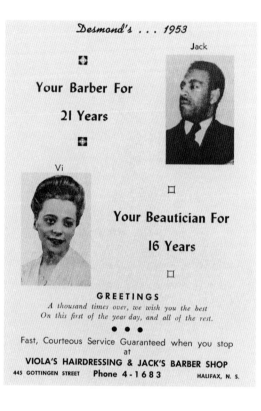

Desmond's . . . 1953

Jack

Your Barber For 21 Years

Vi

Your Beautician For 16 Years

GREETINGS
A thousand times over, we wish you the best
On this first of the year day, and all of the rest.

● ● ●

Fast, Courteous Service Guaranteed when you stop at

VIOLA'S HAIRDRESSING & JACK'S BARBER SHOP
445 GOTTINGEN STREET   Phone 4-1683   HALIFAX, N. S.

Saturdays at Vi's was quite the social event, quite the time. Everyone, just everyone would have to get their hair done on a Saturday at Vi's. On Sunday mornings Cornwallis Street Baptist would be a parade of your hair designs. Your

---

Souvenir calendar, Desmond's, 1953.

hands would ache with washing and shampooing and pressing and curling. The pageboys the French rolls the sleek chignons. Each woman wanted to be unique and you were the artist. You offered tea. You gave your soothing hands to that head, which had had a rough week. You knew that Mrs. Clark's husband was stepping out on her, that Rhoda Murray's son was headed the wrong way, that Glory Spencer had lost her job up in Glace Bay, that all seven children of Mavis and John Deeks had the chicken pox, and that Sylvia Hamilton was planning to run off next Saturday to New York City to be a singer in a band. That was the dream life of all the young girls on Gottingen Street, and Sylvia was determined to live the life. You knew all that Agnes Gordon needed was a little encouragement, a little brightening up to make herself into somebody; that Millie Gains was at the end of her rope with Isaac being late all the time; and you could tell that young one of James and Lettie Howe was hiding a pregnancy under a big coat she wore even on warm days. You knew all this and you knew that people only wanted to strive, to be better than they were.

Secrets and desires you kept like jewels. You had an open fondness for people. That is why your eyes remained bright even in 1955 at the Hi-Hat. No matter what happened you could see the good in it, you could see a positive outcome. The women who came into Vi's admired you for that. You would give them a lift, a feeling of style and charm that their own lives often lacked. The contralto Portia White had her hair specially done at Vi's. That's how classy Vi's Beauty Parlour was.

At Vi's Black women became the ladies they were, leaning back in chairs under heat caps; your gentle hands held the ears down to get the straightening comb at the tightest curls. All week most of the women had been at day jobs doing housework or ironing. Their own hands ached, their feet were talking. They moaned blissfully when they sat down in that chair at Vi's. You worked the oils into their scalps and coaxed kinks onto paper rollers and brush rollers and curling irons. You were careful that the shortest hairs along the hairline were done and you warned customers not to go out uncovered in the rain or snow or stand in a stormy place or else you couldn't be blamed for hair "going back." You added nails and feet to your repertoire. You kept up with new pomades and straighteners and hair greases. You imported Madame C. J. Walker's line of hair care and cosmetics. Cleansing creams, bleaching creams, hand lotions, and hair oils. You lectured on skin care, posture, and beauty secrets.

At the Hi-Hat Club your hands are not visible. What must they look like? Small, capable, strong. Strangely muscular, one suspects. Your nails varnished deep red, the cuticle stripped clean. Your hands lying in your lap, their intelligence hidden. Anyone could see your character in those hands, their wise and sure movement through strands of hair, sorting the different textures, the lengths, and what had to be done. Your hands belie the innocence of your face. It is as if this part of you, your hands, were travelling ahead of the rest of you—their energy, the force and knowledge of them, smoothing a path ahead of everyone, ahead of yourself. Your face reflects wistfulness, something longed for, lost. As if you're saying, "Ah, well, that is the way of the world." Your face is childlike and loving. Whatever is lost there, one can't help but wish it back for you. If only one could. But it is in your hidden hands that we would find the deep resolve of your life.

The Roseland Theatre was just down from the repair shop on Provost. Olivia de Havilland was starring with Lew Ayres in *The Dark Mirror*. You looked at the hand-painted billboard. "To know her is to love her. To love her is to die," it said. Olivia de Havilland. Talk about style. She had a sultry grace you may have admired. A romantic thriller. Just what the evening needed. The Roseland was plush. Beautiful wall murals of roses, cherubs over the doorways, red velvet curtains. Entering the Roseland was entering a place of dreams. Anyone, after passing through the rose-covered door, could find their other best self on the screen. Anyone could live in the celluloid of New York parties and grand staircases, in grand mansions, in ball gowns and tuxedos, in the intrigue of German spies and twisted love, in crazy dance numbers and slapstick humour.

You were a little late, not much, but most people were seated. You gave the cashier a dollar, said, "One down, please." You didn't notice that she gave you a ticket for the balcony with the change. You walked to the house to find a seat. You were ready to become Olivia de Havilland in love with Lew Ayres. A girl was saying something behind you. The ticket taker. It took a minute to register, but she said, "You've got an upstairs ticket, you'll have to go upstairs." Well, you'd asked the cashier for downstairs. Opening your hand with the ticket and the change, you realized the cashier's mistake so you headed back to the wicket. "I asked for one downstairs and you gave me one for the balcony. I'd like to exchange." The ticket seller looked impatient. She shook her head at you and half turned away. You repeated, you said in your most polite way, "Excuse me, I'd like one down, you gave me one for the balcony." You felt odd. You didn't want to misjudge. You didn't want to assume but something was creeping up the back of your neck. A recognition, which no matter how often it happened was a shock. And it happened often enough but it always crept up. When the ticket seller's mouth said, "I'm sorry, but I'm not permitted to sell downstairs tickets to you people," you heard each word separately. It was hard putting them together. The time it took seemed long. You saw the oval of her mouth and you saw the words drop. They were hard and brittle, and when you brought all of your will to listening, they added up to what the ticket seller had said. "I'm sorry, but I'm not permitted to sell downstairs tickets to you people."

You people. You turned your back on her. Her words falling behind you. You walked back into the theatre, those hands of yours clenched onto your purse and your will. Olivia de Havilland's face secret and gloomy loomed on the screen. You took your seat downstairs. You weren't going to let it go this time. Enough was enough. Such an innocent desire. A picture show! Why couldn't a person express one tiny innocent desire without having to watch out. You passed the other girl, she would testify to that. You passed her and took your seat in the house. Lew Ayres smoked a cigarette onscreen. If you were a smoker, you would join him. But you truly did not feel his ease walking across the screen. You felt a shattering, your chest quivered. You felt like crying.

It was then that Dexter Gordon's band slithered into "I Should Care." You sipped your drink. Your sister squeezed your arm. She and Milton had gotten married just a few years gone. You hadn't seen her for a year. It was good to be with her. You both loved this jazz. And Nova Scotia, for all the hurt.

The girl came down to where you were sitting. Her tone was belligerent. She said, "I told you to go upstairs." She tucked a bit of brown hair behind her left ear. She was younger than you. In Vi's Beauty Parlour, a girl as young as she would have called you Miss Viola or Miss Desmond, ma'am. You didn't know then her name was Prima. Prima Davis. You refused to move. You ignored her so she stomped off to get the manager. You sat. *The Dark Mirror* was unintelligible. You heard nothing. You sat. You waited.

You heard their footsteps coming down the aisle. The manager, Harry MacNeil, spoke to you as if you were a child. "You have been told to go upstairs. I demand that you do immediately." He spoke in a low hissing tone at first, not wanting to attract attention. You could not see his face fully in the shadowy flickering half-light of the Roseland. Trying to explain only made him hiss louder. He said something about the right to refuse admission to objectionable people. But you had been admitted, you protested, the girl refused to sell you a downstairs ticket, you explained, she gave you one for upstairs but you never sat upstairs, your eyes, you couldn't see well from there. No matter what you said, no reason could prevail. You spoke softly, thinking virtue and decorum would succeed. Harry MacNeil became angrier and angrier, louder and louder, till there was rustling in the theatre. The voice of Lew Ayres was drowned out by the sound of the patrons. The intrigue of *The Dark Mirror* riffed over the commotion of the manager stalking out of the theatre, threatening to return with the police. The policeman came so quickly. Shock. Shock is all that can be described here. Only later you would recount stoically: "The policeman grabbed my shoulders and the manager grabbed my legs, injuring my knee and hip. They carried me bodily from the theatre into the street . . . I was driven to the police station. Within a few minutes the manager appeared and the chief of police.

They left together and returned in an hour with a warrant for my arrest." That is how you left the Roseland that evening. Harmed.

There's a way that Dexter Gordon has with a saxophone. It is so languid yet so immediate. He plays with the right timbre of melancholy and cynicism. As he plays "I Should Care," you listen in another time, wishing you had just that touch back then at the Roseland Theatre. You were younger then. The wistfulness had not

Viola Desmond relaxing at the Hi-Hat Club in Boston, with her sister and brother-in-law, July 1955.
Viola is in the centre, on the left Wanda (Davis) Neal, on the right Milton Neal.

crept into your eyes. That was the start, no, the confirmation of it. All the plans—the chain of Vi's Beauty Parlours, the young women graduating with diplomas. You loved jazz, you were going to manage a few bands, too. You had already helped a few musicians to patent their lyrics. You had fallen fully into jazz on those days in Montréal and New York. You had been a cigarette girl at Small's Paradise. Heard Dizzy and Bird, Benny Carter and Bud Powell, while you studied in the daytime how to fashion wigs, how to style hair. You were younger and thought that things could be done. Prejudice could be fought.

At the Hi-Hat Club, Dexter Gordon put another spin on that hope. "I Should Care." You did then. Still do. Right there, right there in that jail, the cell next to the male prisoners, it was easy to lose faith. How they could put a gentle-minded woman like you in jail and for what? For what? That question rattled around in you. But faith is a good thing, no matter how rough life feels, your faith brings you through. So you put your white gloves on, they had not taken your purse, you put your white gloves on and you sat straight up and wide awake all night long in that jail cell. The hours passed slowly. Determined to stay awake as a witness, you went over the events of your life that led you to this. It was nothing in particular but an accumulation of moments. If someone had told you yesterday or even seconds before; if they'd said, "Vi, look out now, one day you'll be arrested and thrown in jail for sitting in the white section of a movie theatre," it would not have been believable.

The matron came in now and then, she had a half-sympathetic look. All night the officers kept bringing in more arrested men, drunkards, hooligans. They were none too mannerly. The cell was dingy as crude places are. There was a bunk and blankets, but your resolve would not let you lie down. If they were determined to bring you low, to take every bit of decency from you, you would not let them. The Dodge was at the garage. What would happen to it tomorrow morning? Jack could not have heard. There was no chance to tell him. And the ladies tomorrow, they would be disappointed. There would be no laughing and talking about how Duke Ellington played at the Mutual Street Arena in Toronto just two days ago, or that

Coleman Hawkins played the day you got arrested, and Robeson, can you believe Robeson sang at Eaton's. Refused to sing if it was segregated, he did! That Ruthie Johnson was just crazy for jazz and Duke Ellington and had gone out to Toronto a month ago and vowed to be in the front row. She'd sent news about jumping the jive at the Palais Royale. There would be no catching up on Rhoda Murray's son—truthfully, she should send that boy to his daddy in Toronto so he could teach him how to be a man. Oh, you wished all night that you were there for that conversation.

It must have been about two or three in the morning when it got difficult. There was snoring and cursing from the men's cell, it was all you could do to keep your eyes open and so you set your mind even harder. This was a mistake, a terrible mistake, and as soon as you had the chance you would explain to the higher authorities. After all, there was no law, there was no sign in the theatre. If there had been, you wouldn't even have gone in.

When day broke you took it with relief. You stood up, dusted and straightened your skirt, pulled your gloves close, and waited to be taken to court. There was light signalling morning but it was impossible to say whether it was a sunny morning or a dull one.

New Glasgow woke up to warm itself in front of wood stoves, to cold bodies poured into night-cold clothes. If the day was dry enough, washing could be hung out. It was Saturday. Downtown New Glasgow would soon be bustling. The Roseland Theatre was closed. By mid-morning the ushers would come in and sweep last night's cache of paper bags and soda bottles away, peel off the chewing gum from the bottom of seats and empty ashtrays. The grand proscenium stage, where jugglers and minstrels used to perform a decade or more ago, folded itself in red velvet curtain dropping from ceiling to floor. *The Dark Mirror* had been returned to its can in the projection room. The land of roses painted along the walls lay in mute dimness waiting for the matinee crowd of children. New Glasgow woke up and, after morning coffee and bacon, went on with its life. Some who had been at the Roseland Theatre last night remembered the commotion. They mentioned it again at breakfast.

"What did she expect, after all," the talk went. "Such a shame spoiling a nice evening out. That Olivia de Havilland is so beautiful, I got her eyes, you know." "Why, if I wasn't sitting there, I wouldn't have believed it. Right next to me, she was. To my everlasting surprise."

You stood waiting for the matron. Not hungry, you told her when she offered you tea. You were anxious when they took you to the courthouse. No one would blame you for feeling weak in the stomach. If you'd have drunk the tea, you couldn't keep it down. Anyone would waver between incredulity and fear here. When the daylight seemed never to arrive you must've been ready to give out, to swear that you'd lost your mind; that you were still at the Roseland smothered in celluloid and roses, dreaming like everyone else in the Roseland Theatre.

The magistrate said, "Viola Desmond, you are charged with violating the provincial Theatres, Cinematographs, and Amusement Act. How do you plead?" It sounded funny to you. A nervousness made you want to laugh. Magistrate Roderick Geddes Mackay was looking at you with such utter seriousness, you knew he would not hear you out. Mr. MacNeil from the Roseland, he said, "Sir, she refused to remove herself, she did not pay the tax or the right price." Prima Davis and the ticket seller backed him up. They all said you bought an upstairs ticket paying only two cents tax and then seated yourself downstairs, big as you please. And a ticket for downstairs had a three-cent tax on it. Taxes! No one had said anything about taxes. The girl at the ticket booth had said, "I'm not permitted to sell downstairs tickets to you people." *You people!* That phrase burned itself back into your head but they all kept talking about taxes. You felt alone. There were other prisoners in the courtroom. One for drunkenness, one for assault, one for stealing. You had nothing in common with them except the word *prisoner*. Your small strong hands sweated in their white gloves even though the courtroom was cold. The matron stood close by in case you tried to bolt. You thought that you felt her sympathy, but none of your senses were working so you couldn't be sure. You gathered yourself up when you took the stand. "I am the accused," you said. "I offered to pay the difference in the price between the tickets.

They would not accept it." You said more but that's not in the minutes of the record. And what more you said about Coloured people and all, and the way you were hauled out of the Roseland, causing you physical injury, none of it mattered. You were convicted and fined twenty-six dollars or one month in jail.

Those two days in New Glasgow cost more than money. You sleepwalked through the courthouse door, through the arrangements with the mechanic, and through the rest of the day. The Dodge sedan was still at the repair shop. It looked like a good friend waiting. The Dodge seemed to drive itself back to Halifax. You noticed your white gloves on the steering wheel. You'd forgotten to take them off or you really couldn't bring yourself to take them off. They protected you somehow. You hands didn't tremble as you knew they would if you'd removed their small armour. You daydreamed that it had turned out differently. The car had never broken down. The car had broken down and you had gone to see a movie with Olivia de Havilland and Lew Ayres at the Roseland Theatre, whose walls depicted a land of colourful blooms. The evening had been wonderful and you'd come out of the theatre and gone home. It had turned out differently. There had been no incident at all. The car had made it all the way to Sydney, and New Glasgow had been left behind. You daydreamed all this, time all changed; life all ordinary.

They don't know about this yet on Gottingen Street. It's late Saturday afternoon by the time the Dodge sedan draws up to Vi's Beauty Parlour and Jack's Barbershop. Only then do you take your gloves off. It's not over, you told yourself, no matter the efforts of your body to run and hide. You didn't run off at the Roseland. You stood your ground. Now there was a conviction against your name after all you'd done to lift yourself up. Jack's way of looking at things was to ease yourself along, don't make too much fuss. That was the way of the world, he said. "Take it to the Lord," he'd say. And this time, though he was angry himself, he still said, "You've got to know how to handle things—you can't be too forward." He knew about the Roseland, he did. When he was a boy running errands and working in the drugstore in New Glasgow, he knew they didn't allow Coloureds downstairs.

"Take it to the Lord." That was his motto and it had taken him far. It was the way Nova Scotia was, he said, it was the way of the world. You open your mouth for something like this and whatever little there was would dry up too. So this fuss you wanted to kick up didn't sit well with him.

Remembering this at the Hi-Hat Club in Boston, you smiled. "Hotheaded," he called you. You could smile now of course, but then thank heavens for the good women around you. Miss Pearleen Oliver who said, "Dear God, Viola, what did they do to you?" and took it from there to the Nova Scotia Association for the Advancement of Coloured People. Miss Carrie Best who wrote it up on the front page of her newspaper *The Clarion*. "Disgraceful," she called it. "Jim Crowism."

Wanda always said that you were not a person who liked to lose something righteous. Some didn't agree with you taking it further, said you were "looking for trouble." Who could blame them? They wanted life to be gentle with them, they wanted to walk away, calm it down, act as if nothing happened. But life was rough, not gentle. Something happened every day to prove this.

It took a while. People came together giving money to open the case. After trying to sue the Roseland Theatre for assault, malicious prosecution, and false arrest

The third grade class of Viola Davis, Joseph Howe Elementary School, Halifax.
Viola is in the first row, extreme right.

and imprisonment, the lawyer decided to take the case to the Nova Scotia Supreme Court. It took months and bearing up to the pressure from Jack. It was not his fault, he was just a practical man. Growing up in Tracadie and New Glasgow had taught him some things he couldn't put aside. Shouldn't put aside, when you come to think of it now. Days at the beauty parlour were tense. You could feel Jack's disapproval from next door. At home, things between you came to silence. But you, well, you had faith. You didn't want to live all a bundle of nerves, watching where you sat and where you walked and all the rest. Jack would come around, you thought—people didn't have to just take it all the time, he'd see. Even if they ruled against you, in your heart you would know that you'd taken it as far as it could go.

It's 1955. Wanda and Milton are beside you. The evening is draining away at the Hi-Hat Club on Columbus. Their faces are angled towards the camera taking this picture. You are looking straight into the lens. Your head tilted. You look younger than your years. Is that how we look when we face history dead-on? Youthful and knowing, as if having dipped oneself into a clear stream? Dexter Gordon is on the last notes of "I Should Care." This whole evening you've been thinking about Gottingen Street and Halifax and the places you've wandered since; and it fits somehow into the intricate riffs and squeaks, the driven bass and tender piano. You lost of course. One judge, out of the four, did say that the Roseland tried to "enforce a Jim Crow rule by misuse of a public statute." You still lost. Well, then again . . . Just as this music is a loss and a forgiving.

NOTES

I am grateful to Constance Backhouse whose book, *Colour Coded: A Legal History of Racism in Canada, 1900–1950*, provided some of the details for "One Down." And to Roger McTair for an overheard phrase. I am indebted to Emily Clyke, Eugenie Parris, Wanda Davis Robson, and Constance Scott, Viola Desmond's sisters, for permission to use the photographs, and in countless other ways.

Michelle Berry

HENDERSON HAS SCORED FOR CANADA!

When I first came to Canada in 1975, I knew nothing about hockey.

My father was a baseball fan. We were American. I pronounced some words funny— *orange, milk*—and was called a Yankee by the kids at school. Years later, hockey was some sport that my boyfriends played, a sport that would take them away from seeing me when I was right in front of them. I disliked hockey. Men in my life watched hockey as if their lives depended on it. I was jealous of hockey. And then, not long ago, Rocket Richard died. And the outpouring of grief, the lines of mourners before his open casket in Montréal, the reminiscing on the CBC for days on end, made me stop and wonder. What was this thing, hockey, that everyone was so drawn to—like a cult, an addiction? Canadians I knew got sleepy-eyed and dreamy if you mentioned the Summit Series or the Canada Cup.

When I was approached to write for *Story of a Nation* I couldn't think of a particular event in Canadian history that I wanted to write about. I mulled over some ideas, remembering only that my high school history teacher used to tell us to read

Gladstone Public School in Toronto celebrates the nation's most famous goal.

our textbooks for the hour of our class while he went to the staff room for a smoke. Instead of reading we threw things at each other. Feeling uninformed and anxious, I complained to my husband one night. An avid hockey fan, he turned to me and said, "Nineteen seventy-two. Canada vs. Russia," as if that event was the only thing possible, as if he couldn't even think of one other incident more important in all of Canadian history. "But I hate hockey," I whined. "Even better," he said.

I talked to fans. I watched the videos. I read the books. And one thing everyone agreed upon was that this series, this moment in Canadian history, was one of the greatest moments of all time. This was a defining time for Canadians. It was "Us" against "Them." Our society vs. their society. Capitalism vs. Communism. Kids were taken out of their classes to watch the final game in the gymnasiums and hallways. Offices closed down. My father-in-law told me that a television set was brought into the boardroom in his prestigious law firm. He thought about it carefully and then said to me, "That's the only time we ever brought a television set in to watch anything." A good friend has the entire series on tape. Recently, when he moved to Thailand, he took the tapes with him. I mention that I'm writing this story to anyone and they immediately break into, "Where were you when Paul Henderson scored the goal?" This is the Canadian version of JFK's famous last ride.

Us vs. Them.

A story began to emerge—Canadian farmer, banker, the little daughter who gradually becomes enthralled with the game. The games became the story. I didn't know I was writing this story, of course. I assumed I would write something that would reveal how I felt about the game. But I finished the story knowing that I had somehow become involved, I had somehow seen what everyone else had seen. I understood the moment, finally, and became deeply interested. And in the long run I discovered that it didn't matter whether I liked or disliked hockey. What mattered was the social context of this particular game. What mattered was what Canadians did with the moment and what they did with their memories.

HENDERSON HAS SCORED FOR CANADA!

SHE'S GOT HER SMALL HAND balled tight in his large fist and they are walking towards Maple Leaf Gardens like it was any plain evening other than September 4, 1972. Her whole body is quivering, tight. Her mouth is moving in circles, saying things to herself that no one can hear. Saying, "Jesus, Jesus, Jesus," and "USSR," drawing the *s*'s out like snakes hissing. Maggie doesn't know what USSR means, but she understands that they are the enemy and she is about to see them skate out onto the ice like a pack of wolves. Daddy's holding her hand tight in his and they are joining the crowd now, walking in a flow like a river, to the Gardens.

Maggie says, "Why's it called Gardens? I don't see any gardens."

And Daddy hushes her with a quick tug on her hand. Maggie knows he's still angry at the loss in Montréal and angry at Mommy. He's talking again of Tretiak, of how that goalie, with his flimsy skates and weathered uniform, still managed to kill Team Canada on the first night.

"It was all about saving goals, not scoring them. Canada was stonewalled. They were out of shape and arrogant," Daddy says.

"Mommy wouldn't like it here," Maggie says. "It's too squishy."

"Huh?"

Tight up against the other ticket holders, the crowds surging, Maggie looks

down at her shoes and wishes she had worn something more comfortable, something
good for running. Because if these USSRs are as mean as Daddy says, she's going to
want to start running, bolting it out of the Gardens and into the city streets, through
downtown Toronto. She imagines them with fangs. She imagines them skating
together, feet going back and forth like that street band she saw when they drove to
the city for last year's Santa Claus parade, the skaters marching like devils, their
blades slicing high above the ice.

Last night in bed Maggie had a dream about the USSRs. Last night she could
hear Mommy moving about the kitchen and Daddy's silence like a scream, the house
smelling like dirt and warm air. There was the sound of the wind in the dead corn-
stalks, again like snakes, saying *USSR*, *USSR*, and the chickens in the barn scratch-
ing wildly in the mud.

"Jesus," Maggie whispers when a large man bumps the top of her head with
his elbow.

"Shush," says Daddy. "Where'd you learn to swear? Your mommy teaching
you bad habits?"

They drove all afternoon to get here. They drove past their own measly
cornfields, past their neighbours' farms, left Mommy at the house, alone—"You be
alone when we come back, Janine. I'm warning you." Drove until Maggie fell asleep
sitting up in the front of the truck, bumping and swaying, her nose full of the scent
of hay and clover and chickens. She woke to the sounds of the city, an air brake
squealing, she woke to find her daddy munching a doughnut, sprinkled, holding one
out to her, the truck stopped at a rest station. He was waiting for her to wake up so
she could pee in the stinky washroom. Waiting for her to wash the sleep out of her
eyes, to get that sour, late-afternoon-nap look off her face.

"Good to sleep, grumpy," Daddy said. "It'll be a late game."

Even though it cost a bundle, Daddy brought her here because Mommy said
it'd do her good. Said it'd do him good to get both of them away from the farm for
a while. Away from the stupid corn, which didn't grow this year on the long stalks.

But Maggie somehow knew she meant get away from her. From that something that has to do with Mr. Reynolds from the bank. From Mrs. Reynolds coming by late one evening and talking in low whispers to Daddy and then Mommy walking out onto the porch and the yelling starting. Mrs. Reynolds screaming "house wrecker" and Daddy slamming doors. "What kind of a man are you?" she screamed. "Can't keep hold of your woman."

Mommy told Maggie that the Summit Series was an important step for Canada, claimed that patriotism would make things better somehow, that their faces in the stands would mean something to the rest of the world.

"Don't let them win," Mommy said. *Hush.* "It's bad enough."

Holding Daddy's hand, Maggie doesn't want to be here. She doesn't want to mean something to the world. She wants to be home with Mommy, away from these people, away from the evil that's going to happen in the arena. Stepping into the building behind the burly men, she fears the pack of USSR men she assumes are waiting below the stands, silver blades shining like knives, slashing. She fears Mommy alone at the farm, the house creaking around her.

"The Bay of Pigs," Mommy said, "the Cuban Missile Crisis. And now Vietnam."

"What's that have to do with hockey?" Daddy said and Maggie laughed because she imagined a great body of water filled with floating pigs. "What does any of this have to do with hockey?" And then Maggie imagined the Hudson's Bay Company in town filled with pigs because the Hudson's Bay Company was the only bay she knew and suddenly she wanted a chocolate malted from the third floor by the children's department. She wanted to ride the pink elephant, bucking noisily in the corner by the washrooms. "It won't change what happened to the corn if we go to Toronto."

Mommy lifted her hands up and dropped them. "Things have to get better, Frank."

Silence.

"Seven to three, Frank," Mommy whispered. "All of Montréal in the stands."

Maggie looked at the clock. It was six-thirty, not seven minutes to three. She raised her hand to point out the inconsistency. But they looked past her, through her.

"They'll win in Toronto. The Russians lucked out in Montréal. That's all it was. Blind luck."

"They'll win if you are there."

Daddy said, "Then they should have won with eighteen thousand in the stands in Montréal, Janine. Isn't that right? Two more people aren't going to make a difference. Besides, we don't have the money."

"Go, Frank."

"I'm a small person too," Maggie said. "Almost half a person."

"I didn't think you liked hockey, Janine."

"I hate hockey," Mommy whispered and Maggie echoed, "Me too," just so she could be like Mommy, just so she could say something that made some sense. Because she is a girl and Mommy is a girl and life moves like that, in circles. It's easy if it all makes sense.

And Daddy said, "Hockey isn't the worst thing in the world, Janine. There are things much worse."

"Not in front of the child. Jesus, keep her out of it."

"I don't want to leave you alone."

They are seated in Maple Leaf Gardens, Maggie shaking a little from cold, from excitement, the air a live wire of anticipation around them, circling them. Maggie wanting so badly to know where the gardens are—the pretty gardens. She was promised gardens and saw maple trees and tulips and chrysanthemums. Instead it is cold and bare and white in here. There are no flowers. Not even pictures of flowers on the walls. The attackers, Tretiak, Yakushev, Petrov, somewhere in the bowels of the arena, under their seats, waiting to come out and attack. Russia. USSR. *S*'s. Hissing wind in the cornfields. The smell of cigarettes and cold ice and sweat moving around her, Daddy's white knuckles cupped together.

"Not one crummy flower," Maggie says. "Stupid Gardens."

Mommy saying (always, again) last night at dinner, "Don't bring Maggie into this, Frank. This is our problem. Not hers."

"I'm taking her to Toronto is all," Daddy said, shovelling potato salad on his plate. "We'll go and see the game and then we'll come home. You told us to go, didn't you?"

"You will, won't you? You'll come home? I want you to come home."

"We will. Together. You'll be alone. You'll be alone here at the farm and I'll damn well bring Maggie home."

Mommy somehow satisfied at this. Maggie cringing under the steel in her daddy's voice, sucking the melted butter off her cob of corn, licking the salt and strings. The corn given to them by Mr. Malton on the next farm over. His corn grew big and sweet and healthy. Daddy won't eat the corn. Daddy looks at the corn on his plate and his mouth moves into a tight ball, his chin hard.

Daddy squeezing Maggie's hand tightly as they sit on the hard plastic seats in the arena. As they wait for the game to begin. Maggie doesn't know what is to come. The Zamboni cleans the ice. A Dominion advertisement on the side of the large machine spells out, "Mainly Because of the Meat." Daddy reads it to her because she asks him to. He'll do anything for Maggie. She is four years old, five after Christmas, and the hockey game stretches before her like the rest of her life. Mommy shops at Dominion. She buys meat there. And potatoes and carrots and toilet paper. Mr. Reynolds, his huge bulk filling up the patio screen door, hugging up close to it and peering in at Mommy as she washes carrots in the sink, Maggie playing by the kitchen table, moving Barbie onto the farmer's wagon, taking Ken off because he's been riding long enough. Mr. Reynolds's eyes looking right through her mommy, peering through her clothing and her skin and bones, and her mommy's face blushing red, the freckles standing up.

"How are you doing, Janine?" His voice sending shivers around the house.

The corn didn't do well this year. A bug. A blight. A caterpillar. They won't tell Maggie what it is. They haven't time to fill her in on details. Something happened. Things aren't the way they should be. Mr. Reynolds runs the bank and her daddy owes him a lifetime of money. Mommy invites the man in for a tea and Maggie is told to go out to the barn, she is told to check on the chickens. Mr. Reynolds gives her a lollipop and a pat on the head.

Maggie, in the barn, thinks of Mr. Reynolds's daughter, Marilee, and how

Prime Minister Pierre Elliott Trudeau officiates at the face-off of Game One of the Summit Series in Montréal.

she always has a lollipop sticking out of her fat mouth. Marilee with those red bows in her hair and her face puffed up from eating. Marilee at the grocery store saying, "My daddy says you've got no money for clothes. My daddy says you're going under." And Maggie imagining her daddy swimming through fields of mud. Going under.

Daddy's up on his feet now, shouting something. The crowd is suddenly noisy. There was singing, "O Canada," and then this. Maggie startles and looks down at the men on the ice. Too many men, skating furiously back and forth, chasing a puck. A puck so tiny Maggie can barely see it. And the sounds echoing. The chop of sticks, the swish of blades, the rush of wind. Maggie's breath is sucked out of her. Daddy says something about the four brothers playing, how they'll work together because they are blood—Mahovlich and Esposito.

"Keep your eyes on Tretiak," Daddy says. "Keep your eyes on Phil Esposito."

Maggie is looking for blood on the ice but, again, she can't even see the puck. The men look the same in their clothes, their large bulks hunched over the sticks. They all have sideburns and long hair. Only some of them are wearing helmets. The game started so quickly and her mind was elsewhere and now she's lost the puck amongst the players' legs. The USSRs are not a pack of wolves but a fierce fighting machine, moving together down the ice.

Sound surrounds her. Heads move back and forth. People arching, throwing arms in the air. Maggie didn't know it would be so physical. It's like the playground on a hot summer day, kids moving furiously, the air pushed heavy onto their heads as their eyes, ears, and mouths catch the movement of play.

First period over. Nothing. Maggie breathes out and in.

Everyone worked together. Even the crowd.

Maggie thinks it was magic.

Daddy takes her to the hallway and lights a cigarette.

"What's a house wrecker, Daddy?" Maggie asks.

The smoke creeps from his mouth slowly; Maggie watches it curl.

"Export A" written on the signs hanging around the arena. Maggie recognizes it from the pack in Daddy's front pocket. She knew "McDonald's" when she was fifteen months old, her mommy told her. She would say, "fresh fries," whenever she saw the golden arches. Maggie thinks she's reading but her mommy says she's memorizing. The Zamboni moves gracefully in the arena. Moving only because of the meat, Maggie thinks.

"It's none of your business," Daddy says. "It's not a word you should know."

"But it's two words."

"You're smarter than you think," Daddy says. He ruffles Maggie's hair and she likes his warm hand on her head.

"I'm cold."

Daddy doesn't have to ask if she likes the game. Maggie's eyes shine.

In the second period Esposito scores. Daddy was right. A brother. The sixteen thousand fans all rise together. A great wave. Maggie thinks it's like the corn blowing down in the wind, the stalks stretched forward, bending. The air swirling around them. Whoosh.

"Commies," some people shout. "Reds."

"Jesus," Daddy says. He shakes his head. He is going to say something long, Maggie can tell, but instead he just says, "Come."

Daddy doesn't want to leave her alone in the stands and so Maggie follows him to the washroom and watches as he unzips in front of the trough and pees into the flow of water. He pees with the other men, more than a dozen men, they all watch their urine flow towards a hole in the trough, mixing together. Like pigs standing and feeding on her grandpa's farm in Barrie. Is this the blood Daddy was talking about? Blood brothers. Like animals. Maggie wishes she could join them but there is something distinct about being a girl, something hidden and solitary. Her mommy sits on the toilet and Maggie can only hear the rush of water leaving her body. She can't see the yellow line it makes in the bowl. There are things hidden that Maggie wonders about.

Third period. Canada. Then USSR. Then Canada and Canada again. The brothers working together, using their teammates. Tretiak alone on the other side. Mahovlich falling somehow on top of the USSR goalie and slipping the puck into the net. Maggie sees it all finally. Surrounded by it, it becomes clear to her. Her daddy shouting, on his feet, his face red-pleased and hot. Maggie's breath comes back, steady and simple. Her heart swells, her hands clench. The excitement around her is like the dip in the hill on the road near their house. A quick rise and then sinking, stomach hitting her back, her bones mashed into the vinyl seat where Maggie rides looking out the window at the blue sky and white clouds.

And then everyone is leaving the Gardens in a mass. Horns on the street outside. Black night. Maggie is sleepy. Daddy picks her up and she leans her head on his shoulder. The men around her clapping each other's backs, shouting, "We did it." Maggie hears a tin voice, a loudspeaker, from inside the arena—"restoring confidence in the Canadian people." Her daddy's tight grasp around her body as he walks, a lightness in his step. A whistle in his mouth as they drive the long road back towards the farm. Talking about the game. Play-by-plays. Teaching Maggie what she thinks she already knows. Maggie is too excited to sleep. But then, hours later, Maggie awakes to a guttural choke coming out of Daddy's throat as they drive past Mr. Reynolds's truck, his headlights glowing, passing them on the highway, coming back from the direction of their farm.

The darkness settles into the kitchen where Mommy, her head in her hands, is crying.

"My God, Janine," Daddy hisses.

"There's things you don't know," Mommy says. "You just don't understand."

"They won, Mommy," Maggie says sleepily. "You should be happy." The dead corn in the field bends down in the wind. The chickens scratch the barn floor. Maggie hears this amplified. The silence is loud.

"We won?" Mommy says.

Daddy slams the kitchen door and disappears out into the wind and the blackness.

AND THEN THERE IS WINNIPEG. Maggie watches on TV, curled into a ball on the living-room couch. Tie. Tie score. Daddy wears a tie when he goes into Toronto to apply for a loan.

Vancouver knocks Maggie down. Makes her sad. She's become addicted. She likes hockey more than sugar now, giving up dessert so she can sit and watch the game. So she can watch the flow of people as their heads move back and forth to watch the skaters move. It's her mommy's way of making her healthy, making her pick one or the other. But Maggie would rather be part of this something that will pull them together, that will pull people together. Something this big and strong, a force like a tornado. Sugar means nothing any more. Her mommy puts a fire in the fireplace to save on heating the house. The Russians win and Maggie skulks around the house for days, angry at everyone and everything, smacking the barn cats as they rub against her legs. Phil Esposito almost swore at the fans and Maggie feels like swearing all the time now. She feels like saying the words she hears her daddy saying when he's out in the field.

Daddy's tie didn't work. He says that the man at the bank just laughed at him as he closed the file folder on his big desk.

There are hot days and cold days. There are days where Maggie runs through the withered corn laughing and chasing her friends who sometimes come to play. There are days she huddles under the covers on her bed, afraid to go outside of her room, afraid to hear nothing, a spark about to burn, a bomb about to explode, that silence that fills the house, top to bottom.

The corn is full of holes. It is small. Not fit to feed the chickens even. Daddy walks through the shortened fields each day with a look of pure hatred on his face. Maggie watches as he plucks off the rotten corn and throws it to the ground. He looks like he wants to take his cigarette and burn down the land. Daddy is in the barn with the damn chickens, and Maggie thinks that he might put his foot through one of them, kick it high in the air like the football he sometimes throws with their neighbour on hot summer days. She sees something in his eyes, knows the anger in his voice.

Mommy's at the bank again, asking Mr. Reynolds for more money. She's asking him not to take the house, the fields, the chickens. She's wearing nylons, her hair in a bun, lipstick patted carefully with Kleenex.

The long break after Vancouver, it seemed like forever, where the days and nights flowed into one, where she would hide in the barn in the increasingly cold afternoons and lie in bed at night listening to her mommy trying to talk to her daddy. Listening to her mommy's low rumbling sound. She would wander the fields, keeping behind her daddy, a piece of grass stuck between her teeth, listening for the ins and outs of his breath.

"The Goon Squad," "the Canadian Mafia," the headlines screamed. Skating in Stockholm to get used to the ice, to get their anger and frustration out, chase it away like demons under the bed. Then just as suddenly, Moscow, Moscow, Moscow.

Moscow over the TV set. Maggie sees the strange domes, the spires in the air. Luzhniki Arena. *Luzhniki*. Maggie tries hard to pronounce the word but the word

The Soviet and Canadian teams line up for the national anthem before Game Three of the Summit Series. Played in Winnipeg, the game ended in a tie.

always twists her tongue, curls it, until she can't help but spit. Phil Esposito slips on the ice and then gets up and bows, like a ballerina, a graceful dip. The crowd roars. Jockey, Turtlewax, Motorcraft, Heinekin Beer. Daddy reads the sideboards and tests Maggie's memory.

"Of course they won," Daddy says after the game. "They're on their own home turf."

"What's 'turf'?"

Daddy turns off the TV and settles back into the rocking chair, his hands up behind his head. He rocks quickly.

"Turf is where you live. Turf is what you have here," he points to his chest. "Inside of you."

"Don't be silly, Frank," Mommy says. "Turf is grass, Maggie. Like on a golf course. All the same length."

"There's no grass in Moscow," Maggie says. "I know that. Just big open squares and lots of grey buildings."

"It's a black-and-white TV set, Maggie," Daddy tells her. "Of course everything is going to be grey." And quietly. "Turf can mean many things too complicated for you to understand."

Maggie sees a cow covered in green moss. A moss-cow. She goes to bed at midnight, wakes early, replays hockey in her mind. Wishes she had seen the first game in Montréal. Wishes she had known then what she knows now. The Russians aren't wolves any more, they aren't a fighting machine, they are coyotes, sneaky and unafraid.

It seems to Maggie that everyone is watching hockey. In town the store-keepers have their televisions on the counters. They watch the replays, the commentaries, the breaking news. They talk about Bobby Hull when he wasn't allowed to play in Winnipeg, or Serge Savard when he is hobbled by a hairline fracture. Over and over again, Phil Esposito assures Canadians that the players are giving 150 per cent and Mrs. Mercer at the Becker's store feels good about that. *Tretiak, Tretiak,*

Tretiak. His name uttered with a spit, said in disgust, distaste, but also said with envy and admiration. Players who are enemies every season in the NHL are working together now.

Mommy touches Daddy's head as she passes him in the living room and his eyes water. His cigarette flares red, an angry eye, always glowing. He spends several days helping out on Mr. Malton's farm, cleaning up after the corn harvest, coming home sore and tired, callused and mad. He still won't touch the corn, won't eat it when it's placed on his plate, but Maggie goes through each sweet, buttered cob, back and forth, like she's typing a message to God on her grandpa's typewriter.

Maggie says, "Moscow," to the librarian one day and they both raise their eyes to the ceiling and watch the fan circle amidst the spiderwebbed rafters. The librarian crosses her fingers and Maggie crosses hers. There's a holy feeling in the air. Like an electrical storm coming softly and slowly towards them. Like the rumbling of a train. The librarian stamps her books and lets Maggie out of the library to wait for her mommy on the street.

Two more miraculous wins for Canada and, even though the corn didn't grow, Maggie smiles brightly wherever she goes.

And now it is the final game and Daddy said he would come in after he feeds the chickens to watch with Maggie.

"Don't ask him for anything, Janine," Daddy said to Mommy when she left in the truck for the bank again. "Don't go. I'm telling you. I want you to stay here with your family."

"I have to go, Frank."

"No. Don't go." Daddy pounded on the truck. "Stop this." He almost cried but Maggie chose not to see this. Maggie's mommy chose not to see this too. They both turned a little as Daddy made a stabbing punch-motion at his face to wipe the wet.

Maggie said, "Ask him for a lollipop. He always gives me a lollipop."

Mommy held the steering wheel tightly and turned quickly out of the driveway, away from the farm. Daddy moved out to the barn, his shoulders raised high and tight, his neck stiff. He sniffled like he was coming down with a cold.

"Daddy. It's on," Maggie shouts from the back screen door. "Foster Hewitt is on. He's talking."

"Of course he's talking," Daddy's voice comes clear from the barn. "I'll be there in a minute."

It seems to Maggie sometimes that her mommy and daddy are the only ones around whose lives haven't been overtaken by hockey. It sometimes seems as if they would much rather be doing other things. They would much rather be in the fields or sitting at the kitchen table with coffee, saying nothing, looking everywhere but at each other's face. Maggie's mommy would rather be cleaning the house and changing the sheets on the beds, cooking biscuits and scraping together leftovers into pots to make what has come to be known as garbage soup.

Maggie sits cross-legged on the carpet in front of the TV. Since Game Five, Maggie has fallen in love with Paul Henderson. Number nineteen. It's a childish love. There is no sensation that she is a girl, he is a boy. It has nothing to do with that. It's not the kind of love she feels for Joey Tanner, that tough boy in the playground. It's more like the love she feels for the Friendly Giant and his soothing recorder. An all-consuming, careful kind of love. In Game Five, Henderson knocked himself out on the boards and still he struggled up and continued to play, continued to score. He was determined, like last summer when the chicken pecked the barn cat's eyes and still the cat came at the chicken, mouth open, eyes tearing and bleeding slightly, hissing wildly. Maggie has a love for Paul Henderson that somehow means he will save her, take care of her. He will make sure she is taken care of.

"Can't kick a man when he's down," Daddy said when Henderson lay motionless on the ice. Daddy was sitting on a kitchen stool, looking into the living room, following the game out of the corner of his eyes. Mommy said nothing then. She hummed a tune. Washed dishes in the sink. Her long hair hiding her flushed cheeks.

Daddy comes in from the barn now carrying his hunting rifle. He props it up against the counter. He has grease on his hands. Maggie watches him scrub it off in the kitchen sink, using dish detergent. He leans back against the stove and wipes the sweat from his eyes. His shoulders are still tight. His smile is strange and crooked. Maggie shivers.

"It's on. You're missing the game."

"I'm coming."

Maggie watches her daddy as he crosses in front of the TV and settles on the couch. He lights a cigarette and draws deeply on it. Maggie suddenly misses the Export A advertisements in the Gardens. She wishes she were there, in the arena, with the men and the smells and the sweat and the trough. She wishes she could be there to feel that heavy excitement in the air. The kind of feeling she gets on a swing when she is pushed high into the sky, so high her bum leaves the seat and the chains clink noisily in her hands. She wants to feel the way the crowd moved together, how everyone worked together to make the game happen, to make Canada win.

Penalty after penalty.

"Let's go home," the Canadians in the stands chant when the filthy Russians put the cheating referee from Game Six into the game. Switching officials. Daddy says it's rotten.

"Cheating," Daddy says.

"Not fair," Maggie says, although she doesn't quite understand why. "That's not fair."

"It never is," Daddy says. "Life isn't fair."

A dog barks somewhere outside. From Mr. Malton's farm where they've taken the day off work to watch the game. Daddy was invited there but didn't want to go.

"I might be heading out soon," Daddy says. "Would you be okay by yourself for a bit?"

"No," Maggie says. "This is the last game. You can't leave me alone."

"Just for a bit. Not long."

"Mommy never leaves me alone. You can't leave me alone. It's not fair."

"Mommy's mommy."

"What?"

Maggie imagines Mommy sitting in front of Mr. Reynolds's desk at the bank. She imagines Mommy sucking on a lollipop and smiling nicely.

"I'll only be gone for a little bit. You'll be fine by yourself."

Parise, given a penalty, suddenly lifts his stick to strike down the referee. But then he pulls up from the swinging motion just in time. Maggie sucks in her breath. She is conscious of her daddy's heavy breathing. He is slumped on the couch. His cigarette, ash building at the end, hanging off his fingers, unsucked.

"Look at this," Daddy says. "We're going to lose."

Daddy rises from the couch. He goes into the kitchen and takes the rifle from its space beside the counter.

"Don't go," Maggie says. "Jesus."

"I don't want to lose," Daddy says. "Don't swear."

"We won't lose. If you stay here and watch, we won't lose, Daddy."

"Not even for a minute. I've never been a good loser."

"Don't leave me," Maggie says. "Who am I going to watch the game with? I'm not old enough to be left alone. You're not supposed to leave me alone."

"Just for a minute. It won't be long. I'll come back soon and then we'll go somewhere. Maybe we'll go on a vacation or something. Anywhere you want."

But as he walks towards the side door Maggie can hear Mommy pull into the driveway in the truck. She hears the door slam and Mommy walk, crunchingly, up the gravel path to the house. Daddy stands alone in the kitchen, one hand on the side door, the other hand holding the rifle. His face is sweaty. He looks like Maggie feels when she has to pick between a Popsicle or ice cream. When she wants both, but has to decide.

"Mommy's home. You can go now. She'll take care of me."

Maggie knows the kids at school are watching the game. She knows this because Susan Jessup told her last week at the park in town. She said that the school was setting up a television in the gym and the kids were all going to sit nicely, backs straight, and watch hockey. They were going to sit with straight backs or their principal, Mrs. Pearson, would poke them hard on the shoulder, one by one, and tell them to stand in the hall. Susan said they weren't allowed to talk, they could only watch the game and cross their fingers and pray that Canada would win. Maggie wishes she were there with them, in the large gym she's seen only once—Thanksgiving last year, lines painted on the floor, basketball hoops in the air above their heads, Mommy dropping canned beets into the box by the gym door, beets for poor people who like them—she wishes she could hold Susan's hand and pray quietly when Yakushev ties the game in the second period. Next year Maggie will be in school but by then it will be too late. The game will be over. It will all be over.

Mommy comes, breathless, into the kitchen. She spots Daddy standing still and she rushes over to him, rushes slowly, like running through water at the pool, and she takes the rifle out of his hand. She places it carefully on the kitchen counter and then she wraps her arms around him, wraps his arms around her, rubs his back and touches his hair. She whispers in his ear, soft sounds. Like she's calling in the chickens. A cooing.

Maggie watches the Russians score at the end of the second period. She feels sick to her stomach. She hasn't eaten lunch, no one has thought to feed her, and her stomach is rumbling wildly, sloshing around empty.

"This will help, Frank," Mommy is saying. "This will get us by for a while. Maybe a month or two. We can get jobs then. Get jobs through the winter and then move on. Maybe move away. We could move into Toronto and work there. We can start again. Straighten this whole mess out. I can type, Frank. I can type fast. Your father has that old typewriter in the back room. I can practise until I can type twice as fast as I can now."

She is holding a slip of paper in her outstretched hand. She has moved away from Daddy now and is standing between him and the rifle, holding out this paper as if she's offering him a poisonous snake. Maggie sees the tremble in her mommy's hand. The paper wiggles.

"I want a peanut butter sandwich," Maggie says. "And a root beer."

"I'll make that," Mommy says. "Frank, move. Say something."

Daddy stares hard at the door. His eyes move towards the paper Mommy is holding out. He stares back at the door.

"I'm hungry," Maggie says. "No one feeds me any more."

"I'm back, Frank. Everything is okay."

"Did you get me a lollipop? Where's my lollipop?"

"He just gave me the money, Frank. No strings attached. It's over. He won't take the farm yet. Not yet. We have some time now, some time to—"

"Did he give you a lollipop?" Maggie asks. "He always gives me a lollipop and tells me to go out to the barn. He touches my head. I don't like that. I don't like for people to touch my head. Except Daddy."

"He just gave you the money, Janine?" Daddy's voice is low. A rumble.

"Yes. It's over."

"Quiet," Maggie shouts. "The game is on again. Daddy, come quick."

"He just gave you the money? That's it? Just like that? He didn't want anything for it? Is that what you're telling me? He handed over money and you did nothing, you didn't take off your clothes, you didn't fuc—"

"Shut up." Mommy looks down at her stomach. The paper still hanging on the end of her outstretched fingers. She uses her other hand to flatten the dress she is wearing to her breasts. She breathes deeply. "Yes, Frank. He just gave me the money."

Daddy watches the motion she makes. The way she touches her breasts briefly.

Maggie watches the motion. "Why would Mr. Reynolds want you to take off your clothes?"

Mommy's hand touches the material slowly, touches the mounds of her breasts. Maggie doesn't understand this but somehow Mommy's hands moving over her woman's breasts is a movement that sums everything up, puts the world neatly into a paper package and sends it flying through space.

"Shhhh." Maggie puts her finger up to her mouth and turns back to the game. Canada scores. "They scored! You aren't watching. You both aren't paying attention."

Maggie hears the slap. She doesn't see it. She hears what she later realizes is her daddy's hand moving in a long arch, fast, fully controlled, towards her mommy's face. The sound is like a water balloon hitting the pavement. The sound is like a clap of thunder or like the sound the watermelon made at the farm picnic last year when Mr. Malton's kids threw it off the barn roof. Maggie turns towards her parents and sees her daddy standing in the same position. Her mommy is holding her hand up to her face, a red welt rising, tears coming softly out of her eyes. The paper is lying on the floor between them.

Canada scores again. The light doesn't go on over the net. Maggie turns back to the television. Suddenly, Alan Eagleson bolts out of the stands and tries to get to the ice. The Russian police surround him. The Russian fans whistle instead of boo.

"Look, look," Maggie shouts. Team Canada skate together to free Eagleson. They take him to the Team Canada bench. Maggie starts to cry.

"I don't know why he did that," Maggie says, crying. "I don't know anything. I wish you'd both sit down and tell me what's going on."

"Oh, honey," Mommy says. She walks towards Maggie with her arms outstretched.

And Daddy walks out of the house, the kitchen door slamming shut. He walks out towards the fields. He walks past the barn, through the grass, into the useless corn. Maggie lets her mommy hold her and she cries. She doesn't know why she is crying. She looks up into her mommy's face and sees the slap mark of her daddy's hand. She looks back into the kitchen and sees her daddy is gone.

And then Mommy looks up and into the kitchen.

"Oh my God. Frank?"

She releases Maggie, stumbles towards the door.

"No, Frank. No. Jesus."

"Mommy?"

But the shot is loud. It echoes through the fields. Maggie's mother running quickly, falling, frantic, bumping her hip against the kitchen stool, screaming, out of the house.

"No. No."

"Here's a shot," Foster Hewitt calls. "Henderson makes a wild stab for it and falls."

Mommy running through the horrible corn. Maggie standing now, looking at the TV. Paul Henderson. Looking at the kitchen towards the window over the sink, watching Mommy running. Maggie moves towards the kitchen and then back towards the TV. Towards the kitchen. Back. TV. Kitchen.

Suddenly, Mrs. Reynolds's car pulls up in front of the house. The car door slams shut. Crunch of gravel. Maggie watches as the woman, a sun hat on, her face red and swollen like her daughter's, starts to walk up to the front door. Maggie sees Mommy running. Maggie can see everything. The back window, the front window, the front door, the TV, Paul Henderson skating so hard he looks like he might fly. Maggie looks around, confused, and feels shivers move through her body and the house. A cool breeze, like just before a storm when you know the air is changing and the rain will come crashing down. Mrs. Reynolds pounds heavily on the front door.

Knock. Knock.

"Janine," Mrs. Reynolds shouts. "I know you're in there."

"What was that noise?" Maggie whispers.

USSRs.

Russians.

Hiss.

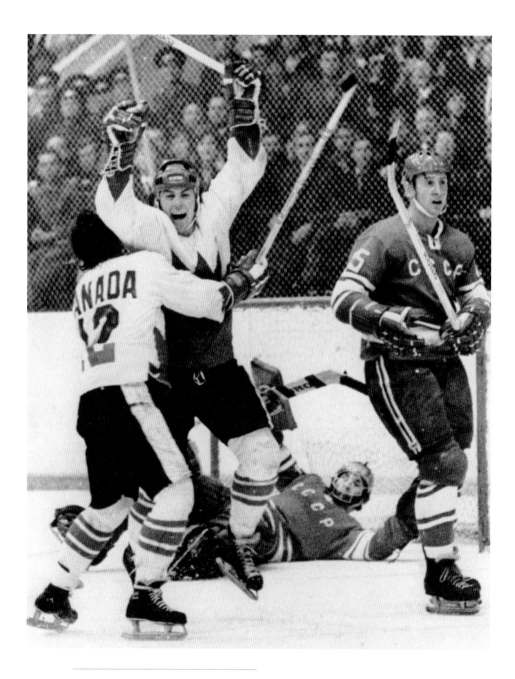

Henderson has scored for Canada!

"Jesus," Maggie says. "Hockey."

Foster Hewitt, breathless now, "Here's another shot. Right in front."

Daddy's rifle is missing from the kitchen counter.

"The Summit Series," Maggie whispers to herself. *S*'s. "Paul Henderson." Words that feel like candy on her tongue.

Maggie doesn't know which way to turn.

TV.

Window.

Mrs. Reynolds at the door.

Paul Henderson.

Daddy.

The rifle is gone.

Mrs. Reynolds knocking hard. Mommy running, chasing something. Both of them screaming something.

"Janine. Open up."

"Frank, No."

Foster Hewitt: "They score! Henderson has scored for Canada!"

"Oh," Maggie breathes. "Bang. We won."

And the silence around her is suddenly a roar.

Hal Niedzviecki

VERY NICE, VERY NICE

I was studying in the U.S. when I first encountered Arthur Lipsett.

A visiting film scholar was lecturing and showing movies. Attendance wasn't required and, in fact, turnout was fairly low. But I went. It was one of those moments when you're not expecting much, but you stumble on to something that completely blows you away. In an instant, you go from barely alive to total attention. You see, I was spending a lot of time telling my fellow students that CanCon was interesting, important, cool. But basking in the ultra-hip of my American art school poseur peers, I was having a hard time dispelling my own lingering doubts.

Enter the visiting professor. He told us about a Canadian whose movies were hard to find. He told us he had gotten his hands on some prints. Familiar phrases like the Sixties and the National Film Board of Canada were used. Ahead of his time. Groundbreaking. Nothing else like him. Most looked bored. But the displaced Canadian in me was fascinated. I scribbled down every word the man said. "Arthur

Filmmaker Arthur Lipsett. Courtesy of the National Film Board of Canada.

Lipsett," I wrote. "Important." The movies ran and I watched them. Riveted.

Soon enough I was back in Toronto, re-energized and committed to publishing and editing my own magazine (*Broken Pencil*, guide to independent culture in Canada) while plotting to research and discover everything there was to know about Arthur Lipsett, a man whose handful of dystopic collage-infused shorts were among the most powerful works of film I had ever seen—and will ever see. I figured I would interview the Lipsett experts, read the Lipsett books, then contribute to the genre by writing my own lengthy Lipsett essay for *BP*.

But I never did.

Why not? Well, for starters, there aren't any Lipsett experts. In fact, few had heard of the guy. He barely seemed to exist, even in the film academia circles and was hardly mentioned in the annals of Canadian cultural history. I should not have been surprised that it took a lecture at an American college to introduce me to his work. Discovering that so few had even heard of Lipsett, let alone were enthusiastic proponents, devalued the project in my mind. I kept promising myself that I would write about Lipsett, but insecurity got the better of me. When I finally found my way back to my favourite Canadian filmmaker, I was surprised to discover that the year was 2001; I was further surprised to find that my pilgrimage back to the legacy of Lipsett would come in the form of fiction, a form so impetuous it almost makes me miss the neophyte I once was, too timid to write a little essay discussing a figure no one seemed to care about.

If I had written my essay on Lipsett, I would have ended it something like this: In 1968, Arthur Lipsett was nearing the end of his short career. The pioneering filmmaker, who worked from within the staid National Film Board, had lost touch with his muse and his employers. Early brilliant short films like *Very Nice, Very Nice* and *21-87* had captured the anxiety of sweeping technological change and ensuing alterations to Canadian life by using a high-speed pastiche of cut-and-paste found footage; Lipsett plundered NFB discards for material and made intricate collages that relied on pace and soundtrack to jar watchers into the familiar strangeness of A-bombs exploding, animals in cages, and the blank faces of urban life. Though remarkably evocative of the sweeping changes of the era, Lipsett's technique would have been more at home on today's Much Music than amongst the gentle animations and earnest instructional documentaries that characterized the National Film Board's golden age. Ahead of his time, Lipsett influenced filmmakers as diverse as Stanley Kubrick and George Lucas, and was even nominated for an Academy Award. But the filmmaker struggled with manic depression, and his ability to fuse questions around the ideology of urbanity and technology with a distinct bleak humour went undervalued and underappreciated. He made his last hopelessly flawed work for the NFB in 1971, and drifted away, all but forgotten.

A fragment from an article I never wrote about a filmmaker whose fragmented films most of us will never see. Pointless? Well, in the ensuing years since I first saw the films of Arthur Lipsett, I've realized that finding a subject to write about that no one else is writing about is a rare thing—something to be coveted.

Which is probably why I've never written anything about another one of my personal obsessions—Rochdale. Topic of books, many articles, and a feature-length documentary, Rochdale College was an eighteen-storey concrete monolith that occupied the downtown corner of Bloor and Huron streets, blocks away from the University of Toronto. When it opened its doors in 1968, it was the largest experiment in communal dwelling and alternative education in Canada and the world. The college quickly became known for its quirky mix of high-rise living and hippy idealism. But Rochdale also had a reputation as a haven for teenage runaways, suburban party seekers, drug dealers, and deadbeats. Plagued by confrontations with the police and the community, it was a place where internecine conflicts erupted about the need for security and financial accountability.

At its height, Rochdale housed U.S. draft dodgers, bohemians thrown out of Yorkville, would-be revolutionaries, university students, as well as a clinic, health food store, recording studio, and even an illegal weekend pizza delivery business. It gave birth to or influenced some of Canada's most important cultural institutions including Theatre Passe Muraille, Coach House Books, House of Anansi Press, and the Canadian Film-Makers Distribution Centre. But it also served as impetus and venue for thousands of arrests, nine deaths (overdoses, suicides, and at least one murder), and millions of dollars in property damage. With its mixture of cultural urgency, deliberate anarchy, and accidental angst, Rochdale was, and still is, the focal point of the Sixties experience in Canada. Genuine icon, Rochdale is Canada's Woodstock and Altamont all rolled into one.

Symbol of an era's impudent daring, Rochdale, like Arthur Lipsett's career, was not so much a great event as a prolonged moment. Pregnant with possibility, these were the incidents that never quite happened in Canadian history. You could say to most people, Hey, a group of kids never really occupied a high-rise in the heart of Toronto with the intention of flouting all rules and expectations and, essentially, starting their own self-contained village, and they would surely agree. You could tell the story of a brilliant Canadian filmmaker who captured the anxiety of the nuclear era by stringing together newsreels and discards found on the cutting-room floor to produce some of the world's most jarring juxtapositions and get not a flicker of recognition. Which is why these are moments, not events: they lack the knockout punch that sees a "momentous" instant inscribed in the textbooks. But however unimportant these incidents—these non-events—were or are, they have stayed with me over the years: the minor moments of a minor nation that nevertheless altered my perceptions of myself and my country, presenting me with a legacy that is like nothing else in Canada, a rift in the fabric, a hole to see through.

Culture is personal as much as it is communal. My fascination with these two relatively obscure moments may be mundane to some, utterly irrelevant to many others. Who cares about something if no one cares about something? That was the question I asked my younger incarnation, talking myself out of writing a Lipsett tribute. And that's the question I have put forward over the years to prevent myself from randomly calling up former residents of Rochdale and asking them inane and intrusive questions. But this denial I feel, this reluctance to truly celebrate and mythologize, is also something that connects Rochdale and Lipsett. Can we applaud a misanthropic filmmaker plagued by depression? Can we pay tribute to a hunk of concrete that housed not just a fascinating experiment, but a failed one? Other countries celebrate their artistic tragedies with reckless abandon, but in Canada we hesitate. Forever diminished by our proximity to meaningless pop stardom, our culture is always displayed to a backdrop of dispelled expectation. But wasn't it that very insecurity that gave rise to Lipsett's terror of human insignificance? Wasn't that insecurity part of the story behind Rochdale's delightfully frustrating refusal to enforce even the most permissive rules? In some odd way, these contradictions have helped me to understand my internal ambivalence where Canada is concerned—an insecurity that has remained with me, with so many of us; an insecurity that, I suspect, will never, ever, go away.

Rochdale closed its doors in 1975, amid riots, forced evictions, police raids, and bankruptcy. Built to hold nine hundred people, the building is estimated to have housed more than five thousand stayed in the building over its seven years. Arthur Lipsett took his own life in 1986. With a renewed interest in the aesthetic of found footage and collage, and an increasing unease about the nature of a dehumanizing technological society, his films have found new younger audiences, and have gradually entered the pantheon of Canadian film.

In the following work of fiction, I imagine what might have happened had the NFB sent Arthur Lipsett to make a documentary on Rochdale College. This is a story based very loosely on fact: the Film Board, the Rochdale, and the Arthur Lipsett I create are, first and foremost, the products of an overactive imagination. I intend this story to be taken not literally, but as an exploration of parallel legends teaching a history lesson somewhat different than the one we're accustomed to: a Canadian history of cultural pioneers traversing the limits of the strictures of modern life.

VERY NICE, VERY NICE

Rochdale College Project, Summer 1968
Final Report Submitted by Arthur Lipsett, August, 1982

I SIT IN THE DARK.

A knock on my office door.

Not now. Now now!

Lipsett, open up. You're in there, I can hear you.

Do not disturb, I say.

Really, Lipsett, there's no point pretending.

I'm not pretending.

Lipsett!

I open the door. Beezly, I say.

He looks over my shoulder.

I step out, into him. He backs up. The door closes. Click.

What is it? I say.

You're wanted for the meeting. In the directors' office.

I don't go to the meetings.

You're wanted.

Is that a new tie? I say.

He looks down at his chest.

I check the lock on my door.

THE FILM BOARD IS A LABYRINTH of scurrying passages. Most stick to the wide, well-lit corridors of documentary and animation. An ill-considered turn down the wrong passageway, and the lights get dimmer, the offices smaller, the studios set behind trick doors that spring like traps. Dark halls lead to locked storerooms stacked with canisters, our films labelled Archive Only or Do Not Open or Danger.

Beezly makes a wrong turn. Assistant to the directors, his presence in unfamiliar territory testifies to the urgency of his summons.

I follow his shadow, blinded by the back of his neck.

He stops, suddenly, at an intersection of peeling ceilings and flickering light bulbs. I bump into him. The sound of dripping water. A musty damp in the air.

Beezly! I exclaim.

Sorry, he says. I seem to have—

Lost your way?

Yes, he admits, looking down at his polished wingtips.

Over here, I say.

A stairway appears.

Beezly fumbles in his breast pocket, attempting to extract some map or directive.

It's a shortcut, I call over my shoulder. A few more steps of descent.

He hesitates.

My body divided, slowly sinking.

The directors are waiting, I call.

Two more steps down.

Hold on, then, he mutters.

THE STAIRWAY WINDS THROUGH brick foundations and into the basement. We put our hands out in front of us, walk gingerly. The air forms rippled shapes in light. Pipes in coils along walls and ceilings. Steam bursts. Beezly jumps.

Careful, I say. Those are hot.

We snake through the detritus of the early years of film. Old crank projectors, cracked lighting umbrellas, and filing cabinets filled to bursting with mice bedded down in memos from the Prime Minister's Office.

In a cramped hall jammed with mothballed props, mostly kaiser uniforms from the First World War, Beezly panics, grabs my arm.

See here, he says. I really think we should—

Be getting back?

Yes. He gulps.

The directors are waiting, I say.

He nods.

We hear a noise. A wail followed by a long syncopating groan. Drawn-out symphony of glottal anguish, the crescendo perpetually mounting, never reached.

It's coming from over there, Beezly says.

A staccato shriek, piercing highs punctuated by long gulps of air.

Beezly leads. I follow.

Glookman projects large oblong shapes twitching and sweating in the manner of a virus under a microscope. Gradually, a single organism consumes the other smaller shapes. It bloats up, skin rippling. The image gets larger, threatens to creep off the white square screen, the mental workings of a B movie blob harnessed in some abstract tribute to the consumptive methodology of the nuclear age.

The pulsating entity bursts.

Beezly falls back.

A shiver of wet molasses coating the screen.

I touch my forehead. Just sweat.

Glookman switches off the projector, the spinning wheels of his eight-track recorder.

Ah, Lipsett, he says. Finally. I've been working on the soundtrack. What do you think?

Potent, I say.

He gazes at Beezly.

Beezly opens his mouth. Closes it.

Glookman nods. I'll begin again, he says. Silence, please. The projector spews tiny atoms shuffling politely against each other. Glookman issues a slow moan.

I slip away.

THEY FIND ME IN EAGLESON'S garbage, squinting at discarded footage of an Eskimo squaw giving birth.

I used to make movies.

A woman on the street, her face a rigor-mortis grimace of makeup. Six seconds is enough. Office buildings and sky. Claustrophobic sharp points cutting us off. Sky and sun gone. The dizzy-angled city. A monkey in a cage. A scientist in a white coat waving his fingers in front of a simian face, making a coochy-coo noise. Twelve seconds, the first time. A rocket ship blasting off to space. The voice counts backward, you know the voice. Ten, nine eight . . . A crowd, a pigeon in a park. Three men pretending to shoot each other in the woods. The men have beards, wear leather vests. One of them is me. All of them are me. The monkey again, shorter this time, just his sad oval eyes, and the scientist. Coochy coochy-coo. A newscaster voice, Brylcreme man behind his desk. This is the beginning, he says. He says it again. This is the beginning. Bang, I fall down dead. There's no sound. Bang, I fall down dead, quiet. Monkey jumps in her cage. Coochy Coochy. The rictus smile, same as the monkey's. An operator wearing her headset, plugging the right lines into the right holes. Despite the pace, she looks confused. Doesn't she look confused? Bam! I'm dead. Bam! We're all dead. This is the beginning.

I used to make movies.

Say, Lipsett, the directors start, as if accidentally meeting me on the way to the water cooler.

There are ten, fifteen, twenty directors. They wear black suits, scalped hair with a bit too much up front, matching horn-rimmed spectacles. They are clean-shaven, smell of Aqua Velva, sport thin ties. They talk in a round robin, never more than two or three words per person.

Lipsett, they say, surrounding me.

I blink.

I'm alone.

Lipsett!

A hand on my shoulder. I look up. Housely.

Arthur, really! Haven't you heard a word I've said?

I shake my head.

I've been looking for you everywhere. We were waiting for you. All of us. All the directors. You didn't arrive. It's okay. I covered for you. Arthur, uh, can you kindly, step out of—we're wondering what you did with our assistant—

Beezly?

My voice surprises both of us. They think of me like my films: mute, incapable, silent babble, future anachronism, a time they hope will never come. Housely wants to be different. He wants to be my friend. He wants to know the truth.

Look at this, I say, brandishing my scrap of celluloid. Who discards this? Is it Eagleson? That hack Eagleson?

Housely flinches. Eagleson's their favourite, makes upbeat shorts on the lifespan of the blackfly and natural fishing in the trout streams of Saskatchewan.

Really, Lipsett. I'm trying to—well, look, Arthur, let me be frank with you.

Yes?

I'm, I mean, I'd like to think of myself as your friend.

I nod.

Arthur, my support for your work, it's become, well—as you know, I'm a great admirer, fantastic stuff, but some of my colleagues, the other directors, they, well, it's a question, Arthur, of the direction of the Film Board, I'm afraid.

The direction?

Yes, well, Arthur, as I'm sure you've noticed, we're an institution entrusted with portraying a certain vision—

Tuktu and the Magic Bow? Tuktu and His Clever Hands?

Well, yes, frankly, Arthur, those are—

Tuktu and His Nice New Clothes?

Really, Lipsett! I don't think that's accurate. We pride ourselves on the diversity of subject matter. We don't shy away from the larger issues. But one must, I mean, there's only so much of your kind of—the concern, Arthur, is that your current project, uh—

Fluxes.

Yes, well, it's a bit—

Too dark?

Yes, well, for myself, I think, Arthur, that you really are unique, your vision, it's really—and I'm sure that, in other circumstances, the other directors would—I mean, we do explore that world, the works of Mr. McLaren, those wonderful —

Cartoons.

Yes, well, Arthur, it's not just animation. Why, just this year, there are several dramatic films articulating modern . . . positions.

The one about the farm and nuclear war?

Let me tell you, that is shaping up to be an excellent production. Not that your work isn't—I mean, it's a question, as the directors have articulated, of the proper balance, the use of, characterization, some narrative, this *Fluxes*, which I fully support, but really, Arthur, it's, I mean, it's been three years and the film is—I mean, three years, Arthur! The directors feel that you need a change.

A change?

Quite.

I can feel myself sinking deeper into Eagleson's scraps.

Arthur, I'm not here to reprimand you. I'm hear to provide you with, the directors have, well, there's an opportunity to make a contribution, an assignment of significance, provided that we have your assurance as to your understanding of the values of the Film Board, the values of this country, such an assurance being, of course, mandatory, within the context of further discussions regarding your future—

Look, Housely, I blurt. If you don't mind—I'm—we're all—busy men. I drag my fingers down my stubble cheeks.

Housely fingers his black tie.

Lipsett, Housely says, suddenly grasping my arm between his wet palms. There's a new mood, on the streets, we're told, the youth, a street level . . . You understand. We're told there is a centre, in Toronto, perhaps you've—at any rate, a giant co-operative experiment of some sort. We're told that's where they gather.

They?

Yes, Housely says.

I WALK INTO ROCHDALE COLLEGE.

It has no air.

The smell of youngsters, their exuberant odours and self-contained spontaneous ejaculations replicating the torpor of an institutional buffet.

I stand in the lobby, with its graffiti-covered No Smoking signs, its This Is Not Your Bedroom, Please Clean Up After Yourself magic-marker banners and mimeographed announcements for a free school session on Transcendental Meditative Communism. A boy with no shirt, ribs in stitches, sits cross-legged in the corner, strumming on the rusted strings of an old guitar. Sallow-eyed slumberers wrapped in buckskin-fringed jackets and stray scraps of blanket snore in time. The door to the building opens. Sunlight. Blinding me. I reach down and pluck a pair of sunglasses off a sleeping moon-faced kid desperately attempting a goatee. He doesn't stir. I put the glasses on. I sniff the air. I can't see. The press of bodies, the scent of newness—sawdust, insulation, wet paint—the fresh odour of progress lingering under the collective stench of bitter sweat sweetened with the honey exhale of smoke.

Near me, two girls giggling. I put my hands out, step forward.

Something hard stabs my side. I fall forward. The sunglasses slip off.

The girls laugh.

A huge man in a cowboy hat, his arms straining around a giant filing cabinet. How about a hand? he says.

We haul the cabinet upstairs. I step over an intertwined couple, asleep in a makeshift warren. My arms ache, my back throbs.

The man in the cowboy hat opens a door. We carry the cabinet down a long hall (all the halls are long here). Sweat burns into my eyes. We stop in front of a door. Just hold on, will you? He props the cabinet on my chest.

I try to say something. Grunt.

Yonge Steet, ca. 1975.

He fumbles with a complicated array of locks. I teeter back. The cabinet twists in my arms. The top drawer bursts open, smashes my forehead. It rains pebbles. The drawer, I remember thinking, is filled with pebbles.

I'M LYING ON MY BACK, my throbbing head in a soft lap smelling of lilac and tobacco.

He's cute.

Do you think we should keep him?

Yeah, let's keep him!

My eyes closed, I think of smooth rocks raining down my cheeks, fossilized tears.

Do you think he's okay?

Sure, he's okay.

I dunno, he hasn't moved.

Should we try and wake him up?

A chest straining against a white peasant blouse. Long strands of brown hair drowning me. If only. A smooth arcing neck. Weeping willow, I try to say. A hard disc rolls from my mouth, down into my throat. I claw at my beard, gag.

The girls turn me sideways, pound my back.

I choke out a small stone.

I FIND DAVID TYPING, finger hovering over stiff keys. David wears jean shorts and a Campus Co-op T-shirt dyed ugly shades of purple, pink, and brown. I knock on his door. He peers through the currents of light and smoke that flow ceaselessly through the building. A single lamp casting a petulant net. He sighs, puts aside his typing, clears a giant stack of papers off a wooden chair with no back, and beckons me to sit.

I need a room, I say.

There aren't any rooms, he says.

It doesn't matter, I say.

You don't think so? David is sleepless, curious, obsessed.

I could go elsewhere, I say.

We aren't turning you away.

Aren't you?

This is Rochdale. We don't turn anyone away.

Why not?

The collective will. Rochdale is a democracy. It's a co-operative. It's about openness. We have open doors. The kids come here. Everyone comes here. Anyway, there's no way to stop them.

You could lock the doors.

They would just smash them.

Who would?

I would.

David reaches into a desk drawer, pulls out a hammer. Puts it on the desk. He smiles.

I nod, understanding. What can I tell him? That the government has sent me to make a film, to etch the official record, to swirl into the cybernetic spiral of my own hopeless aspirations? Send a freak to film the freaks, and if he never comes back, so much the better —isn't that right, Housely?

Can I sleep in your room? I ask.

Sure, man.

I SPEND THE FIRST WEEKS quietly going about my business. Nobody asks me why I'm here. I tell everybody why I'm here. They nod attentively, fixed smiles—Cool, man. Then they lose interest. It's the same for all of us. We're here because they sent us. We're here because we don't have anywhere better to be. We're here to make great art.

I attend the free school, learn to chant and fashion inedible delicacies out of foliage found on the shores of the Humber River. I swear an oath against wars and governments. After smoking a very large bowl of hashish, I help a brigade of volunteers paint a communal toilet blood-red. The Film Board delivers a camera, tripods, lights, film. I store their equipment with the arts and crafts centre, leave it for co-operative use. Never see it again.

My mind works in the background, a lurid film strip showing scenes of unexpected, heartbreaking clarity. A man in space. A new prime minister. National unity. Canada on the world stage. A crowd frozen in mid-cheer. The end of the beginning.

One morning, I return to David's room to find several people conducting a seance over my meagre heap of possessions (a change of clothes, a picture of my mother). They've arranged everything in a stack, each item folded with touching exactitude. My mother as a young woman, smiling on top.

They turn to stare at me. They are sexless, bald, calm.

We like your stuff, they say in unison. I think I might weep.

That same day, I find myself unexpectedly awake, my heart pounding.

It was a party. Everything here is a party.

I lie on David's bed.

A knock on the door.

Blood spews through my veins. I make fists, flex my arms.

The door opens.

A group troops in. Black suits and stiff slicked-back hair. My staff, the twelve eager would-be directors Housely promised me in accordance with Film Board protocol. Is a movie that never gets made still a movie? What if you make it and never show it? What if you leave it in the sun to fade, strip by strip? Close your eyes, watch the images leach into the air, pollution from a rocket's exhaust.

I convene a brief meeting.

I'm sorry to say that I won't be needing you.

They smile.

Naturally, I say, I wish you well in your chosen profession.

They shuffle their feet. Someone coughs.

Ah, sir, inquires one bright-eyed youngster. Where will we, uh, how long are we supposed to—?

Their grins are stricken. Why? They will continue to receive their pay courtesy of the federal government, the taxpayers, the much-beloved queen.

If you have any questions, I say, ask Housely. Montréal headquarters.

—

That's it. Go on. You're dismissed.

They file out. Midnight in the summer of lost love. What can I teach them? Let them grow up, get jobs, become our brightest and best, unhindered by the delusions of light seeping through film. Or else let them join the rest of the red-eyed minors labouring late, carving chunks out of their minds, lowering themselves into the dark deaths of their collective suffocation. It seems like freedom, but the gloomy light and bricks remind me of somewhere else. I haven't given up, I tell myself. I've done enough. My film is finished. They don't know what's it like. To watch the start of something come apart between your fingers.

Rochdale seems to have no windows.

Don't come looking for me, my directors.

I SLIP THROUGH THE BODIES, crave the warm feeling of my head in a pillowed lap. I am back in the room where the girls giggled and a filing cabinet showered me in escarpment tears. It's been a long time since I've been held. My mother is dead. They took her picture with them when they left.

That familiar giggle, next to me.

I turn to her.

Hey, she says. She trails her index finger down the rise of my face, from my ear to the arc of my chin. Remember me?

She's wearing my sunglasses.

I picture her on a beach after the war. The only person left alive. You'll be in the next one, I want to tell her. You'll be the mother who strokes my head through

the dark storm of fever. You'll be the girl who dances around the office, in her own wonderful world. You'll be the last survivor of some terrible conflict no one really understands.

She puts her hand on my shoulder.

Rosie! she says. She says it like she can't believe it.

Well, well, Rosie says. What do we have here? He returns to the scene of the

Gathered around the sculpture of the "Unknown Student" outside Rochdale College, May 16, 1970.

crime? Rosie is awesome in his cowboy hat, embroidered-beaded cowboy shirt, fake-fur vest, and long black trousers with gold piping. Sergeant Pepper meets Pierre Trudeau meets the pimp on the twelfth floor.

He reaches over us, opens the top drawer of that filing cabinet, now empty. He takes the sunglasses off my willow's face, lowers them in gently. He slams the drawer shut.

Rosie examines me with the air of an indifferent patrician.

Ha ha. He laughs at me. Willow laughs too, her breath sweeping my ear.

They call me the Churchman, Rosie says.

Why?

Because I get them higher.

Closer to God?

Like that. Ha ha. Funny, funny man.

LSD was discovered by accident, I say. In 1943 by a Swiss pharmaceutical researcher.

There aren't any accidents, Rosie says. That's what I told the judge. I said, You just go ahead and try. Because I can't be rehabilitated. I stepped beyond the law, and I would do it again. This is who I am. There aren't any accidents. I walked out of there and nobody tried to stop me.

What will happen if they come back to arrest you?

Rosie laughs again. Willow sways. The air in separate granules. Bits and pieces. Rosie swallows. It'll be heavy, he says, continuing his conversation with himself. You know what I mean?

Rosie gives us a sheet of tabs.

Wandering the halls, I see the monkey scream and a rocket propels me up into the atmosphere. I die.

A wet hand grabs me, pulls me into a closet.

Shh, she whispers.

Why?

We're hiding. She giggles. If I could, I would run away.

At night, the building is contrast: fluorescent light fixtures with their beaches of barren institutional illumination; candle islands, havens of soft incandescence. Between the islands and the stark sands connecting them, patches of swampy forest, permeable darkness where we can lose ourselves.

We can't stay here, she whispers.

Can't we?

No, no . . . they'll see us. She says it like she's about to burst out laughing.

We slip back into the hall, follow the shadows, the veils of smoke, candles heaving thick black stains, a flash of pale fluorescence I see her white skin, her hair a tangle of wet branches.

This way, she says, pulling me. In the stairs, a single bulb flickering. Pentagrams and peace symbols sprayed on walls. Footsteps coming towards us.

Oh shit, kiss me, she whispers.

I embrace her, pushing us against the wall, covering her body with mine.

The footsteps pass.

Wow, she says. That was him.

Who?

Who? she laughs. C'mon.

We move through halls, candles and electric light, smoke, shadow clouds. Bodies attached to faces lit up for an inhaling instant, then darkened again.

We're high. Far up the building, near the top. The upper floors of Rochdale are meant to be the classrooms and communal spaces. They were never finished. The work is not continued. We move past ramshackle lean-tos, Hendrix and Freak Brothers posters, exposed insulation.

Red roaming eyes. The smell is sour then sweet. Music coming out of everywhere, kaleidoscopic notes dried out, set on fire, burned to ashes. I think of Glookman, howling in the bowels of the Film Board.

Willow tows me into a crevice where the ceiling seems absent. We lie down on a naked mattress, stare up, imagining stars but seeing the shaded currents and flickering beacons of the ascending floor. The patterns of darkness. My own dreams through the lens, what can't be cut up and spliced together. What if Rochdale really is something alive?—ecosystem biosphere, building launched into the heavens, all that teeming possibility.

Why did you come here? she asks.

I couldn't help it. I shrug. Why did you?

I dunno. It's like, I just had to. My parents—they—but I knew, you know?

Sure, I say. So how long will you stay?

I don't know. A while.

Was that your boyfriend, on the stairs? I ask.

No. Kinda.

How old is your boyfriend?

Older.

Older than me?

No!

Has he met your parents?

Yeah, right.

Do your parents know where you are?

Yeah. Kinda.

Willow puts a finger on my lips. Like a stain.

She gets a cigarette. Lights it.

Above us, footsteps.

She settles against me.

I like you, she says. You're cute.

When she takes off her jeans, what do I say to her?

What would you say, Housely?

MY BEARD GROWS LONG, my eyebrows creep upwards. I believe I've achieved a certain simultaneity, the illusion of arrival, adopting the attitude of my young compatriots, external change a kind of stasis, the same everywhere, but different.

Images careen. My hands work, shredding paper, skin, celluloid.

I smoke pot with seventeen-year-old runaways from Truro, Nova Scotia, and Lethbridge, Alberta. With draft dodgers from Georgia, I listen to the Band, the Stones, Bob Dylan's electric lyrics. My heart shot into space, orbiting time capsule.

A knock on my door. Actually David's door. But no one comes looking for him here. Ever the fateful coordinator, he spends his days attempting to organize self-perpetuating brigades of volunteer plumbers into unclogging the boggy toilets; nights, he leads shivering freshmen inductees into the college of laboratory transcendentalism back from the by now well-mapped terrain of the bad trip.

Come in, I think I say.

The knocking stops.

Mr. Lipsett?

The visitor steps in, stoops in front of me. I lie on a dirty mattress in my underwear. My skin clings to me.

Uh, Mr. Lipsett? It's Ephraim, one of your students, with the Film Board. Are you—okay?

I nod, open one eye.

Actually, this former student of mine says, I'm called Elf now.

Do I smile? Yellow teeth through a patchwork beard.

I came to thank you. You were right, man. You really helped me. My whole life has changed. There's so much happening out there! And I was going to waste my time making movies. You were right. I see that now. A bunch of us, we're going to Ottawa for the really big rally.

Elf's voice rises in enthusiastic candour. I keep an eye open, focused on the wall.

Then we're going to drive to Washington. We'll be part of a Canadian delegation, against the war. Allen Ginsberg is coming. We're going to meditate. Sit-in. They're going to levitate the Pentagon. We've got to use other ways to communicate. Not guns. The mind, man. The mind. I'm thinking of staying on there. I'd really like to get involved. You were right, man . . .

Once, I had an office in a basement. I matched pictures to their visceral moment, isolated, stripped down, flesh picked away leaving only the bones: A mouth. A stone window. A dream. An explosion. A desert. A desert on the edge of the mountains. A desert on the edge of mountains overlooking the ocean. A mouth. A mouth and teeth. A book. An education. A desire. A loneliness. A nudie bit. A businessman. A mother. An Eskimo child. A window. A stone. A squat in the snow. A mouth. A man. An explosion.

Very nice, I tell Elf. Very nice.

I TAKE THE LONG WAY, through unfinished halls and dark passageways. I am stopped, harassed, hugged. There are rumours. I'm a narc. I'm a madman. I'm a prophet. I spend my nights alone. I am a camera.

Pushed from behind, tripped. A press of bodies, a punch to the stomach. A blow to the back of my head.

When I come to, I am lying on my back. Women surround me. They wear long skirts. They carry babies on their hips.

What is this? I say. I try to get up. A foot on my chest.

Stay where you are.

I stare. Pipes. Steam and the gurgle of water. I'm back in the basement. The women loom over me.

Who are you? I ask.

A blonde kicks me. Arthur Lipsett, isn't that correct?

Yes.

Age?

Thirty-two.

Profession?

Senior editor at the National Film Board of Canada.

That sounds important. What do you do?

I edit movies.

Including your own?

Yes.

Can you tell me about your movies?

I hesitate. She doesn't. Her heavy boot.

Okay. I grunt. I breathe deep. The women around me, waiting. As if what I'm going to say really matters.

They're about absence, I finally whisper. The absence of a past and a future.

We've seen your movies, the woman says. And I quote: *I don't think there's a deep concern about anything. People forget what happened on Tuesday. A politician can promise anything, and they will not remember what they have been promised.* You come in here. Consort with a drug dealer. Screw a teenage runaway. Take a room that does not belong to you.

The pipes rush through. The floor is cold. The ceiling low.

The foot on my chest presses down. I can feel my ribs.

You're just like the rest of them, she says. She sounds disappointed.

Yes, I croak.

Will you make a film? A film about Rochdale?

I shake my head. No.

They surround me. Kick. A baby gurgles. Drops of warm water from the swelling pipes. Everyday women pining for the end of nations.

I FIND DAVID IN HIS OFFICE.

Paper castles, towers on his desk, document dungeons burying the floor.

He nods, distracted.

Look at this, he says. He shows me a death threat. From the boys in blue, he says.

How do you know?

A detective delivered it.

He sighs.

Are you afraid? I ask.

I can see his throat swallow.

They're against us. They don't want us to succeed. They think there's a real world. They want to rub our noses in it. They want to break our noses.

He knocks over a spire of papers. They flutter down: *Past Due. Warning. Notice of Nonpayment.*

They want money, David says. I can't give them their goddamn money. Collect the rent, they say. From who?

He laughs.

Are you afraid?

David looks at me, only just noticing I'm there.

Don't leave, he says. Something's going to happen.

ACID. Peaceniks from out west. The big rally, Vietnam, nuclear war, Ottawa, Washington, Moscow. A lecture on holistic farming. The details elude me. We're on the top floor. Makeshift huts. Dirty mattresses. Hidden protocols. Theft is rampant. Trash heaps. Tie-dyes drying. Rules but no laws. I feel at home. I should leave.

Someone shouts, The pigs are arresting David!

The riot starts at the top.

This is what I see: flashlights, mist.

Dark shapes in a phalanx, engulfed in the eerie quiet.

Rosie's cowboy hat teeters. The piping on his pants arcing in the air.

Police. A rock. The cop raises his flashlight. Crunch, a cardboard box collapsing. The fire alarm kicks in. There's a world out there, Housely, country of eager workers riding the bus to the future. Our exhaustion mocks them.

Then it begins in earnest. Stones. The filing cabinet's payload. Bottles. Walls wet with liquid detonation.

Not the plants! I hear someone yell.

A voice counting backwards.

Police and sheriff's agents encountered opposition when they attempted to evict the residents of a commune on the 17th floor of Rochdale College, May 31, 1975.

A gun in my hand. The hand of a bearded skinny man.

Nowhere to go. A spaceship launching. Grassy knoll. Lapping river.

My legs carry me. Down the stairs. People rush. Up and down. Yelling. They've taken David. No. Not David. They're beating Rosie. Rosie's dead. David's dead. I creep past, unnoticed. Slip into a small gaping crevice. A room just big enough for a mattress. A room with a hole instead of a ceiling. Through that hole come the cries: the peacenick chant of Die, Pigs, Die; the high-pitched plea of David: I'm okay, it wasn't me, everybody just—

Swinging flashlights, hallway brush fires, strobe visions of my fragile willow, thin arms pressing a tiny suitcase to her chest.

This is the movie I'll never make: A house. A shack. An igloo. An Eskimo squaw giving birth. A man. A man with a gun.

August 10, 1982

Director Housely
Office of the Directors
National Film Board of Canada
Montréal, Québec

Housely,

Each moment takes me away from who I was.

I apologize for the lateness of this report, required by the Ministry of Protocol and Cultural Expenditure no longer than six weeks past a terminated appointment.

But it's been years, hasn't it?

I have retired to a small cottage.

There is the structure, the grassy slope dotted with trees, the water a river of perpetual motion.

I dream of this place, having seen it before, defiled by the blood of a man with a beard and a monkey in a cage, made barren by the wasted exhaust of a rocket on its way to the stars.

Housely, the film burns, spiralling into itself.

At night, my pistol under my pillow. I draw my legs to my chest, bend my head into my knees, wrap my arms around, and curl down to sleep.

Note from the Bureau of Canadian Film Records:
Project Status: Incomplete
Employee Status: Terminated; deceased
Status of Footage: Indeterminate
Film Board Representative Explanatory Assignment Failure Memo Proviso: Pending
Final File Status: Open; incomplete

Thomas King

WHERE THE BORG ARE

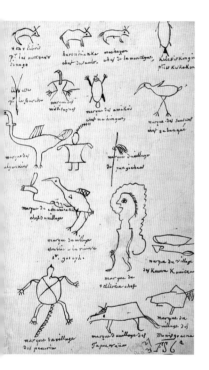

In the first place, writers will write about anything that piques their interests or stirs their passions.

I like to write about Indians. Natives. Aboriginals. First Nations. Take your pick.

However, I hate history. Or to be more exact, I resent the fact that history enjoys a reputation of being truthful while fiction is seen as pure fancy. As I see it, the two are more or less the same, stories we make up as we go along.

A couple of summers ago, I took a car trip with my son, Benjamin, who was thirteen at the time, and my daughter, Elizabeth, who was ten. The idea was to mosey through the West, stopping here and there, on our way to California to visit my mother.

Above: Signatures of First Nations chiefs on the great Peace of Montréal, August 4, 1701. As a signature each chief drew his tribe's totemic animal.

Previous: Cree children attending an Anglican Church Missionary School in Lac La Ronge, Saskatchewan, March 1945.

One of our stops was at the Custer Monument near Harden, Montana. You know, the place where General George Armstrong Custer made his famous "last stand." Now you may wonder why a family of contemporary Indians would bother to stop at a site that honours a military egotist who made a really stupid decision and was caught by the same Indians he was trying to catch.

Yes. Exactly for those reasons.

I had been to the Custer Monument before, and when I was there that first time, I went to one of the open-air lectures that the rangers at the park give on the Battle of the Little Big Horn. That lecture was all about how Custer had been out-numbered by the Lakota and the Cheyenne and how he and his men had fought bravely to the end.

Yawn.

However, when my kids and I got to the Custer Monument, things had changed. Instead of one lecture, there were two. One was given by the ranger while a second lecture was being given by an Indian. Both lectures were given at the same time and the audiences were separated by no more than fifty yards. Which meant you could sit in one lecture, and if you listened closely, you could hear the other lecture.

Did they agree. Nope.

So when I began looking around for a great moment in Canadian history to write about, I wanted to find a moment that had some real fluidity to it, a moment that had some real problems with interpretation, and a moment that meant something to Native people. But as I cast about among my friends, Native and non-Native, the only moment anyone could come up with was Louis Riel and the Red River and Northwest rebellions, or, as Maria Campbell calls them, resistances.

Too predictable.

Now, to be sure, the Indian Act is not your normal moment in history, but that's what makes it appealing. Unlike other moments, moments that have been bronzed and hung from the rear-view mirror of Canada's family sedan, the Indian Act has always been a loose, nervous thing, changing in subtle and dramatic fashion, as it winds its way through the country.

Like the landscape.

The act itself is an endlessly argumentative moment, where new sections contradict old sections, where disparaging language can run to encouragement and back to slander in a generation. Where punitive requirements that were meant to destroy communities and nations, and promises that were never meant to be kept, rise out of graves to hurry and harry our beloved Canadian (dare I say it) mosaic, which, as it stands on the brink of the new millennium, imagines itself absolved of the mistakes of the past through its many acts of political and public contrition.

And is now free to repeat them.

In short, the Indian Act is the best kind of historical moment for a novelist who does not trust history, for it is a historical moment in constant motion, with only the vaguest of notions of where it is going, with only the vaguest of understandings of where it has been.

WHERE THE BORG ARE

BY THE TIME MILTON FRIENDLYBEAR finished reading Olive Patricia Dickason's *Canada's First Nations* for a tenth-grade history assignment, he knew, without a doubt, where the Borg had gone after they had been defeated by Jean Luc Picard and the forces of the Federation. And he included his discovery in an essay on great historical moments in Canadian history.

Milton's teacher, Virginia Merry, was not as impressed with Milton's idea as he had hoped. "Milton," she said, in that tone of voice that many lapsed Ontario Catholics reserved for correcting faulty logic, bad grammar, and inappropriate behaviour, "I'm not sure that the Indian Act of 1875 is generally considered an important moment in Canadian history."

"Why not?"

"But I am positive that there is no significant correlation between the Indian Act and 'Star Trek.'" She said this with the natural assurance that the well-educated are able to manage, even though she had never read the Indian Act and only knew about "Star Trek" because her husband watched it every night while they ate dinner.

"But it's all here," said Milton. "Pages two hundred and eighty-three to two hundred and eighty-nine."

"Your handwriting could use some attention," said Ms. Merry, and she wrote a note on Milton's paper in thin, delicate letters that reminded him of the doilies on the back on his grandfather's easy chair.

When Milton got home from school, he showed his paper to his mother who sat at the table and looked at the grade for a long while. "Sixty per cent's not too good, eh?"

"Ms. Merry said I had a vivid imagination."

"What's this about neatness?"

"That's because she's a Borg."

His mother read the paper, and when she was done, she nodded thoughtfully. "Maybe you should go and talk to your grandfather."

Milton liked his grandfather a great deal and would have liked him just as much if he did not have a thirty-six-inch television set that was hooked up to the biggest satellite dish on the reserve.

"Hiya," said his grandfather. "You're just in time."

"'Star Trek'?"

"You bet."

"Are the Borg in this episode?"

"Who knows," said his grandfather. "It's always a surprise."

The episode did not have anything to do with the Borg. It was about a hypnotic space game that would have turned the *Enterprise*'s crew into automatons had it not been for the quick thinking of Data and Wesley.

"I wrote a paper on the Indian Act," Milton told his grandfather as they waited for "The Simpsons" to come on. "For my history class."

"Oh, ho," said his grandfather. "I've heard about that one, all right."

"My teacher didn't think that it was a great historical moment."

"That's probably because she's not Indian."

"But I read this really neat book, and guess what?" Milton waited in case his grandfather wanted to guess. "I think I know where the Borg went after they were defeated by Jean Luc Picard and the forces of the Federation."

"Boy," said his grandfather, "that's probably the question of the century."

Milton took *Canada's First Nations* out of his backpack and put it on the coffee table next to his grandfather's recliner. "Everybody's been looking for them somewhere in the future, right?"

"That's right."

"But if this book is correct, I think the Borg went back in time."

"Ah," said Milton's grandfather.

"Into the past."

"Ah."

"Europeans," said Milton, and he turned to page two hundred and eighty-four in the history book and pointed to the eighth word of the first line. "That's where the Borg went."

Milton's grandfather looked at the word just above Milton's finger. "Holy!" he said, and he sat up straight and hit the mute button.

"That's right," said Milton. "'Assimilation.' According to this book, the Indian Act is"—and Milton paused so he could find the right tone of voice—"an assimilation document."

Milton's grandfather picked up the book and turned it over.

"It was written by this woman," said Milton. "A university professor."

"Those women," said Milton's grandfather. "They know everything. Is she Indian?"

"She's Métis."

"Close enough," said Milton's grandfather. "Does that Indian Act say anything about resistance being futile? That would sure clinch it."

"So, you think I'm right about the Borg having come to Earth and taken over."

"It makes a lot of sense," said Milton's grandfather, "but I suppose we better get a copy of this Indian Act and read the whole thing before we jump to conclusions."

WHEN MILTON GOT HOME, his mother was waiting for him. "So," she said, "what did your grandfather think of your idea?"

"He liked it."

"You know, stuff like that might hurt people's feelings."

"It would explain why Dad took off."

"It would, would it?"

"Sure," said Milton. "He was assimilated."

The next day, after school, Milton went to the library and looked up the Indian Act. There were all sorts of listings for Indians, but the act itself was not there. Milton looked under "Borg," too, but it wasn't there either.

"I'm looking for the Indian Act," Milton told the woman at the desk. "Do you know where I can find it?"

"Is it a . . . play?" asked the woman.

"I don't think so," said Milton, though he didn't know exactly what it was. "It's got to do with history."

The woman went to work on her computer and in a matter of minutes found the act. Milton was impressed.

"It's not hard," the woman explained. "This computer is connected to all the rest of the libraries in the province and to the National Library in Ottawa."

Milton began to feel a little queasy. "Sort of like a . . . collective?"

"Exactly," said the woman, who did not particularly look like a Borg. "Do you want me to request a copy of the act for you?"

"Oh, yes," said Milton.

"Is this for a school assignment?"

"Yes," said Milton.

"Research is fun, isn't it?" said the woman.

"It certainly is," said Milton.

THE INDIAN ACT DIDN'T ARRIVE right away. By the end of the second week, Milton figured that the Borg were on to him and that he might wind up disappearing the same way his father had. But when he got home from school the next day, his mother told him that the library had called. "They said to tell you that your Indian Act thing is in."

Milton raced down to the library. The woman was still sitting at the reference desk, and she smiled when she saw him. Beside her on the floor was a stack of rather large, very old-looking books.

"The Indian Act," she said, and she leaned over and gave the stack of books a pat.

"All that?" said Milton.

"No," said the woman. "These are the Revised Statutes of Canada for particular years. The original Indian Act is in the 1875-1876 volume. This one contains the revisions for 1886. This one is for 1906. There are a couple for the 1950s and one for 1970."

"Wow!"

"The Indian Act was revised a great many times."

"So it probably represents a great moment in Canadian history."

"I don't think so," said the woman. "Most great moments in Canadian history have holidays."

Milton looked at the stack for a few moments. "Okay," he said, and he began to stuff the books into his backpack.

"Oh, you can't take them out of the library," said the woman. "These are government documents. They don't circulate."

Of course, thought Milton. The Borg wouldn't want their secret to get out.

"But you can Xerox the parts that you need."

"How much is Xeroxing?"

"Ten cents a sheet."

Those Borg, thought Milton, as he hauled the books to one of the long tables by the window. They don't leave much to chance.

Milton spent the rest of the afternoon reading in each volume and taking notes. It was a long laborious process, but he was determined not to let the Borg and their "ten cents a sheet" rule deter him. That evening, he showed his grandfather what he had found.

"What do you think?"

Milton's grandfather got up and stretched his legs. "I don't know," he said. "It sure sounds like the Borg."

"All the stuff about assimilation must be Borg," said Milton. "Look at this. 'Every Indian who is admitted to the degree of doctor of medicine, or to any other degree, by any university of learning, or who is admitted, in any province of Canada, to practise law, either as an advocate, a barrister, solicitor or attorney, or a notary public, or who enters holy orders, or who is licensed by any denomination of Christians as a minister of gospel, may, upon petition to the Superintendent, *ipso facto* become and be *enfranchised*.'"

"Whoa," said Milton's grandfather. "That could certainly limit the choices Native people might want to make."

"It sure could," said Milton. "I don't think I want to be . . . 'enfranchised.'"

"It sounds better than 'assimilated,'" said his grandfather, looking at Milton's notes. "But it's probably the same thing."

"So," said Milton. "What are we going to do?"

"It may be more complicated than we imagine." Milton's grandfather closed his eyes for a moment and then opened them. "Look at this section. 'The Governor in Council may authorize the Minister, in accordance with this Act, to enter into agreements on behalf of Her Majesty for the education, in accordance with this Act, of Indian children.' Now that sounds more like the Vulcan than the Borg."

"You think so?"

"Sure," said his grandfather. "The Vulcans were always the intellectual ones."

Milton stood up and walked around in a circle. "You mean it was the Vulcans who came back in time?"

"It gets worse." Milton's grandfather sighed. "Look at this."

Milton leaned over his grandfather's shoulder. "'Management of Indian Moneys'?"

"And these." Milton's grandfather ran his finger down the notes that Milton had taken. "'Descent of Property.' 'Sale of Property.' 'Rent.' 'Sale of Timber Lands.' Who does that sound like to you?"

"Oh, no." Milton paled. "Ferengis?"

"Yep," said Milton's grandfather. "Sounds like we might be dealing with the Ferengis."

"And the Ferengi Rules of Acquisition?"

"Let's check it out." Milton's grandfather went to the bookcase and came back with a small notebook. "I've been keeping track of the Ferengi Rules of Acquisition in case there was something worth knowing."

"How many are there?"

"At last count, there were two hundred and eighty-five."

For the next little while, Milton and his grandfather went through the Ferengi Rules of Acquisition, looking at each one carefully.

"Maybe you're right," said Milton. "Look at this. Rule Twenty-six. 'The vast majority of the rich in this galaxy did not inherit their wealth; they stole it.'"

"And Rule Twenty-seven," said Milton's grandfather. "'The most beautiful thing about a tree is what you do with it after you cut it down.'"

"And Rule Forty-two. 'Only negotiate when you are certain to profit.'" Milton's grandfather shook his head. "Boy, I sure wish I had known about this before we signed those treaties."

Milton felt a shiver go up his spine. "Look at Rule Sixty-one."

Milton's grandfather ran a finger down the page. "'Never buy what can be stolen.'"

"You're right," said Milton. "The Borg didn't come back in time. And neither did the Vulcans. It was the Ferengis."

The next day, Milton stayed after class and apologized to Ms. Merry. "I was wrong about Europeans being Borg," he told her.

"It's all right," said Ms. Merry. "I'm sure it was an easy mistake to make."

"They're really Ferengis."

WHEN MILTON FINISHED WRITING "Racism hurts everyone" on the blackboard fifty times, he went back to his grandfather's house to talk with him.

"I've been thinking," said Milton, "and something doesn't make sense."

"That's the trouble with life," said his grandfather. "Television is a lot simpler."

"It sure is," said Milton.

"So," said his grandfather, hitting the mute so you could still see what Captain Cisco and Dax and Quark were doing on "Deep Space Nine," "what doesn't make sense?"

Milton put the Indian Act and the Ferengi Rules of Acquisition on the coffee table side by side. "We know that the Borg and the Vulcans and the Ferengi have little in common."

"That's true," said Milton's grandfather.

"I mean, the Borg want to assimilate everyone. The Vulcans want everything to be logical. And the Ferengi are only concerned with profit."

"I see your point," said his grandfather. "Europeans seem to have many of the bad habits of all three."

"They could be Klingons, too, because the Klingons are warriors and because Klingons love to fight simply for the sake of fighting."

"Don't forget those tricky Romulans," said Milton's grandfather. "Now that I think about it, those treaties have Romulan written all over them. What else does that Indian Act say?"

"Not much," said Milton, and he made a face. "It has a bunch of stuff about who's an Indian and who's in charge of Indian affairs and how you can get an Indian declared mentally incompetent."

"Boy," said Milton's grandfather, "if you were a Romulan, that would be a handy thing to know."

"So, what should we do?"

"Maybe you better talk to your teacher," said his grandfather. "And see if she can help us."

MILTON WASN'T SURE HE WANTED to talk to Ms. Merry again, but he was very sure he didn't want to get her upset and have to spend the afternoon writing on the blackboard.

"Hello, Milton," Ms. Merry said with a cheery chirp, when Milton stopped by after school the next day.

"I have this problem," said Milton, glancing at the blackboard. "I was hoping you could help me with it."

Ms. Merry listened patiently as Milton explained what he had learned about assimilation and the Indian Act and how the Borg, or the Vulcans, or the Ferengis, or the Klingons, or quite possibly the Romulans figured in the history of North America. Along with his theories on space travel, wormholes, and time warps.

"Christopher Columbus was not a Ferengi," said Ms. Merry. "He was an Italian."

"But you told us that he kidnapped Indians from the islands of the Caribbean and sold them in the slave markets in Seville."

"Yes, he did, but that doesn't make him a Ferengi."

"Who else but a Ferengi would try to sell people?"

"Milton," said Ms. Merry, "do you remember what I told you about racism?"

"Racism hurts everyone."

"That's right."

"I told my mother, and she mostly agreed with you."

"Mostly?"

"She said it hurts some people more than others."

THAT WEEKEND, Milton's mother had to go to Edmonton for a conference. "You can come with me, or you can stay with your grandfather."

"Are you going to be near the West Edmonton Mall?"

"No."

Milton's grandfather was in the backyard setting up his tipi when Milton arrived with his backpack and his sleeping bag.

"Nothing like sleeping out under the stars," said his grandfather.

"Like the old days, right?"

"Right."

"Before television, right?"

"You bet," said his grandfather. "Here, give me a hand with this."

"What is it?"

"An antenna. If you hook it to one of the lodgepoles, it really improves the reception."

"We moving the big television outside?"

"No," said his grandfather. "It's too heavy."

Watching "Star Trek" on the seventeen-inch portable wasn't quite the same as seeing it on the big screen. But it was cozy inside the tipi, and during the commercials, if you looked up, you could see the stars.

"Look what I found," said his grandfather, and he handed Milton a magazine. "I went to the doctor's office the other day and there it was."

"*Maclean's?*"

The banner headline on the cover said, "Abuse of Trust," and one of the stories was about the George Gordon Residential School in Saskatchewan.

"Residential schools," said his grandfather. "That's one of the places where Europeans tried to assimilate Indians."

"Are we back to the Borg, again?"

Milton's grandfather sighed and opened the magazine to page eighteen. "Look at this. It says here that in 1879 the John A. Macdonald government decided to set up boarding schools in order to remove Native children from their homes to begin assimilating them into white culture."

"And in 1894," said Milton, reading ahead, "Ottawa passed an amendment to the . . ." Milton stopped for a moment to catch his breath.

"That's right," said his grandfather, "an amendment to the Indian Act making attendance for Native children mandatory at these schools."

"Wow!" said Milton. "So it was the Borg, after all."

Milton's grandfather turned off the television and pulled the flap to one side. "Come on," he said. "I want to show you something."

It was a moonless night, and the sky was aquiver with stars. Milton's grandfather walked to the edge of the bluff overlooking the river and sat down on the prairie grass. "I think I know what happened," he said. "I think that Europeans and Jean Luc Picard and the Federation are . . . one and the same."

"That's silly," said Milton, who did not really think of his grandfather as silly. "Europeans can't be part of the Federation."

"The Prime Directive, right?"

"That's right," said Milton. "The Federation's Prime Directive was never to interfere in the affairs of another race."

Milton's grandfather picked up a stick and drew a circle in the dirt. "You ever watch Sherlock Holmes on A&E?"

"It's a little slow," said Milton. "Mum likes it."

"Sherlock Holmes says that the way to solve a crime is to eliminate all the possibilities, and then whatever remains, however improbable, has to be the answer." Milton's grandfather paused and gestured towards the sky. "There's one."

Milton looked up in time to see a shooting star streak through the night.

"That's probably how it happened," said his grandfather. "That's probably exactly how it happened."

Milton was getting a little cold, and he was a little sleepy, and he had lost track of what his grandfather was trying to tell him. "We have anything to eat?"

"I got some apples."

"Any popcorn?"

Milton's grandfather shook his head. "Have you ever wondered why Europeans and the crew of the *Enterprise* look a lot alike."

"Yeah, that is a little weird," said Milton.

"Europeans don't look like the Borg. They don't look like the Ferengis or the Klingons or the Vulcans or even the Romulans."

"Too bad Europeans aren't as nice and considerate as the crew of the *Enterprise*. I'll bet if Jean Luc Picard had come to North America instead of Christopher Columbus, he would never have kidnapped Indians and sold them to other Europeans as slaves."

"Christopher Columbus did that?"

"Sure," said Milton. "You could make pretty good money selling slaves."

"Well, I guess that settles it," said Milton's grandfather.

"It does."

"You're a smart boy," said his grandfather. "How would you explain a race of people who look exactly like Federation officers, but who want to assimilate everyone and make a profit at the same time?"

If Milton had had any hair on the back of his neck, he was sure it would be standing on end.

First Nations representatives meeting to discuss provisions of the Indian Bill to amend, consolidate and clarify the Indian Act, February 1951.

"Remember that episode when the Borg were racing towards Earth?"

"And everyone was chasing them?"

"Klingons, Ferengis, Vulcans, Romulans. And Jean Luc Picard. Everyone travelling through space at incredible speeds."

"Warp ten at least."

"They go faster and faster. The Borg out in front. The Federation right on their heels." Milton's grandfather paused, so Milton could catch up.

"Like a shooting star."

"Exactly." Milton's grandfather nodded. "And then . . . something happened."

"Something?"

"An accident. An explosion. Maybe a wormhole collapsed."

"A wormhole! You think a wormhole collapsed and caught everyone in a high-energy gravity field?"

"Maybe it was a faulty temporal time warp," said Milton's grandfather. "Who knows."

"But everybody would have been . . . crushed."

Milton's grandfather shook his head. "Or they were phased into particle streams, and their atoms were mixed and merged. Borg, Klingon, Vulcan, Ferengi, Romulan, even John Luc Picard and his crew."

"You mean they were . . . reconfigured?"

"And when the dust cleared, what do you got?"

Milton sat back and took a deep breath. "Europeans."

"Only thing that makes any sense," said his grandfather.

"This is worse than I thought," said Milton.

"I never did buy that story about Columbus sailing the ocean blue," said his grandfather.

"So what are we going to do?"

Milton's grandfather got up and brushed off his jeans. "Not sure there's anything we can do. I'll bet Europeans don't even remember it happening."

"You know what this means, don't you?" said Milton glumly. "I'm probably going to have to write my paper over again."

FOR A BORG/Klingon/Ferengi/Vulcan/Romulan/Federation molecular composite, Ms. Merry was remarkably understanding. "No," she told Milton. "You don't need to do your paper over again."

"I know you can't help it," Milton told Ms. Merry. "It's just that I don't want to be assimilated."

"Then you should probably stop watching so much television," said Ms. Merry.

AT THE NEXT COMMUNITY MEETING, Milton's grandfather got up during the open-microphone period and read Milton's paper out loud. It was a big hit, and afterwards several people came up and said how nice it was to have a scholar on the reserve. Milton was flattered at first, but after he'd had a few cookies and some time to think, he felt a little depressed.

"What's wrong?" asked Milton's grandfather, as the two of them walked home under a spacious starlit sky.

"I don't know," said Milton. "Doing that paper on the Indian Act and discovering what happened to the Borg was fun, but what good does it do to know that Europeans were created by a freak accident in deep space."

"Probably not much," said his grandfather. "But look on the bright side. Now that we know the truth, having Europeans around won't seem nearly as bad as it once was."

"You think so?"

"Sure," said Milton's grandfather. "They invented television."

"That's true."

"And those ice-cream bars covered with dark chocolate are pretty good, too."

"They certainly are."

Milton's grandfather stopped and looked into the sky just as another shooting star flashed through the night. "And don't forget the Borg."

"The Borg?"

"Sure," said Milton's grandfather. "Europeans are no great shakes, but think how bad things would have been for Native people if the Borg had gotten here in one piece." The old man paused for a moment and a frown began working its way across his face. "Unless, of course, we're wrong."

"Wrong about what?"

Milton's grandfather wrinkled his forehead. "Of course. That's what they want you to think."

"Who?"

"The Federation."

"Jean Luc?"

Milton's grandfather sighed and sucked at his lips. "When has the Federation ever lost a fight? When have they ever lost anything?"

Milton thought about this for a moment. "Never."

"So, what if the deep-space accident never happened." Milton's grandfather was chuckling now. "What if the Federation attacked the Borg and defeated them long before the Borg got to Earth."

"You think the Federation attacked the Borg?"

"Why not. The Federation likes to fight as much as the Klingons."

"Yeah, but they never start the fights. The bad guys always start the fights."

"And they like logic, same as the Vulcans," said Milton's grandfather. "And they acquire things at almost the same rate as the Ferengis."

"Yeah," said Milton. "That's true. But what about the Prime Directive? The Klingons and the Vulcans and the Ferengi and the Romulans don't have a Prime Directive."

"Lot of good it does," said Milton's grandfather. "The Prime Directive says you're not supposed to interfere with another culture, but Jean Luc Picard and Data and William Riker and councillor Troy are always sticking their noses into other people's business."

"They can get a little pushy," Milton agreed. "Especially Riker."

"'To boldly go where no one has gone before,'" said Milton's grandfather. "Sounds like nosiness to me."

"That's just exploration talk."

"You know," said Milton's grandfather, "now that I think about it, the Prime Directive sounds an awful lot like the federal government."

"Our government?"

Milton's grandfather slapped his hands together. "You know what I think? I think that the Federation destroyed the Borg and then, when no one was looking, they ambushed the Klingons and the Ferengis, the Vulcans and the Romulans, one by one, until there was no one left in the universe to oppose them."

"But why would they do that?"

"So they could have the universe all to themselves."

"But, Grandpa," said Milton. "The Federation are the good guys. Good guys wouldn't do something like that."

The smile on Milton's grandfather's face slowly faded, and the old man's shoulders sagged a little. "Holy," he said softly. "You're right. Boy, what was I thinking? I guess I got a little carried away."

"It's okay, Grandpa," Milton took his grandfather's hand. "It's an easy mistake to make if you don't know what you're looking for. All you have to remember is that, in most cases, the bad guys look like lizards or devils or scary people with dark skin and snaky hair."

"And the good guys look like Europeans?" said Milton's grandfather.

"Sure," said Milton, "Who else would they look like?"

THE FOLLOWING MONDAY, Milton stopped by Ms. Merry's room to give her the good news and to ask her, in light of all the extra work he had done, if she would consider changing his grade.

"Collapsing wormholes and molecular realignment?"

"My grandfather thought it might be a tear in the space-time continuum, but he doesn't watch as much 'Star Trek' as me."

When Milton's mother saw the new grade, she was pleased. "There's probably no one else on the reserve who knows as much about the Indian Act as you do. I never would have realized that it was such an important document."

Milton settled on the couch. Yes, he thought to himself as he ran through the channels until he got to the space station, the Indian Act was an important document. Certainly important enough to have its own holiday. And who would have guessed, Milton mused as he watched Jean Luc Picard save another primitive civilization from destruction, that it would turn out to be the key to understanding the universe.

A young Mi'kmaq boy runs past signs from a peaceful demonstration of women and children in Burnt Church, New Brunswick. Protests were held in response to the federal fisheries department's limitation on the number of lobster traps members of the Burnt Church band could place in the ocean as the contentious issue of Native treaty rights continued. October 10, 1999.

ILLUSTRATIONS AND PHOTOGRAPHS

CM: Cumberland Museum
CTA: City of Toronto Archives
CP: CP Picture Archive
GA: Glenbow Archives
G&M: Globe and Mail
NAC: National Archives of Canada
NFB: National Film Board of Canada
PANL: Provincial Archives of Newfoundland and Labrador

ATWOOD: pp.6-7, p.20, jacket NAC C- 077769; p.8 CP- 167357; p. 15 NAC C-026063; p.18 NAC C-105765.

MAILLET: pp.24-25, p.31 NAC C-024549; p.26 NAC C-024550; p.36 NAC C-019584; p. 42 NAC C-003020.

MANGUEL: pp.44-45, p.62, jacket NAC PA-099557; p.46 NAC C-000728; p.53, jacket NAC C-004572; p.56, jacket NAC C-001732.

CARRIER: pp.64-65, p.88, jacket GA NA-949-54; p.66, jacket NAC PA-013284; p.73, jacket NAC PA-013304; p.82 NAC PA-016239.

MACFARLANE: pp.90-91, jacket NAC PA-127034; p.92 CP 1043197; p.100 NAC PA139674; p.107, jacket PANL A12-60; p.115 NAC PA-198.

TURNER: pp.118-119, jacket CM C-165-2; p.120 CM C-110-5; p. 125, jacket CM C-110-2; p.136 CM C-70-4; p.142 CM C-110-1.

FINDLEY: pp.144-145, p.168 GA NC-20-2; p.146 CP 1242930; p.154, jacket NAC PA-3683; p.161, jacket NAC PA-931; p.173 NAC 80027.

SAUL: pp.176-177, jacket courtesy of the author; p.178 NAC PA-132467; p.181 NAC PA-131271; p.184, jacket NAC PA-132651; p.191 NAC PA-141890.

BRAND: All photos of Viola Davis Desmond courtesy of her sisters: Mrs. Emily Davis Clyke, Mrs. Eugenie Davis Parris, Mrs. Wanda Davis Robson and Mrs. Constance Davis Scott.

BERRY: pp.214-215, jacket © The Record, Kitchener; p.216, jacket CP 1308161; p.223, jacket CP 44420; p.228 courtesy of Brian Pickell; p.238, jacket CP 825724.

NIEDZVIECKI: pp.240-241, p.267, jacket G&M 14189; p.242 NFB; p. 254 CTA SC118 Item 191; p. 259, jacket G&M 67232.

KING: pp.270-271, jacket NAC PA134110; p.272 NAC C-075209; p.286 NAC PA184376; p.291, jacket CP 1174478.

MARGARET ATWOOD is the author of more than thirty books of fiction, poetry, and critical essays. Her novels include *The Handmaid's Tale*, *Cat's Eye*, *The Robber Bride*, and *Alias Grace*, winner of the prestigious Giller Prize in Canada and the Premio Mondello in Italy. Her most recent novel, *The Blind Assassin*, was awarded the 2000 Booker Prize. Her work is acclaimed internationally and has been translated into thirty-three languages. She is the recipient of many literary awards and honours from various countries, including Britain, Italy, France, Sweden, and Norway, as well as Canada and the United States. Margaret Atwood lives in Toronto, with writer Graeme Gibson.

MICHELLE BERRY is the author of two critically acclaimed short-story collections, *How to Get There from Here* and *Margaret Lives in the Basement*, and the novel *What We All Want*. Her second novel, *Blur*, will be published in Canada and the UK in Spring 2002. She has published short fiction in magazines and journals throughout Canada, is a reviewer for *The Globe and Mail*, teaches at Ryerson University and has served on the board of PEN. Berry lives in Toronto.

DIONNE BRAND won the Governor General's Award for Poetry and the Trillium Award in 1997 for *Land to Light On*. Her novel *In Another Place, Not Here* was shortlisted for the Chapters/Books in Canada First Novel Award and the Trillium Award, and was published in the US and the UK to great acclaim. Her latest novel, *At The Full and Change of the Moon*, received rave reviews internationally as well. She has also written a non-fiction work, *A Map to the Door of No Return*, published in Fall 2001. Dionne Brand lives in Toronto and Vancouver.

ROCH CARRIER has written novels and short stories, including *The Hockey Sweater*. He has had the privilege of travelling extensively across Canada and is fascinated by its untold stories. Currently, he is the National Librarian of Canada, where he is dedicating himself to providing Canadians with free access to information for a better democracy.

TIMOTHY FINDLEY, born in Toronto in 1930, now divides his year between Stratford, Ontario and Provence. After an international career as an actor, he came to prominence as a writer with his 1977 novel, *The Wars*. Since then, his fiction, plays, memoirs, and film and television scripts have won numerous awards. Findley is an Officer in the Order of Canada, a member of the Order of Ontario and, in France, Chevalier de L'Ordre des Arts et des Lettres.

RUDYARD GRIFFITHS has been the chief executive officer of The Dominion Institute since it was established in 1997 by a group of young people concerned about the erosion of a common memory in Canada. Prior to founding the Institute, he worked as a policy analyst for the Department of Foreign Affairs and in corporate communications.

THOMAS KING is a writer best known for his novels, *Truth and Bright Water* (1999), *Green Grass, Running Water* (1993), which was nominated for the Governor General's Award, and *Medicine River* (1990), winner of the Alberta Novel Award and the Josephine Miles, Oakland PEN award. In addition, he has written a collection of short stories, *One Good Story, That One* and two children's books: *A Coyote Columbus Story*, nominated for the Governor General's Award, and *Coyote Sings to the Moon*. He currently writes and performs in the CBC radio show "The Dead Dog Café Comedy Hour." Thomas King was born in 1943 and currently resides in Guelph, Ontario with his partner Helen Hoy and their two children. He teaches Native literature and Creative Writing at the University of Guelph. His short stories have been anthologized throughout North America.

DAVID MACFARLANE is the author of the bestselling novel *Summer Gone*, which was shortlisted for the 1999 Giller Prize. His book *The Danger Tree* received the Canadian Authors' Association Award for Non-Fiction. He is a regular columnist for *The Globe and Mail* and has won six gold National Magazine Awards as well as a National Newspaper Award and the Author's Award for Magazine Writing.

ANTONINE MAILLET is the celebrated author of many published works including fourteen novels, thirteen plays, numerous translations and a children's story. She is the recipient of many literary awards and honours including the Governor General's Award and the Chalmers Award. She is a Companion of the Order of Canada and Commandeur de l'Ordre des Arts et des Lettres de France. Antonine Maillet was born in Bouctouche, New Brunswick, the heart of Acadia. She now lives in Montréal.

ALBERTO MANGUEL is a Canadian writer, novelist, translator and editor, acclaimed for several award-winning works, including *A History of Reading* (a *Maclean's* Best Book of the Year, a *Times Literary Supplement* International Book of the Year, a *Globe and Mail* Notable Book of the Year, and winner of France's Prix Médici), *The Dictionary of Imaginary Places*, *Meanwhile, in Another Part of the Forest*, *Black Water* (Volumes I and II), *News from a foreign country came*, and most recently, *Reading Pictures*. He was born in Buenos Aires, lived in Italy, France, England, and Tahiti, and he became a Canadian citizen in 1985.

CHRISTOPHER MOORE is a distinguished historian and writer who specializes in presenting history to general audiences. He is the author of *Louisbourg Portraits*, winner of the Governor General's Award for Non-Fiction; and co-author of *The Illustrated History of Canada*, *The Story of Canada*, and most recently, the bestselling *Canada: Our Century*.

HAL NIEDZVIECKI is editor of *Broken Pencil*, the magazine of zine culture and the independent arts. He is the author of the novel *Ditch*, the short story collection *Smell It*, and the macabre retelling of *Charlotte's Web*, *Lurvy*. He is also the author of a pop culture commentary *We Want Some Too*.

JOHN RALSTON SAUL is the author of *On Equilibrium* (Penguin Books) and of four novels including *The Birds of Prey* and *The Paradise Eater* (Vintage Canada).

MICHAEL TURNER's first book, *Company Town*, was nominated for the Dorothy Livesay B.C. Book Prize for Poetry. His second book, *Hard Core Logo*, was made into an acclaimed feature film and he received a Genie Award for his contribution to the movie's soundtrack. He is also the author of the screenplay-cum-novel, *American Whiskey Bar*. His most recent novel, *The Pornographer's Poem*, was awarded the Ethel Wilson B.C. Book Prize for Fiction.